Visual Intelligence

Visual Intelligence

Microsoft Tools and Techniques
for Visualizing Data

Mark Stacey

Joe Salvatore

Adam Jorgensen

Visual Intelligence: Microsoft Tools and Techniques for Visualizing Data

Published by
John Wiley & Sons, Inc.
10475 Crosspoint Boulevard
Indianapolis, IN 46256
www.wiley.com

ISBN: 978-1-118-38803-7
ISBN: 978-1-118-43936-4 (ebk)
ISBN: 978-1-118-41752-2 (ebk)
ISBN: 978-1-118-70750-0 (ebk)

Manufactured in the United States of America

10 9 8 7 6 5 4 3 2 1

For general information on our other products and services please contact our Customer Care Department within the United States at (877) 762-2974, outside the United States at (317) 572-3993 or fax (317) 572-4002.

Wiley publishes in a variety of print and electronic formats and by print-on-demand. Some material included with standard print versions of this book may not be included in e-books or in print-on-demand. If this book refers to media such as a CD or DVD that is not included in the version you purchased, you may download this material at http://booksupport.wiley.com. For more information about Wiley products, visit www.wiley.com.

Library of Congress Control Number: 2013932100

About the Authors

Mark Stacey, entrepreneur, CEO and founder of Aphelion Software, works tirelessly to cross the business/technical boundaries in Business Intelligence, and consults in both Sharepoint and SQL. He is a frequent speaker at SQL, SharePoint, and BI industry events, tweets at @MarkGStacey, and blogs at http://markgstacey.net.

Mark works with data at scale in industries such as vehicle tracking, mining, finance, insurance and retail, and has developed data warehouses in both SMP and MPP, built Master Data Management solutions, and created real time analytics systems for multiple customers. Mark is currently developing a predictive analytics platform to help predict accidents. He lives by the motto "Data Driven Decisions." This is his second book, after *SharePoint 2010 Business Intelligence 24-Hour Trainer* (Wrox, 2011).

Joe Salvatore has over 15 years of Information Technology experience and presently is a Business Intelligence Architect with Pragmatic Works Consulting. He specializes in data access architecture, data integration especially extract transformation and load (ETL), and Microsoft® business intelligence solution design and development.

Joe is an accomplished SQL Server author and contributor to *Professional SQL Server 2005 Administration* (Wrox, 2006), *Professional Microsoft SQL Server 2008 Administration* (Wrox, 2008), and *Microsoft SQL Server Reporting Services Recipes: for Designing Expert Reports* (Wrox, 2010). He was the lead technical editor for *Professional Microsoft SQL Server Reporting Services 2012* (Wrox, 2012).

Joe is a Microsoft Certified Professional with IT Professional (MCITP) certifications for SQL Server 2005 and 2008 Business Intelligence Developer, as well as having Technology Specialist (MCTS) certifications for SQL Server 2005 and 2008 Business Intelligence Development and Maintenance.

He attended data warehousing worldwide innovator Ralph Kimball's Dimensional Modeling in Depth and Data Warehouse ETL in Depth classes, and regularly attends industry conferences such as the Microsoft Business Intelligence Conference and the Professional Association for SQL Server (PASS) Summits.

Joe designed content areas for Microsoft Certified IT Professional Exam 70-446 Designing a Business Intelligence Solution by Using Microsoft SQL Server 2005, and participated in an invitation only design review of Katmai (SQL Server 2008).

Adam Jorgensen is the President of Pragmatic Works and a Director at large for the Professional Association of SQL Server. As a Microsoft SQL Server MVP he has extensive experience with SQL Server, SharePoint, and analytics over the past 13 years. His focus is primarily on helping organizations and executives drive value through new technology solutions, management techniques, and financial optimization. He is especially focused in the areas of OLAP, Cloud and Big Data, and working on solutions to make those technologies real for the enterprise.

He regularly speaks in person and virtually at industry group events, major conferences, Code Camps, and SQL Saturday events on strategic and technical topics. He has co-authored white papers and books on business Intelligence, among other topics.

Prior to his work with Pragmatic Works, Adam garnered extensive technical and managerial experience in industries including automotive, manufacturing, software, education, security, and retail. He has delivered high-performance, highly available systems as well as niche specialty systems for a variety of clients around the world. These systems deliver critical operations and analytics for firms like Toyota Motor Company, Dealer Track, American Auto eXchange, NASDAQ, Goldman Sachs, Deutsche Bank, Clipper Wind Power, Rayonier, and Microsoft.

About the Contributor

Dan English, is a Microsoft SQL Server MVP and the Business Intelligence Practice Manager at Superior Consulting Services in Minneapolis, MN. He has been developing with Microsoft technologies since 1996 and has focused on data warehousing and business intelligence since 2004. Dan has presented for the Minnesota SQL Server user group, the Microsoft Minnesota BI user group, Minnesota TechFuse, along with SQL Server and SharePoint Saturday events. He is also an avid blogger and tweeter.

Dan holds a Bachelor of Science degree in Business Administration from Minnesota State University Mankato. He is an MCITP: Business Intelligence Developer 2005 and 2008, a Microsoft Certified Technology Specialist (MCTS) for Microsoft SQL Server Business Intelligence—Implementation and Maintenance, and also Microsoft Office SharePoint Server 2007—Configuring.

Dan and his wife Molly live in Minnesota and have two children, Lily and Wyatt.

About the Technical Editors

Kathi Kellenberger, is a Senior Consultant with Pragmatic Works. She enjoys speaking and writing about SQL Server and has worked with SQL Server since 1997. In her spare time, Kathi enjoys spending time with family and friends, running, and singing.

Shawn Harrison, is an experienced BI trainer and developer for Pragmatic Works. He has extensive experience in in SSIS, SSRS, and computer networking technologies. He has helped hundreds of customers with SSIS, architecting, and developing solutions. Shawn contributes to the SQL Server community and has presented at community events around the country.

Credits

Executive Editor
Robert Elliott

Project Editor
Tom Dinse

Technical Editors
Kathi Kellenberger
Dan English
Shawn Harrison

Production Editor
Daniel Scribner

Copy Editors
Nancy Sixsmith
Charlotte Kughen

Editorial Manager
Mary Beth Wakefield

Freelancer Editorial Manager
Rosemarie Graham

Associate Director of Marketing
David Mayhew

Marketing Manager
Ashley Zurcher

Business Manager
Amy Knies

Production Manager
Tim Tate

Vice President and Executive Group Publisher
Richard Swadley

Vice President and Executive Publisher
Neil Edde

Associate Publisher
Jim Minatel

Project Coordinator, Cover
Katie Crocker

Compositor
Maureen Forys,
Happenstance Type-O-Rama

Proofreader
James Saturnio, Jennifer Bennett,
Word One

Indexer
Johnna VanHoose Dinse

Cover Image
Ryan Sneed

Cover Designer
Andrew Donaldson

Acknowledgments

I'd first like to thank Christina Leo (`@christinaleo`) for her help in creating this book—her aid in crafting an understandable chapter was invaluable. I'd also like to thank Dan English for stepping in at the last minute to help us get the book finished on time—a true life-saver. Finally, Matt Horn (`@maxui`) and Andrew Donaldson, for their contributions on the HTML5 code and visualizations.

—Mark Stacey

I want to thank my team at Pragmatic Works and the incredible SQL Server community that drives this spirit of learning. That spirit provides the market for books like these and for opportunities for those of us who want to write to deliver collective knowledge in a beautiful format like this new full color book. A special thanks to our team at Wiley—Bob Elliot, Tom Dinse, and all the publishing and marketing folks who make this possible. Lastly, thanks to Mark and Joe for letting a reformed DBA tag along on this amazing project. Thanks guys!

—Adam Jorgensen

No worthwhile effort is accomplished without the loving support of so many important people. I wish to extend my most sincere gratitude to my Lord and Savior who challenges and inspires me to be mindful of the greater good. My family, wife Linda and two sons Andrew and Matthew, deserve mention for their loving commitment through some challenging times when they would prefer to have me around for family activities rather than writing for yet another technology book. Mark Stacey and Adam Jorgensen were fantastic co-authors and were largely responsible for ensuring this book meets our high expectations. Lastly, thanks for the top-notch efforts of all the managers, editors, reviewers, and without whom our efforts would be less than the stellar results that have been achieved.

— Joe Salvatore

Contents

Introduction

Visualization, both in the form of traditional business intelligence (BI) and as infographics (such as those of *The New York Times*) has become a vital part of communication in business, in the media, and in government.

Much work has been done on the art and science of visualization, and just as much has been done on specific technology implementations. However, less work has been done on the intersection between these, making it difficult to choose the best tool to implement a specific visualization. *Visual Intelligence: Microsoft Tools and Techniques for Visualizing Data* bridges this gap, helping you to choose the right visualization and the right tool to implement the visualization, and then to guide you in the best way to implement that visualization.

OVERVIEW OF THE BOOK AND TECHNOLOGY

This book focuses on the Microsoft platform. With the ubiquity of Microsoft products such as Excel, and to a smaller extent SQL Server and SharePoint, almost everyone has access to a Microsoft tool. Indeed, anyone working on a Windows PC can freely download SQL Server Express and gain access to Reporting Services.

The biggest challenge in the Microsoft BI platform is the spread of the capabilities across the platform. With products from the SQL team and the Office team often overlapping, it can be challenging to know when to use one tool as opposed to another, and there is often a tendency to try to make just one tool (most commonly Excel!) fit all use cases. In this book, you find out how to avoid this pitfall and choose the correct tool for the task at hand.

HOW THIS BOOK IS ORGANIZED

In order to visualize data, you need to understand why visualization is a good representation of the data. This involves a good understanding of the data you are analyzing, a good understanding of which visualizations are appropriate, and an in-depth knowledge of what your toolset is capable of representing visually. Part 1 of this book starts with a review of the history and science of visualization, explaining what research has discovered about human perception, and how this science can be applied to building a visualization.

Part 2 explains how to bring data into the platform to do visualizations. Building on the basics covered in Part 1, we give you an overview of the capabilities of the Microsoft platform and dive into the shortcomings that can be solved using custom code. We take some time to explain the place of Silverlight and how it is being changed with the advent of HTML5, and we show you an approach that enables you to build for either platform. We also discuss the future of Microsoft user interface (UI) technologies using XAML.

The real value of the book is in Part 3. Each chapter in the part explains a particular family of visualizations, starting with the science behind the visualization and what types of data it is appropriate for. This section of the book is appropriate for any person regardless of the technology he is using. The part continues by helping you choose the best technology on the Microsoft stack; we provide practical real-world implementations along with code samples.

PART 1: INTRODUCTION TO DATA VISUALIZATION

Chapter 1 introduces the concept of visualization, and differentiates between data-driven visualization and infographics. It also discusses the place of 3D.

Chapter 2 talks about designing a visualization, and what techniques need to be applied as you decide what effects to use.

PART 2: MICROSOFT'S TOOLSET FOR VISUALIZING DATA

Chapter 3 discusses the Microsoft toolset and introduces you to the various tools.

Chapter 4 explains the basics of building a data set to support your visualization.

Chapter 5 discusses the tool everyone loves (or loves to hate)—Excel. It also covers the data-processing tool embedded in Excel 2013: PowerPivot,

Chapter 6 introduces the new data exploration tool called Power View.

Chapter 7 covers the dashboarding and performance management tool called PerformancePoint.

In **Chapter 8** you get an introduction to Reporting Services.

Chapter 9 covers the custom code development tools—the future of Silverlight (or lack thereof) is covered, followed by HTML5, and building web services to supply datasets.

PART 3: VISUAL ANALYTICS IN PRACTICE

Chapter 10 focuses on scorecards and indicators; it explains how you can use them to monitor your business.

In **Chapter 11**, you find out how to analyze data that changes over time.

Comparing data points is one of the fundamentals of visualization, and in **Chapter 12** you work through the different ways of doing so.

Chapter 13 covers a subject that has been at the core of many BI tools—slice and dice, also called ad hoc analytics.

Chapter 14 covers a visualization that has become much more important in the modern world of social media: relationship analysis.

In **Chapter 15**, we cover the art of embedding visualizations in tables.

Chapter 16 talks about visualizations that are not covered in depth in this book. Many of the visualizations are very useful, but they are not built into the Microsoft toolset.

Appendix A is a cheat-sheet to help you choose a visualization tool based on the visual you want to achieve.

Appendix B is a DAX (Data Analysis Expressions) function reference. DAX is used by both PowerPivot and the Tabular mode of Analysis Services, and you will find it is greatly useful for data analysis.

WHO SHOULD READ THIS BOOK

The target reader for this book is a data professional who needs to present data. By *data professional* we mean anyone who works with data—from sales managers and accountants to BI professionals.

The primary audience is people with a moderately technical inclination who are comfortable learning new technologies and/or adding to the understanding they already have of the technologies. A basic knowledge of Excel will suffice for many of the implementation examples, and this book starts by introducing you to new tools.

The secondary audience is those people who, despite not implementing any visualizations themselves, need to understand how to choose a visualization, such as journalists who need to present data to their readers. This audience includes business analysts who need to know what visualizations to choose for development, and anybody who reads modern publications, consumes infographics, and needs to know how to interpret them.

INDUSTRY AND TECHNOLOGY TRENDS

BI, and its front-facing discipline visualization, is changing from a back-office activity of mega-corporates to a mainstream activity conducted by small companies, bloggers, journalists, and departments in a company. This has been partly driven by a change in the world to a data-driven culture and is driven partly by an improvement in the tools—both in capabilities and in affordability.

There are two major changes in the technology space that inspired this book: One is Microsoft specific, and the other is a general sea change. The release of Microsoft SQL Server 2012 is a driving force for end-user adoption. Data integration visualization tools, in the form of PowerPivot and Power View, are coming to the less technical end user for the first time. In the world as a whole, the adoption of a standard web-based technology, HTML5, for the presentation of highly interactive user interfaces, has led to the wholesale adoption of more interactive data graphics, which are automatically cross-platform.

Both of these changes allow more people to implement data visualization, but they also require some re-education on the part of existing implementers.

TOOLS YOU NEED

This book covers the entire Microsoft stack, and different tools are shown throughout. You don't need any of the tools listed in the following sections to understand the material that's presented in the book, but the implementation examples do require them.

VERSIONS

Excel is the most important tool, and the examples shown are all built in Excel 2013. Most of the implementation samples work with Excel 2010, and a good portion also work with Excel 2007.

The PowerPivot add-in is required for Excel 2010. Excel 2007 requires an Analysis Services instance from SQL 2012 because PowerPivot is not available for that version of Excel. Excel 2013 requires the Professional Plus Edition to use PowerPivot.

SQL Server 2012 is used for the Reporting Services component, as well as for the databases that contain the data—both SQL databases and Analysis Services. SQL Server 2008 R2 Reporting Services can do most of the visualizations listed, but 2012 is required to install any of the samples.

The PerformancePoint examples require SharePoint 2010 Enterprise Edition, but they work without modification in SharePoint 2013.

EXCEL AND POWERPIVOT

Excel has always been the world's foremost data-analysis tool for the end user, and with the advent of the PowerPivot add-in it has become even stronger. We work primarily on Excel 2013 (with and without PowerPivot), but we highlight when a particular visualization also works on earlier versions. Most of the work in PowerPivot will be possible in Excel 2010 as well.

POWER VIEW

Power View is part of the SQL Server 2012 release, and it's also embedded in Excel 2013. PowerView's greatest attraction is its integration of animation components to show changes over time.

REPORTING SERVICES

Reporting Services is the reporting tool provided with SQL Server. It focuses primarily on the developer market. With rich customization abilities, in some ways it's the most powerful of the Microsoft visualization tools, but it comes with a commensurately steep learning curve.

SQL SERVER ANALYSIS SERVICES (MULTIDIMENSIONAL AND TABULAR MODELS)

Writing SQL queries to access data is not something the average person wants to do. Analysis Services provides a user-friendly layer as well as query acceleration that makes developing visualizations a quick and easy process.

SQL Server Analysis Services (SSAS) comes in two flavors: multi-dimensional (MDM) and tabular (BISM or Business Intelligence Semantic Model). The multi-dimensional model has not changed significantly from SQL 2008 to 2008R2 and 2012, so all code samples provided work in SQL 2008. Tabular is a new version released with 2012, and so SQL 2012 is required for those examples.

SHAREPOINT TECHNOLOGIES: PERFORMANCEPOINT AND EXCEL SERVICES

Excel Services is the web-based version of Excel, and as such all Excel Services discussions are the same as Excel.

PerformancePoint is the dedicated monitoring and analysis tool provided in SharePoint, and forms a large component of this book.

CUSTOM CODE: C#, SILVERLIGHT, XAML, AND HTML5

There are some places where the Microsoft toolset falls short. In those cases, you have to write some code. The book covers the use of non-Microsoft HTML5 libraries such as InfoVis. These sections are explicitly highlighted, and you can skip them if you're part of the non-developer audience.

The custom code samples used in the book cover several different technologies, and we include a discussion of the strengths and weaknesses of each technology. A chapter on the future of Silverlight (and the presentation language called XAML that is used both for Silverlight and other Microsoft presentation technologies) with the advent of HTML5 is included in the book, along with guidance to help you future-proof against the changeover from Silverlight to HTML5.

C# is covered as a way of providing a data provider to front end-only technologies such as Silverlight/HTML5, and for a code sample we provide a generic version that you can use for any of the visualizations in this book.

WHAT'S ON THE WEBSITE

Data for the implementation examples that you will work through have all been obtained from the Organization for Economic Development (OECD) at `http://stats.oecd.org/`. The data samples have been provided in SQL database form, as Analysis Services backups, and PowerPivot workbooks.

We have provided finished versions of all implementation examples.

In addition, code samples for the C# web service and the HTML5 visualizations are included in more detail than covered in the book.

The data sets, implementation examples, and code samples are available from this book's page at `www.wiley.com/go/visualintelligence`.

PART I

INTRODUCTION TO DATA VISUALIZATION

In this part

CHAPTER 1

Fundamentals of Visualization

When we talk about visualizing data, it is important to understand that any representation of data other than simple text is visualization. The very first visualization was a tabular representation of numbers, and tables are still a very powerful visualization—indeed the most common. Tables, however, are not the most appropriate visualization for every type of data—visualizations such as bar, column, and line charts; scorecards and key performance indicators; network maps; and custom graphics drawn by an illustrator are all visualization techniques that, when used appropriately, convey the meaning of data better than a simple table.

This book explores the different visualization types and, more importantly, how to choose a visualization based on the data you have.

These explanations apply to any business intelligence application, but we perform implementation examples using the Microsoft stack—starting with Excel, the world's most widely used Business Intelligence (BI) tool and then covering the entire toolset. We also explore the new world of custom visualization techniques using HTML5.

This book is divided into three parts: this first part introduces you to the subject of visualization; the second part introduces you to the tools you will use; and in the third part, you dive deeply into the individual visualizations, learning when to use them, which tool to use, and how to build them using the appropriate tools.

In this first chapter, you learn how to differentiate between *data visualization* and *artistic visualization*. Each has its place, but it is important when presenting data to focus on data presentation and not just make the visualization presentation pretty. Typically, three-dimensional (3D) rendering is an example of choosing form over function, but it can be done right, with form properly serving function, and you will learn how.

THE FIRST VISUALIZATIONS

The very first visualizations (other than tables) were the time series and bar charts you are probably very familiar with. Although earlier versions exist, the art of line and bar charts was created in the form we are now familiar with by William Playfair in the late 1700s. Other related developments, such as the development of graph paper, also occurred in this time period. The invention of lithography aided the widespread adoption of visualizations, and new forms of visualization such as the pie chart soon followed. All these developments were paralleled by the huge strides taken in cartography, and the graphic techniques required to render these maps were used in the visualization space. William Playfair's first bar chart is shown in Figure 1-1.

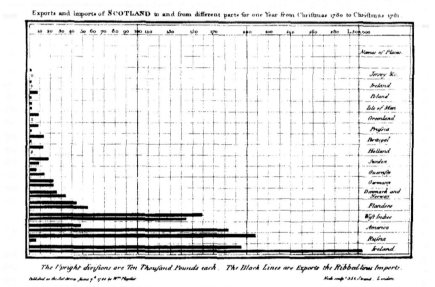

FIGURE 1-1   *The very earliest bar chart from William Playfair*

DATA VISUALIZATION VERSUS ARTISTIC VISUALIZATION

The goal of *data visualization* is to present data to either provide a more intuitive understanding of the data or show it in a way to view a large amount of data in a smaller area. *Artistic visualization* is designed to present a piece of data in a way that appeals to people and hence engenders interest in the data being presented.

There is obviously an overlap between these goals, but it is important when developing data visualizations to remember that the goal is to present data more meaningfully, not just to make it prettier.

Figure 1-2 shows an artistic visualization—it is exceptionally pretty, but it contains a minimal amount of data.

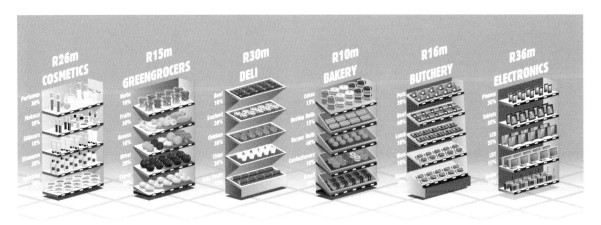

FIGURE 1-2 *An infographic where the pictures don't add value*

Figure 1-3 follows the same theme, but has been enhanced to be data rich. It shows how graphics can be used to enhance data presentation:

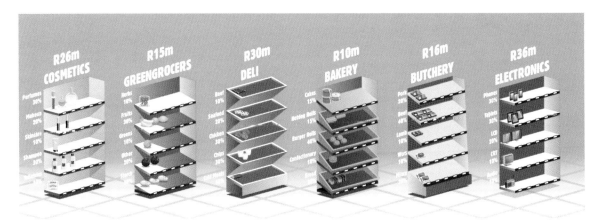

FIGURE 1-3 *The same infographic crafted as a data driven graphic*

Of course, as pretty as these graphics might be, they are very space-consuming. Figure 1-4 is a traditional BI chart showing the same data.

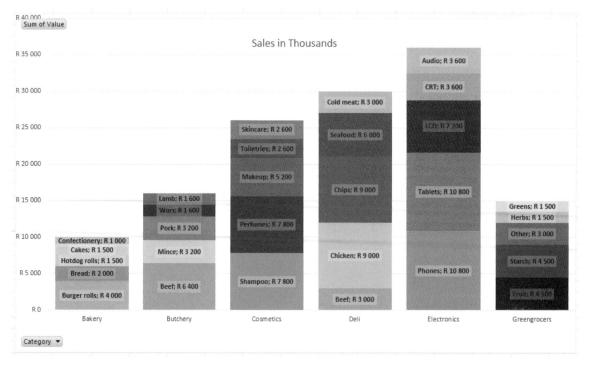

FIGURE 1-4 *A stacked bar chart*

Although not as flashy, this chart shows it's utility quite quickly: the different categories can be compared to each other at a glance, while still allowing for comparisons of the components of the categories. In addition, comparing cakes and pork in this graph, it is apparent that pork is a much bigger sale amount, although they are the same percentage of their category. Labels for the actual amounts have been added in lieu of percentages; either could be used, but comparing values is more meaningful for cross-category comparisons here.

Now that you have looked at these graphics, you should keep the following questions in your mind each time you develop a visualization:

- Does this visualization contain more data than an equivalently sized table?

- Is the data presented in this visualization easier to comprehend than an equivalent table?

- Do the artistic elements add meaning?

- Have I added any gratuitous elements that don't add meaning or distract from the meaning, such as 3D effects, animated transitions, or gratuitous images?

At the point of answering these questions, consider then whether you are producing an infographic or a data visualization.

THE PLACE OF INFOGRAPHICS

The distinction between an infographic and a visualization is a narrow one, but can be put simply as follows:

- An *infographic* is a graphic used to convey a message that is known before the creation of the infographic.
- A *data visualization* is a graphical aid used to discover a message buried in data.

It is clear from these definitions that a data visualization can be published as an infographic. But data visualizations are often interactive and dynamic, so if the message changes (for instance, the sales figures that are being reported on show a decrease from June to July), the data visualization updates automatically and shows the new figures. Whereas an infographic designed specifically around showing how well the sales team performed in June still shows the same figures because an infographic is typically simply a flat graphic.

The reason for flat and non-interactive infographics typically being the case is rather simple: infographics are often handcrafted one-offs, and the level of effort involved in creating a data visualization that performs image transforms similar to those done in a tool such as Photoshop can be challenging. However, this work is valuable because it means that an infographic does not become stale and out of date; it stays up to date as the data changes. (You read more about how to do this using HTML5 in Chapter 9 and throughout Part 3 of this book.)

To reiterate the questions mentioned previously: When you create a data visualization, you enable the discovery of answers through the data presented, and as such the data presentation should be as rich as possible.

USING 3D EFFECTIVELY

The use of three dimensions in visualization is a controversial topic. 3D effects are used in many ways: to add flash by creating an illusion of depth; as an additional dimension to represent another data point; and for representation of true 3D objects, such as machinery or topography. In this chapter, you learn how 3D can distort the meaning of your visualization. This applies to other types of visualization as well, so take care in any visualization that you do not create an equivalent distortion!

This section delves into the pitfalls of the various approaches used in charts and graphs, and goes through one of the approaches to solve the problem of parallax.

THE ILLUSION OF DEPTH

Figure 1-5 shows a typical Excel chart—and as you see, the default chart formatting leaves much to be desired. (You learn how to address many of Excel's formatting issues in later chapters.) The main issue with the 3D representation here is the distortion of the values: Compare June 2011 to October 2011, and work out whether they're the same. You need to look between September 2011 and November 2011, and May 2011 and July 2011. We deal with this particular flaw in the chart in later chapters.

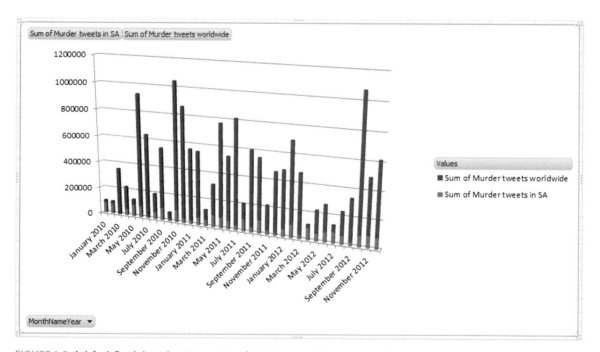

FIGURE 1-5 *A default Excel chart showing a misuse of 3D, distortion of figures by stacking values, and poor axis label choice*

Reading the values off this chart can be done by following the lines and thinking about them: they look fairly similar. But the top of the October column is slightly below on the image, so you could be forgiven for thinking October is about the same or a little more. It turns out that October is 2.64% less than June: 553849 versus 539566. You see this by carefully following the lines drawn above it, but it is not as intuitive as showing the columns starting from the same baseline.

An additional issue is that the height of the columns is also distorted. January 2010, with a value of 101586, has a height of 22 px; whereas December 2012, with a value of 618987, has a height of 132 px. The ratio of the values is 6.077, and the ratio of the heights is a ratio of exactly 6—a distortion of almost 8%!

It is clear that adding perspective in this manner must be approached with caution, if done at all.

ADDITIONAL DIMENSIONS

A better use of 3D is to show an additional dimension, as shown in the Excel graph displayed in Figure 1-6.

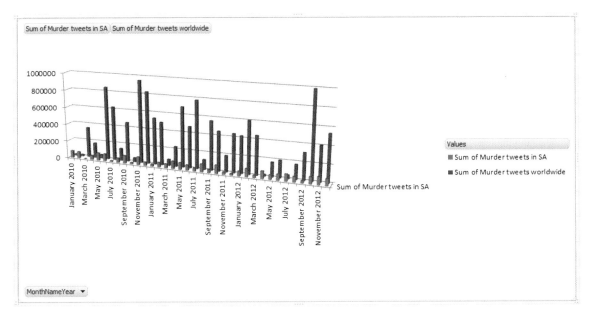

FIGURE 1-6 A better use of the third dimension

In this chart, the third dimension is being used to break up the numbers by the country dimension. Although it is better because the third dimension is no longer simply stacked and indeed carries data, this representation still carries all the flaws of the previous chart.

The solution in both of these cases is truly that three dimensions are not required to adequately represent the data points. A stacked bar chart in 2D is a better representation and is more efficient in terms of space. The third dimension would be great if it could be used in addition to stacking and add a dimension otherwise not present, but unfortunately, basic tools such as Excel do not allow for this functionality. In Excel, the one solution is to choose "Right angle axes" in the Rotation menu to get the chart shown in Figure 1-7.

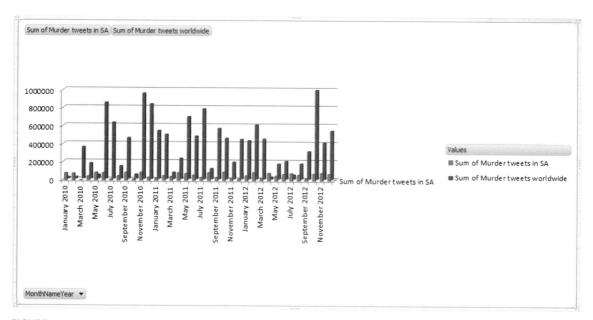

FIGURE 1-7 *Flattening out the chart*

A DESCRIPTION OF THE PROBLEM AND A PROPOSED SOLUTION

The reason why these distortions occur is that although an object is created in three-dimensional space, a further transform is applied to represent it on the two-dimensional screen on which we view it. This transform projects the edges of the 3D dimensional object against your screen, applying a shrinking factor to the height (as in the first example) and width to give a sense of perspective.

The solution in these examples is to provide a faux 3D transform—keeping the relationships of the heights to one another identical and distorting the shape to present a 3D view.

Figure 1-8 is an example of such a graphic on a country map. Note that the countries are extended vertically rather than in three-dimensional space.

The way the extension of the countries is achieved is through a transform—essentially each country is the base of a column graph, and as such the height of the country can be read as the height of a column.

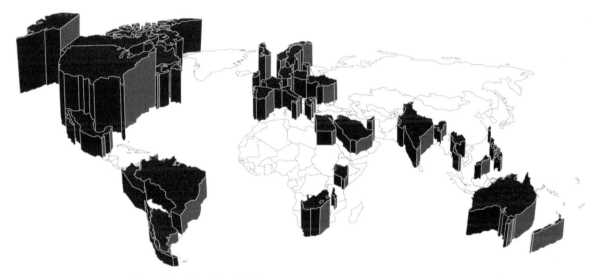

FIGURE 1-8 *A prism map illustrating a false 3D projection*

If you are using a tool with predefined three-dimensional transforms, I urge you to hesitate and think through the utility of using them before you apply them. They often add no value and also easily distort the values presented.

SUMMARY

In this chapter you learned to distinguish by their intended purposes between a data-driven graphic (a true visualization) and an infographic: visualizations enable you to discover facts in your data, whereas infographics are designed to communicate a message.

You also learned about one of the ways visualizations can misrepresent data, with the hope that you will apply this thinking to the visualizations you learn throughout this book. In Chapter 2 you learn the principles of choosing a specific visualization to match the type of data you are working with, to prepare you for the details that come the chapters that make up Part 3 of this book.

CHAPTER 2

Designing a Visualization

Designing visualization is not a simple case of picking one from the list that a tool supports. The right visualization conveys the right message, whereas the wrong visualization might confuse the message you are trying to send, or even convey the wrong message. An example of this is a 3D pie chart in which the 3D distortion shows one slice of a pie as the largest even though it isn't the biggest piece. Another example is a line chart that shows discrete values, such as murder rates, across countries but the interpolation between the countries makes no sense. Each visualization is covered in later chapters; this chapter shares the background of why you should choose different visualizations.

GOALS OF VISUALIZATION

The goal of a visualization is to make it possible to answer questions—even questions you didn't know you should be asking until you saw the pattern of the data in the visualization.

Example questions include:

- How are my sales figures trending over time?
- What is my most profitable product line?
- Who is the best sales person in the company?
- How does seasonality affect my stock levels?

Temporal analysis is the place where the advantages of visualization first become easily apparent. Someone reading two lines on a graph can predict where the lines will cross or diverge by glancing at the graph. (Read more in Chapter 11.)

Visualizations answer questions by highlighting patterns and outliers. For example, changing the color of an element that is significantly different from its neighbors, tracking the relationship of two lines over time, comparing two columns that are side by side are ways to graphically illustrate a pattern that may not be immediately apparent.

In Figure 2-1, an early chart of the "radar" or "polar" type, comparisons of causes of mortality are compared in the Crimean war. The red areas are used for war wounds, blue areas are for preventable diseases, with black for all other causes. It is immediately apparent that disease significantly outweighs any other cause of death on average. Indeed, barring September, war wounds are still outweighed as a cause of death by all other types.

The chart in Figure 2-1 easily illustrates, at a glance, a weighty amount of information. The chart visually describes how the deaths from war wounds grew and how quickly they grew, but it also shows how the increase in disease-related death outweighed the war deaths. Both causes of mortality grew earlier and carried on growing after the war wound deaths started decreasing.

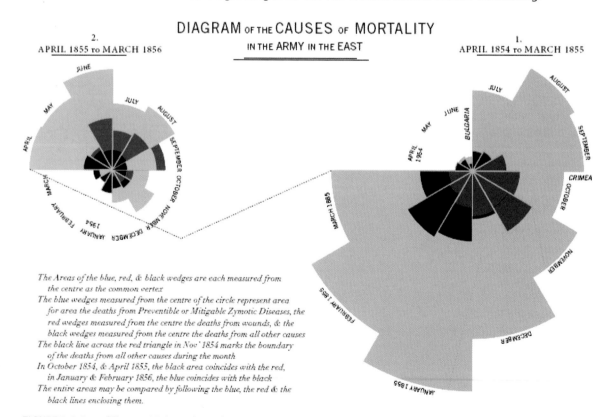

FIGURE 2-1 *One of Florence Nightingale's early charts*

However, as with many of the chart types developed prior to this, there are failings. Although the pattern of growth and decline is easy to see, the absolute values of the deaths are not easily discernible. Being able to quickly get to an absolute value that can be compared to other charts and data sources is a key goal of data visualization.

To summarize, the possible goals of visualization are

- To present more data than otherwise possible
- To illustrate patterns that are not immediately apparent
- To answer questions posed by a viewer
- To compare values
- To show changes over time
- To easily extract the underlying data points used
- To draw a viewer toward a visualization
- To create a quick mechanism to view a value

Visualizations such as these use color as a fundamental: it must be noted that this will not work as effectively for color-blind people, or when figures are printed in gray scale. In addition, a clearer indication of what each color indicates would be useful—the descriptions are embedded in the paragraph without a color key.

HUMAN PERCEPTUAL ABILITIES

Human visual perception is not as clear-cut as you might think. The perceptual difference in the size of a full moon just above the horizon versus the full moon directly overhead is the most commonly known instance of how an optical illusion can trick you. The moon is in fact the exact same size in terms of angular diameter, or what fraction of your visual field it takes up. Knowing and taking into account perceptual differences are key to creating visualizations that communicate the intended message.

You have already discovered how the use of 3D imagery in visualizations can be misleading—partly due to the technologies used to represent it and partly due to our perceptual abilities—but there are additional pitfalls you need to be aware of.

The most important pitfall is context—the shapes around a visualization may distort the message of the visualization. An extreme example is shown in Figure 2-2.

The two lines in Figure 2-2 are, in fact, the same length. Of course, you are unlikely to end up with such an extreme example in your visualization, but the use of a gradient background or a watermark could lead to more subtle, but just as misleading, misinterpretation. Using grid lines, as in Figure 2-3, aids the viewers' comprehension.

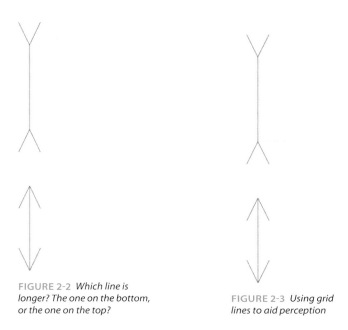

FIGURE 2-2 *Which line is longer? The one on the bottom, or the one on the top?*

FIGURE 2-3 *Using grid lines to aid perception*

Another key to human perception is choosing an unambiguous dimension upon which you show values. On the left in Figure 2-4, it is immediately apparent that we are measuring the difference in height. In the middle pair and on the right, it is immediately apparent that we are using angle. But which of these changes in the angles is equivalent to the left-hand change in the height?

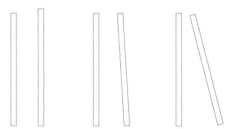

FIGURE 2-4 *Changes in angles versus changes in height*

Technically, either of them could be deemed equivalent. The right side is angled at 14.4 degrees from vertical, or 4 percent of 360 degrees, and the middle is angled 3.6 degrees, or 4 percent of 90 degrees. As it turns out, most people, whether due to training in school or a natural proclivity, tend to perceive the middle figure—represented as a percentage of the difference between vertical and horizontal—as closer in difference to the change in height.

A change in area in a column, as shown in these figures, is harder to read. The area in each of the three columns in Figure 2-5 are equivalent, and can be perceived as such after a little mental ninjitsu. At first glance, though, your eye rebels at seeing them as the same.

This difficulty comes in trying to equate change in two different dimensions with each other. A rect-angular shape is by far the easiest to do this with. Attempt to determine the relationships between the circular shapes in Figure 2-6 using area and not radius.

FIGURE 2-5 *Doubling and halving widths and heights to keep the areas the same*

FIGURE 2-6 *Evaluating the area of circles*

The answer may be surprising: the radii are 20, 28, 34, and 40. The areas, based on π * (radius squared) are 1256.63, 2463, 3631.38, and 5026.55.

Not an even stepping, but that is hard to pick up.

This problem is compounded with pie charts. Attempting to dissect a circle and determine the constituent percentages is even more difficult. You might be saying, "But we can use the angles to tell the difference!" Alas, although the human eye is skilled at judging the angle from vertical or horizontal, judging intermediate angles is something at which humans are not so skilled, as you can see from the examples in the figures. Read more on this issue in Chapter 12 about comparison visuals.

Use lengths and heights rather than area. Use straight lines and slopes rather than circles, except as markers.

STRATEGIC, TACTICAL, AND OPERATIONAL VIEWS

Strategic, tactical, and operational views have been around since the early days of military action. They reflect a real need for different levels of an organization to have a different type of view of the data flowing within that organization.

In any intelligence application—from the military uses in which the techniques evolved to the business intelligence (BI) applications you are more likely to be familiar with—the reason for having a view of data is to make a decision and/or take an action. The key difference among strategic, tactical, and operational views is the level of detail required in the view and the magnitude or importance of the decision being made.

In the retail world, an example strategic decision is the decision to open a new store. A decision like this is typically collaborative, with many people contributing to making the decision. A market research firm may be engaged to discover and compare the demographics of the possible areas in which the store could open; the Finance Department evaluates the cost of doing business in those areas and does profitability projections; and product managers supply their knowledge of what products would work well in each store. All of these data are collated and discussed. It takes some time, and—most likely—many meetings to make a decision to open a new store, but an organization does not usually have to make very many strategic decisions.

The other aspect of strategic views of data is monitoring. While the new store project is being evaluated, the CEO and other executives need to know, at a glance, that the business is still performing optimally, or at least adequately. The executives need to know which of the existing regions, and which stores within those regions, are doing poorly so that an intervention can occur immediately. The strategic view is at an aggregated level, and it offers the ability to drill into more details. See Figure 2-7 for an example.

An operational view, such as what's shown in Figure 2-8 on the other hand, is at a detailed level. For example, in the same retail organization, a credit controller at a store may be considering a request from a customer to get a credit extension for a specific purchase, and will run a report showing the customer's payment history and credit rating. The presentation style of this type of detailed data is typically very different from the high level view used in the strategic level. In direct contrast to strategic decisions, operational decisions are made frequently. Individually, they have very little effect on the organization, but in aggregate they spell the difference between success and bankruptcy.

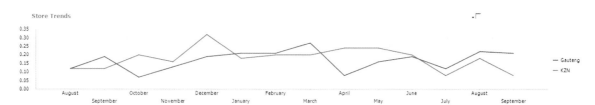

FIGURE 2-7 *An example of a strategic view with drill down*

FIGURE 2-8 *An example of an operational report*

Tactical decisions are the middleground between strategic and operational decisions. For the most part, in the preceding example scenarios, the decisions being taken into account and the data being monitored are known ahead of time; tactical decisions are often about data exploration more than just pure monitoring or evaluating a detail view. For instance, a product manager may need to decide which products need to be held in extra stock over the festive season. The product manager examines the product's sales data and its seasonality, and might also examine data from fashion labels that highlights which products will have strong marketing campaigns. The key here is more interactivity and flexibility than in the other views. Decisions and actions arising from tactical business intelligence (BI) typically sit between strategic and operational in terms of both their business impact and the quantity of them. An example of a tactical report is shown in Figure 2-9. This report provides an interactive view of sales and profit, broken down by month and by brand, and with a slicer for region. The view allows for additional analysis by changing each chart element according to the other chart elements that are clicked on—for instance, when clicking a particular brand, each column for the months will be split up by that brand. This is covered in more depth in Chapter 6.

The Microsoft business intelligence toolset loosely follows this model: PerformancePoint dashboards match to the strategic level; Excel, PowerPivot, and now Power View match to the data exploration of the tactical level; and Reporting Services is often used for operational-level reports. This correlation is not very strong and is explored further in Chapter 3.

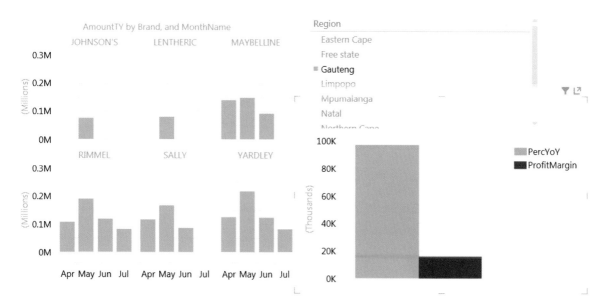

FIGURE 2-9 *An example of a tactical report being used for data exploration. Clicking on one chart or slicer will filter the other charts.*

GLANCE AND GO VERSUS DATA EXPLORATION

We've explored the use of monitoring (which can also be called glance and go), specifically for strategic views, and exploration specifically for tactical BI, but of course there is a large overlap. Strategic views can include exploration, and tactical views can include monitoring.

It's time to explore the different use cases. "Glance-and-go" BI, which is often called *monitoring* and is epitomized by colorful indicator icons, has for many years been the poster child of BI applications. Figure 2-10 shows an example with colorful indicators that are presented on a scorecard with drill-down and drill-across capabilities.

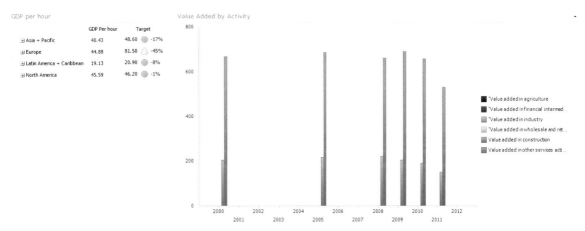

FIGURE 2-10 *An interactive scorecard, with indicators. Clicking on an indicator will filter the chart on the right.*

For a long time the use of vehicle-type gauges and dials, such as those shown in Figure 2-11, were immensely popular for a long time, but they're luckily fading into oblivion now. This format that resembled a vehicular dashboard seemed like an ideal way of showing business information in a manner that people were familiar with. However, a key failing of these types of dashboards were that they showed little information. A gauge is designed to show a continually changing figure, and it is ideal for continual monitoring; information such as speed, engine revolutions, and oil temperature are measured up to thousands of times per minute, and keeping an eye on a gauge is a good mechanism for viewing this velocity of data. However, business rarely changes this frequently; Indeed, much financial data is only relevant as of the last month end, and the gauge is a poor representation of this data.

Title	Sales Amount	Sales Quota	
European Sales Manager	$98,323	$117,000	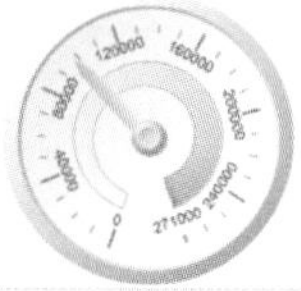
North American Sales Manager	$249,400	$271,000	
Pacific Sales Manager	$26,580	$33,000	

FIGURE 2-11 *An early example of a "gauge" in a dashboard. Note how only one number is communicated.*

Glance-and-go visualizations thus need to be at once "information dense" (or, to use another term, data rich) such that enough data are presented to enable a viewer to know whether more investigation is required, but sparse enough that the data do not overwhelm. A guided maximum of seven data points is suggested, with the extension that multiple axes of seven points can be used. For instance, you might have seven indicators each for Month-To-Date, Year-To-Date, and Year-over-Year. This would be viable in a scorecard, but depends on the visualization. Figure 2-12 shows a good example of a monitoring scorecard, including drill-down information.

Store Metrics

	Yesterday	Yesterday (LY)		Company	Rank (YD)	District	Rank (YD)	Wk To Date	Wk To Date (LY)		Month To Date	Month To Date (LY)		Year To Date	Year To Date (LY)	
⊞ Sales Amount	$7,162	$7,986	● -10%	●	53	●	5	$24,567	$28,375	● -13%	$101,685	$115,066	● -12%	$2,864,050	$2,926,156	● -1%
DSW Sales	$1,450	$908	● 60%	●	147	●	9	$2,863	$1,859	● 54%	$10,251	$11,643	● -12%	$294,367	$298,026	● -1%
⊞ Fab Finds Sales Amount	$585	$722	● -19%	●	47	●	5	$1,824	$1,116	● 64%	$7,550	$3,217	● 135%	$156,293	$52,363	● 198%
⊞ Clearance Sales Amount	$708	$275	● 158%	●	9	●	4	$2,038	$2,392	● -15%	$9,123	$11,083	● -18%	$385,854	$200,289	● 93%

FIGURE 2-12 *A scorecard with key performance indicators (KPIs) and time-based measures*

Glance-and-go visualizations are often accompanied by interactive elements. Drilling down on the KPIs to see what figures make up the number that is not meeting target and drilling across to a second element, such as a line chart, to give detail about how the KPI has trended over time are two of the most common. In addition, capabilities such as interactive slice and dice are often incorporated to aid discovery of the data behind the KPI. For instance, a retail organization analyzing poor sales in a region may want to drill down to a store that's performing particularly poorly, check the store's performance trend over the last year, and bring in a list of any marketing campaigns run in that store for that period.

NUMBER OF DATA POINTS IN A VISUALIZATION

The suggested number of data points in a visualization is four to seven. Of course, this doesn't mean that you should only have seven dates in a line chart; instead the limit is suggested so that you only have a maximum of seven series plotted over time. This limit applies to any kind of visualization and is based upon the human ability to keep only a certain number of items in focus at any given time.

Be careful not to confuse this data discovery portion of glance and go with data exploration!

The key difference between the data discovery based on glance-and-go visualizations is the intent. In glance and go, you know what question to ask—for instance, "Have sales targets been reached?"—and typically which follow-up questions need to be asked, such as the following:

- Which stores missed their sales targets?
- Which product categories are performing poorly?
- What marketing campaigns were run in that period?

In data exploration, the questions are unknown, and the visualization is explored until a pattern is discovered. The patterns to be discovered may be correlations such as similar products being bought together or seasonality of purchasing patterns.

USING COLOR IN VISUALIZATIONS

Preparatory to discussing the use of color in visualization, it's important to understand the way color is perceived in the human brain. Despite the popular education of red/green/yellow as primary colors, the three primary colors in the human eye, and not coincidentally, in the computer monitor are red/

green/blue, or RGB. Several things are important about the RGB encoding scheme for colors on computers:

- RGB does not adequately cover the spectrum of visible light. To test this, simply compare a photo of a sunset to the real sunset, and the differences between the two will be very apparent.

- Human perception of color is skewed. Red, green, and blue are the most readily perceived colors because they match to the cones in the eye, but not in direct proportion. Reds and greens are much stronger than blue, and the cones are more centered in the eye, whereas blue is more in the surrounding areas of the eye. This has led to the use of red and green in most indicators, mostly notably traffic lights.

- The differences between rods and cones in the eye are beyond the scope of this book, but a nice explanation is available at `www.cis.rit.edu/people/faculty/montag/vandplite/pages/chap_9/ch9p1.html`.

The default color schemes implemented by the Microsoft toolset can be problematic. Both Excel and Reporting Services allow for a great deal of control over the colors used, but PerformancePoint and Power View do not. The website `http://colorbrewer2.org/` (shown in Figure 2-13), gives great recommendations for different color scenarios.

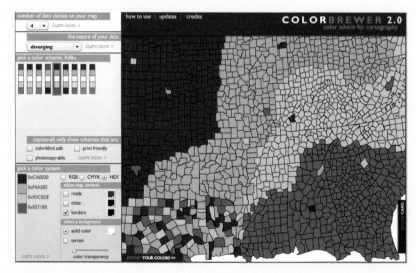

FIGURE 2-13 *Colorbrewer*

What should you use color for? Color can be used to highlight and separate different series, to show a value along an axis, or as a quick visual cue to show crossing a threshold.

Looking at Figure 2-14, you can see that differentiating between the series is relatively easy based on the use of colors.

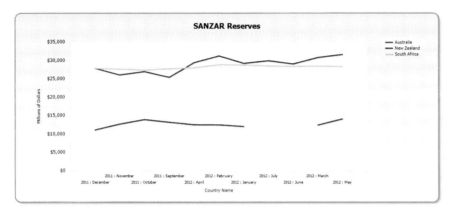

FIGURE 2-14 *Chart contrasting the 3 SANZAR countries' reserves over time*

Showing a value along an axis can take many forms, with shapes in forms such as heat maps, bubble charts, and geo-spatial maps. In all these cases, the color is used to indicate a value along a range, with the most common ranges being green ➤ yellow ➤ red, or blue ➤ orange ➤ red. Figures 2-15, 2-16, and 2-17 show these different charts.

It is important when choosing these color ranges to make sure that the number of colors chosen and the values being displayed are congruent. Choosing a four-color range when there are five different possible values easily leads to confusion when two disparate values are displayed using the same color.

In the same way, choosing the intervals between the colors is important. Having one value widely divergent while using an even interval, as in Figure 2-18, bunches up colors toward one end of the spectrum and possibly hides variances in the values. Figure 2-18 shows the five European countries with the highest national reserves, and Switzerland is much higher than the rest, which can't be distinguished by color.

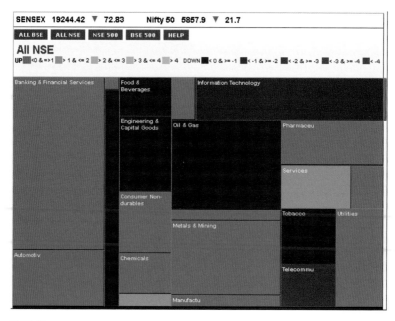

FIGURE 2-15 *Heat map example*

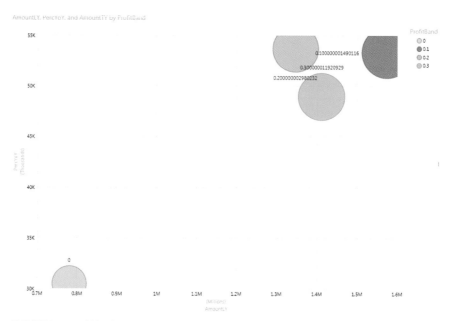

FIGURE 2-16 *Bubble chart example—color is based on profit margin, banded into ten percentiles*

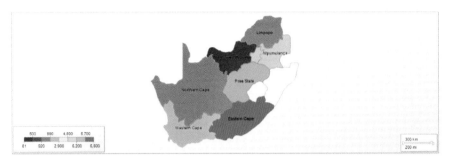

FIGURE 2-17 *Geo-spatial example*

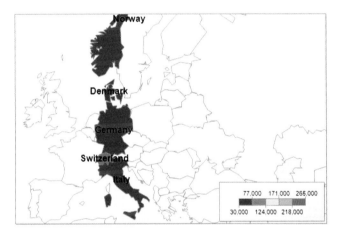

FIGURE 2-18 *Divergent values*

The solution in these cases is to choose intervals carefully and, knowing your data, apply a wider range to the first color. Figure 2-19 shows this approach with the same data. The variances are much clearer, and color has been used to rank the countries.

You can think of indicators as a subset of the display of colors along an axis, with predetermined shapes in a predetermined grid rather than colors on a map. The convention of red is bad; yellow is a warning; and green is good. Just red and green is very typical and should only be diverged from with much thought. One example of a divergence may be to show red for values less than last year, and black for values greater, which is a system that more closely matches accounting conventions. Figure 2-20 shows an example of a scorecard using red/yellow/green for figures against targets and red and black for values against the previous year.

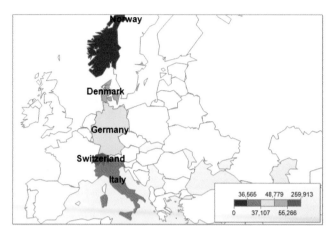

FIGURE 2-19 *A better spread*

	Sales This Month	Quota This Month		Sales Last Month		Sales LY This Month	
⊟ Sales		●		●		●	
⊞ Europe	$1,339	$1,099	◖ 22%	$1,396	◗ -4%	$460	● 191%
⊟ North America	$3,304	$2,190	◖ 51%	$2,825	● 17%	$2,096	● 58%
⊞ Canada	$833	$406	● 105%	$527	● 58%	$513	● 62%
⊟ United States	$2,470	$1,758	◖ 40%	$2,298	● 7%	$1,583	● 56%
Central	$317	$312	◖ 2%	$324	◗ -2%	$231	● 38%
Northeast	$220	$258	△ -15%	$183	● 20%	$179	● 23%
Northwest	$782	$174	● 349%	$746	● 5%	$182	● 330%
Southeast	$220	$248	△ -11%	$234	◗ -6%	$230	◗ -4%
Southwest	$931	$709	● 31%	$811	● 15%	$761	● 22%
⊞ Pacific	$600		◇	$460	● 31%	$206	● 191%

FIGURE 2-20 *A scorecard using colored shapes to indicate performance*

USE OF PERSPECTIVE AND SHAPE

Perspective and shape may appear different, but in the two-dimensional world of visualization, shape is the only way to show perspective, and thus we treat them as the same.

There are many ways to use shape in visualizations. The one you will be most familiar with is to use the shape of an object as it appears in the physical world as a representation. Examples of this are the use of shapes of countries as used in maps, representing real objects in infographics as well as the 3D representation of objects, or using an object as a metaphor for a size. Figure 2-21 shows an example of using the height of buildings to represent a measure. An interactive version of this is available at www.pwinfographics.net.

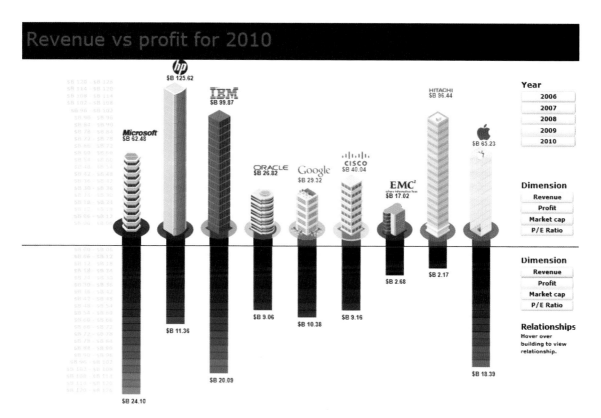

FIGURE 2-21 *A column chart implemented using buildings instead of columns*

Other ways of using shapes in visualizations are similar to the ways you can use color: as ways to differentiate between series; as ways to illustrate a point along an axis; or as a quick way to differentiate crossing a threshold. Figures 2-22, 2-23, and 2-24 show an example of each of these.

Although this seems similar to the use of color, it's important to note that the number of discrete values, often called the set of domain values, which is available to us when using shapes is much less than when using colors. For instance, the human eye struggles to differentiate between a septagon (seven sides) and a nonagon (nine sides), whereas nine different shades of green are easy to differentiate. The number of different shapes that allow for ranges—such as equilateral polygons, stars, and crosses—is also much smaller than the number of colors.

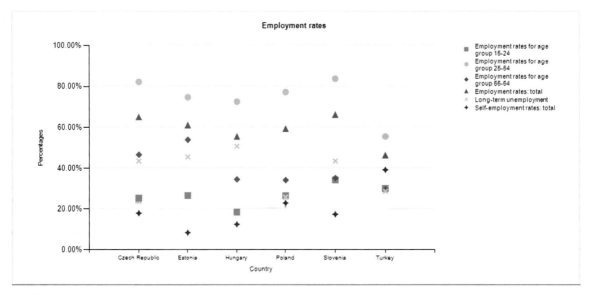

FIGURE 2-22 *A scatterplot using different shapes for each set of values. The use of both color and shape is useful.*

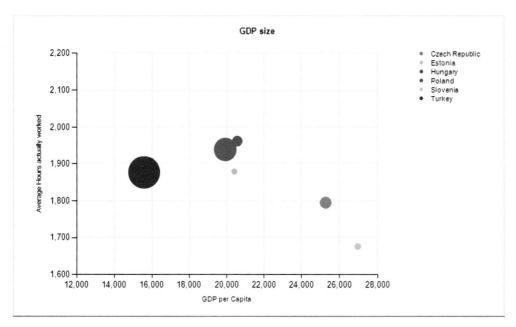

FIGURE 2-23 *A bubble chart using the size of the bubbles to show the magnitude of the visualized values*

Activity Progress Table

Actions ▾ ⟳   ⏮ ◀ 1   of 1 ▶ ⏭   ⇩   FindNext 100% ▾ ⊞

Key

Target Date   ★

Achieved Milestone   ✓

Past Completion Date   ❗

STP8.1.1 : Upgrading households in informal settlements with access to secure tenure and basic services
ACT8.1.1.1 : Activity 8.1.1.1

Milestone Name	Target Date	2010/11				2011/12				2012/13			
		Q1	Q2	Q3	Q4	Q1	Q2	Q3	Q4	Q1	Q2	Q3	Q4
Identification and categorisation of informal settlements in all provinces	2011/03/31 ❗	50%	50%	50%	★ 30%								
9 confirmed provincial project lists	2011/03/31 ❗			10%	★ 30%								
Assess existing projects for compliance against delivery agreement target	2011/03/31	0%	★ 5%										
Confirm pipeline of new and existing projects	2011/03/31		★ 20%										
Planning, land acquisition and service provision to 20000 households	2011/03/31		★ 10%										
Planning, land acquisition and service provision to 100000 households	2012/03/31 ✓		216%						★				
Planning, land acquisition and service provision to 140000 households	2013/03/31		0%									★	
Planning, land acquisition and service provision to 140000 households	2013/06/01		0%										

FIGURE 2-24 *Ticks and exclamation points used to show crossing a threshold*

Sizes, on the other hand, are much easier to comprehend, but you must take care in how the sizes are represented. The use of area versus diameter to represent sizes could be challenging to read. Look at Figure 2-26 for two values that are 25 percent apart, using diameter and area. Which looks most like a 25 percent increase?

It is a good idea to indicate what differentiator you have used when it is ambiguous. If you have bars increasing in one dimension only—for example, the lengths are changing—it is not necessary to state what differentiating characteristic you are using, but when a circle's size is increasing, visually indicating which dimension is being used is helpful to a user.

FIGURE 2-25: *Doubling a circle by diameter versus doubling by area*

SUMMARY

In this chapter you learned about the elements to consider when choosing and designing your visualization, balancing illustrating data by using color and shape. This knowledge will be used as the basis of the chapters in Part 3 of this book, guiding you to choosing a specific visualization.

PART II

MICROSOFT'S TOOLSET FOR VISUALIZING DATA

In this part

CHAPTER 3

The Microsoft Toolset

Microsoft was a late entry to the visualization market. Although it had a strong and early entry to the online analytical processing (OLAP) market, for the most part it relied on third-party vendors to do the front-end work and focused in the early days on the database work, allowing vendors such as Panorama and Proclarity to take the lead. More recently, as Microsoft wanted to take more control of the market, it started to develop and buy more of the front-end toolset. Microsoft's purchase of Proclarity and later Report Builder marked a strong entry into the front-end market, but it was paralleled by a strong independent entry in the form of both strengthening the Excel visualization tools and developing a tool called Business Scorecard Manager (BSM), which evolved into PerformancePoint and was eventually subsumed into SharePoint as PerformancePoint services. Reporting Services, originally aimed squarely at the technical user from a developers' point of view, has evolved into a self-service tool aimed at the business user. In this chapter, you find out about the history of the Microsoft toolset and discover how each tool fits in the tool bag.

Microsoft purchased Report Builder 1 from Active View, and later purchased a product called Radius from 90 degree software that became part of Report Builder 2.

A BRIEF HISTORY

The history of Microsoft's business intelligence (BI) toolset is in two parts: the history of the analytic tools is first and begins with Microsoft's purchase of the OLAP engine from Panorama, which happened in 1996. In the initial days, Microsoft focused on building SQL Server, and allowing third-party vendors such as Panorama and Proclarity to build the front-end tools. The chart in Figure 3-1 shows the release versions for each analytic database. It's important to note that even the analytic databases embedded in SharePoint and in Office are in fact developed by the SQL team and, more importantly, require a separate installation. Read more about the evolution of these products in the "Database Tools" section.

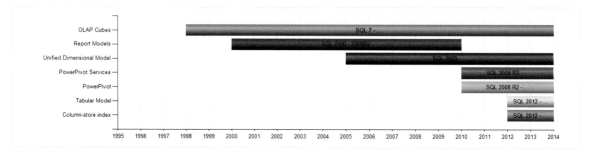

FIGURE 3-1 *A timeline of the Microsoft backend tools*

Development of the front-end toolset started much later, and it has a much more diverse path. Figure 3-2 shows the introduction timelines and evolution of each tool currently available from Microsoft.

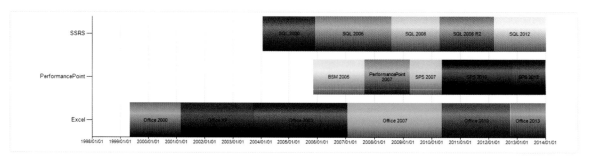

FIGURE 3-2 *A timeline of the Microsoft front-end toolsets currently in use.*

CRYSTAL REPORTS

Although you might be thinking that Crystal Reports has been omitted, it is not truly a Microsoft BI product. It did come bundled with Visual Studio for several versions, but Crystal Reports was always a non-Microsoft reporting solution. It is currently owned by SAP/Business Objects.

Excel introduced pivot charts in Office 2000. Pivot charts are hardly true BI, yet they are quite likely the single most prevalent subset of BI. With the ability to connect to cubes in Analysis Services, this combination of tools was truly the first Microsoft BI stack.

The next entrant to the BI field was Reporting Services. Released as an add-on to SQL 2000 in 2004, Reporting Services was aimed squarely at the developer demographic; it required that you have Visual Studio and a fair degree of technical expertise. Reporting Services served as replacement for the venerable Crystal Reports.

Both Excel and Reporting Services have kept their names but, as discussed in the following paragraphs, the dashboard toolkit has had a much more checkered history. One caveat: Reporting Services now includes Power View, a break from the earlier naming.

Business Scorecard Manager (BSM) was the first iteration of this tool. It provided the ability to connect to multiple types of data sources, and incorporated Key Performance Indicator tools (read Chapter 10 for more details), as well as some graphing capabilities. Much like PerformancePoint today, much of the power of BSM 2005 was only provided when connecting to Analysis Services as a backend.

PerformancePoint 2007 was Microsoft's foray in the world of Enterprise planning. With three different products (each with its own installation) sold as a single product at a fairly hefty price point (by Microsoft standards—it was well priced compared to the competition), Microsoft struggled to sell massive volumes of this product. The three products were PerformancePoint Monitoring (the predecessor to PerformancePoint services that is discussed heavily throughout this book), PerformancePoint Planning, and Proclarity.

PROCLARITY

Proclarity, a major third-party solution provider, was bought by Microsoft in April 2006 and sold as part of PerformancePoint 2007. The product line was discontinued along with PerformancePoint planning.

The planning product was deemed too complex for most organizations because it required multiple skills across various Microsoft technologies, and the product was deemed too expensive to obtain solely to have PerformancePoint. Consequently, Microsoft started bundling PerformancePoint with the SharePoint 2007 Enterprise license from April 2009. This move, although derided by those who had implemented the planning product, was a good one for the monitoring toolset.

The SharePoint 2010 release incorporated PerformancePoint Services as a baked-in service application, making administration and installation much easier.

SharePoint 2013 adds theming and makes administering security simpler.

The tool history in Table 3-1 gives some highlights the released feature set. With Excel especially, this is a small subset of the changes.

TABLE 3-1 Tool history

TOOL	VERSION	FEATURES ADDED
PerformancePoint	BSM	Initial release
PerformancePoint	2007	Dashboard Designer with Office Ribbon
		Click-once client install
		Drag-and-drop design
		Multiply connected filters
		Analytic charts and grids
		Scorecard aggregation formulae
PerformancePoint	2010	Pie charts
		Multimetric (multiple column) KPIs
		Decomposition tree
		Content integration into SharePoint
		Connect to SharePoint filters
		Dynamic hierarchies with drill down/up
		Dynamic selections
		Time intelligence
		Calculation engine
		Value filtering
		Reusable filters
PerformancePoint	2013	SharePoint theming
		Kerberos not required for role-based security
Excel	2000	Pivot charts
Excel	XP	Task panes
Excel	2003	Lists
		Auto filter
		SharePoint integration
		New statistical functions
Excel	2007	Ribbon UI
		1 million-row workbooks
		XML format
		Lists upgraded to tables
		Conditional formatting limits raised from three
		Unlimited color pallet

TOOL	VERSION	FEATURES ADDED
Excel	2010	Slicers
		PowerPivot available as an add-in
		Sparklines
		64-bit Excel (essential for big PowerPivot workbooks)
		Faster conditional formatting
Excel	2013	PowerPivot built in
		Power View built in
		Recommended charts
		FlashFill
SSRS	2000	Initial release
SSRS	2005	DatePicker
		Multi-value parameters
		Report sorting of data
		XML Data provider
		64 bit
		Report Builder 1 and Report Models (*Note:* RB1 and RB2 are actually different products, not versions of one product)
SSRS	2008	Report Builder 2 for self-service reporting
		Performance improvements
		Tablix
		Gauge
		Text formatting
SSRS	2008 R2	Shared data sets
		Report parts
		Integrated GIS capabilities
		Azure, PDW, and SharePoint List data sources
		Sparklines
		Indicators
		Atom rendering extension
		Aggregation expression enhancements
SSRS	2012	Alerts
		Power View

DATABASE TOOLS

Many people working in the SQL Server world don't understand the need for analytic databases. Especially in organizations with either small databases or really good SQL developers, some of the benefits are not immediately apparent.

The first benefit of analytic databases is related to performance, and this benefit is typically the one that blinds some SQL developers to the other benefits. SQL databases are really good at row-by-row work, but not as good at doing aggregations. Summary tables have often been used to solve the issue of aggregation, and OLAP was one approach to this.

OLAP

OLAP stands for Online Analytic Processing, coined in a 1993 white paper by Edgar F. Codd. The generic term for working with Multi-Dimensional Analysis (MDA) is cubes, but this has been mostly used to apply to OLAP cubes. There are subsets of OLAP: MOLAP is Multi-dimensional OLAP; and ROLAP is Relational OLAP, in which the queries are passed through to SQL; and Hybrid OLAP (or HOLAP) is a hybrid of the first two.

OLAP (and hence Microsoft's OLAP product, Analysis Services) provides performance benefits by aggregating data according to user defined hierarchies. For instance, the designer of the cube defines a date hierarchy as rolling up from Day to Month to Year (YMD), and the OLAP engine creates aggregations at each level—for example, summarizing sales for the day, for the month, and for the year. Other hierarchies across multiple dimensions such as the organization or location dimensions are also created and aggregated. This can lead to a problem called database explosion (where the size of the database increases exponentially), and thus needs a fair degree of skill to optimize.

Partitioning is another performance enhancement technique in Analysis Services. This works by splitting the data into partitions (for instance by region or by month), and then queries are optimized, either by reducing the size of the data to be queried when it exists within a single partition, or by allowing parallelization when the data is split across multiple partitions.

An alternative method for accelerating queries is to use a column store database. Whereas SQL is a row store and stores data in rows, pages, and extents, column stores instead store each column independently. This has benefits in terms of not having to scan over all the attributes of a row when scanning for large aggregations. It's a big benefit when a lot of attributes are present, as in a typical data warehouse scenario.

Figures 3-3 and 3-4 show the differences between a column store and a row store.

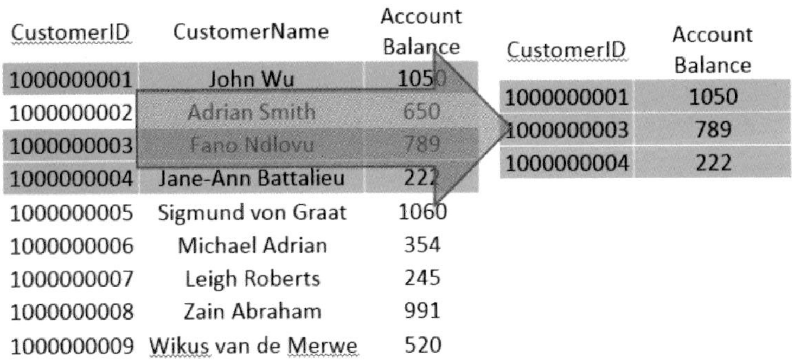

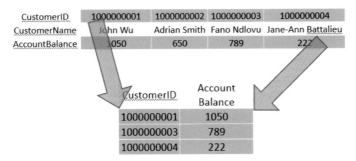

FIGURE 3-3 *How a row store selects data*

FIGURE 3-4 *How a column store selects data*

An additional benefit of column store databases is the compression that's achievable. As similar data is stored contiguously, both dictionary compression and run length encoding are successful techniques. Read more on this at Daniel Abadi's excellent paper, which you can find at `http://db.csail`
`.mit.edu/projects/cstore/abadi-sigmod08.pdf`.

Another key benefit of column store databases (as proven in the Abadi's paper, as well as in much other research) is that denormalization is not as necessary for performance reasons in a column store. This is the reason the latest version of Analysis Services has a "tabular" mode (or at least that it is called that).

The final reason for the Microsoft column store being so fast is that it is stored in memory.

With the advent of much better performance on SQL Server, including the introduction of a column store index that has all the benefits of the engine spoken that was previously described, the other benefits of using an analytic database become much more important.

The second benefit of analytic databases is the creation of what Microsoft once called a Unified Dimension Model, and now calls a Business Intelligence Semantic Layer. This layer abstracts the naming conventions of the underlying database and allows for meaningful, business-friendly naming, as well as abstracting the structures, aggregations, and calculations. The main benefit of this is that a single maintenance point is created. If the calculation of Net profit changes, it can be maintained in a single place and not have every single report require changes.

The third benefit of analytic databases rolls on from the second: Report writers and self-service users do not need to know the underlying structures or how to write SQL queries against them, nor do they need to know the calculations used. Instead, if they are working in a tool such as Excel, they can simply drag the Net profit measure onto a pivot table and then drag the location hierarchy onto the rows and have a basic report with drill-down capabilities.

In today's world, with the hardware capabilities available, the second and third benefits are often greater than the first—at least in the enterprise space that has a BI team.

In the organizations that don't have BI teams, an organization's ability to build its own "analytic databases" or cubes is important. This is where the tool PowerPivot comes in.

PowerPivot was first introduced as a downloadable add-in for Excel 2010 and an installable add-in for SharePoint (run from the SQL 2008 R2 install) called PowerPivot Services. The engine running underneath both of these is the Microsoft column store implementation then called VertiPaq—the same column-store you have just read about.

In the SQL 2012 release, these options were expanded to include an Analysis Services instance that doesn't require SharePoint. The engine was renamed xVelocity (a naming choice this particular author doesn't like—Vertipaq was a better name in my opinion). One of the biggest advantages of this shared engine across the tools is that a model can be designed in PowerPivot, shared across a team by saving to a SharePoint library, and then imported and optimized by importing into Visual Studio.

Table 3-2 summarizes the toolsets available for databases with SQL 2012.

TABLE 3-2 Toolset for databases as of SQL 2012

TOOL	ENGINE	QUERY LANGUAGE	NOTES
Analysis Services— Multi-dimensions	OLAP	MDX (DAX now supported)	Still has capabilities such as writeback, actions, and parent-child hierarchies that have yet to make it into tabular mode. In addition, the memory requirements are much lower.
Analysis Services—Tabular	xVelocity	DAX, MDX	Standalone xVelocity engine. Performance is great as long as workload fits in RAM, but massive degradation when paging starts to happen Distinct counts are much improved over SSAS-MD Quicker development time
PowerPivot Services	xVelocity	DAX, MDX	A tabular Analysis Services instance that is also connected to SharePoint
PowerPivot	xVelocity	DAX, MDX	An instance of the xVelocity engine inside Excel, with a backup of the database stored inside Excel. This backup can be extracted and restored to an SSAS tabular instance
Column Store Indexes	xVelocity	SQL	An instance of the xVelocity engine running as a non-clustered index on SQL Server. As of SQL 2012 SP1, these are non-updateable (they need to be rebuilt for any changes) and can't be clustered.

THE PLACE OF EACH FRONT-END TOOL

Chapter 2 introduced the concept of strategic, tactical, and operational views, with a statement that the tools loosely match to the following concepts:

- PerformancePoint is the strategic tool, allowing for monitoring of business metrics and some analysis when the values are out of band.

- Excel is the tactical tool for data exploration. It is split into two pieces, with PowerPivot being the data integration tool, and Power View being the visualization tool.

- Reporting Services fits in as the operational tool, showing detailed data.

In reality, this view is off-kilter, with quite a lot of overlap.

Historically, these tools were developed by different teams within Microsoft, which is why there's some overlap. Table 3-3 shows the differences in the tools.

TABLE 3.3 Front-end tools

TOOL	PROS	CONS
PerformancePoint	Scorecards: High-level overview, drill down Analytics : Interactive	Not totally customizable
SSRS	High fidelity Advanced visualizations Drill down/drill through—can be dynamic, requires more work	Interactivity requires work and even then is limited
Excel/Excel Services	Fully customizsable High fidelity	Loses fidelity in Excel Services Not as interactive with other SharePoint components
Power View	Very interactive—data exploration Animations	Not a great deal of control over visualizations Requires a model for visualizations Gimmicky GUI

It is very important to keep in mind that each tool has its place. It is not the case that an organization will only choose a single tool and implement everything on it. This is commonly the case with either Excel or Reporting Services as they have been aimed at different users. Instead, it is vital to choose the appropriate tool for each task.

PerformancePoint is really strong at the monitoring and guided analysis tasks. The designer of the report knows what needs to be monitored—for instance, sales per store—and also knows that when an out-of-band value occurs, the person looking at the value is likely to analyze the cause through a finite set of choices. For instance, the person is likely to take the sales figure and break it up by date, salesperson, or product to determine exactly where the problem is coming from.

Reporting Services is used for reports and visualizations that are likely to remain mostly static—for example, a monthly management report, an engineer's report, or a spatial visualization. The data that feeds these reports are dynamic, but the interactivity is limited.

Excel (and this author includes PowerPivot and Power View in this description) is an interactive experience for users who might not know up front how they will combine and analyze the data and instead want to discover meaning in data.

These roles map to the retail example in Chapter 2.

When to use PerformancePoint:

- An analysis services cube (multidimensional or tabular) is available.
- Glance-and-go dashboards are required.
- Users are likely to need to change the view displayed.
- Integrating Reporting Services or Excel within a report is required.

When not to use PerformancePoint:

- Control over aspects such as color is required.
- Dashboards need to be printed.

When to use Reporting Services:

- Specific visualizations, such as ranges and maps, are required.

- High visual fidelity is required.

- Reports need to be printed.

When not to use Reporting Services:

- Dynamic measures are required.

- Slice and dice capabilities.

- Anonymous access is required.

When to use Excel:

- Interactivity is required.

- No cube is available (build one through PowerPivot).

- A higher level of control over individual chart elements is required (for example, drag-and-drop positioning of chart labels).

- Possibly the fastest development using pivot tables and charts.

When not to use Excel:

- Guided interactivity is necessary—it's better in PerformancePoint.

When to use Power View:

- Animation is required.

- Cross-filtering between charts.

When not to use Power View:

- When any control over chart formatting is required—it is even more limited than PerformancePoint.

INSTALLING THE SAMPLE DATABASES

The two samples are in SQL server database format and in Analysis Services tabular mode. You need SQL 2012 for both.

To restore the SQL database, open Management Studio, right-click Databases, and choose Restore. Select the Device radio button, and click the ellipsis to see the screen in Figure 3-5.

Click Add, browse to the `VI_UNData.bak` backup file, and click OK. Type **VI_UNData** in the Database Name field and restore the database.

For restoring the Analysis Services database, ensure that you have Analysis Services running in tabular mode (you may well need to run the SQL install again if you chose all the defaults because multi-dimensional is installed by default), and connect to it in Management Studio.

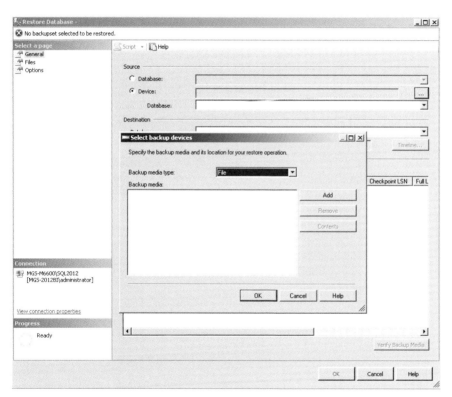

FIGURE 3-5 *Restoring a SQL database*

You need to copy the backup to a folder that Analysis Services can access. You can check what these are by right-clicking the instance and then clicking Properties. The information tab has a line item called `BackupDir` as in Figure 3-6. Copy `OECD_Data.ABF` to this folder.

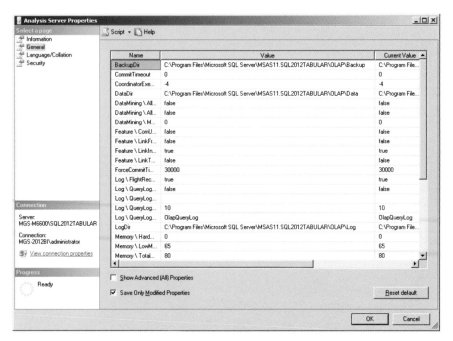

FIGURE 3-6 *Analysis Services backup directory location*

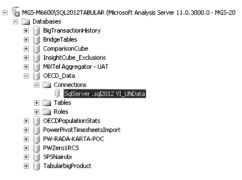

FIGURE 3-7 *Changing an Analysis Services Connection*

Right-click Databases and choose Restore. Browse to OECD_Data.abf in the backup folder, and then type in the name of the Database (OECD_Data), and restore it.

Your final step is to connect this cube to the SQL database you restored previously. Right-click Databases and choose Refresh to show the database you just restored. Open OECD_Data.abf, expand the connections, and then double-click the connection as shown in Figure 3-7.

In the Connection Properties dialog box, click the Connection String property and then click the ellipsis next to it to see the connection string builder shown in Figure 3-8.

Set the connection to your SQL database and test the connection. If you get an error, you may need to edit the security settings on your SQL Database. Start by going Start ➢ All Programs ➢ Microsoft SQL Server 2012 ➢ Configuration tools ➢ SQL Server Configuration Manager. Click SQL Server Services and check what account Analysis Services is running under, as shown in Figure 3-9.

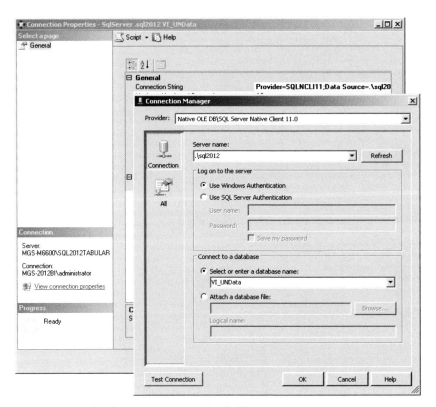

FIGURE 3-8 *Analysis Services connection string builder*

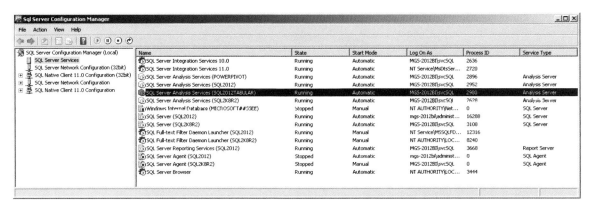

FIGURE 3-9 *Analysis Services Service account*

Now, go to your SQL database and expand Security and then Logins, as in Figure 3-10. If the login exists, double-click it; otherwise, right-click and choose New Login.

If you created a new login, first search for the login you identified in the configuration screen, and choose it.

Next, go to the User Mapping tab and, as shown in Figure 3-11, select the VI_UNdata database. Ensure that the database is checked, and that the db_datareader role is selected.

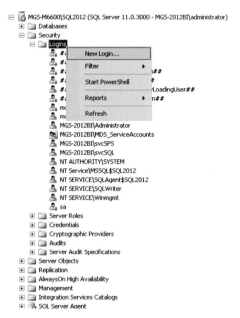

FIGURE 3-10 *SQL Server logins*

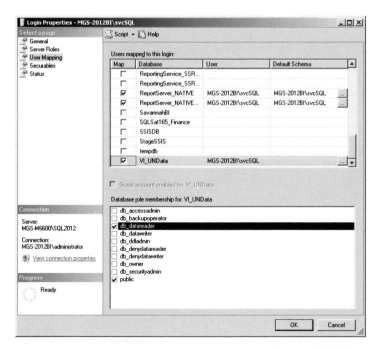

FIGURE 3-11 *SQL Server username mapping*

This process allows Analysis Services to access the database, so go back and change the connection appropriately.

SUMMARY

This chapter discussed the background of the Microsoft tools that you work with throughout this book. The remainder of the chapters in this part of the book take you through the tools themselves in detail, laying the foundation for creating visualizations as well as guiding you in choosing a tool to create your visualizations.

CHAPTER 4

Building Data Sets to Support Visualization

This chapter focuses on the building of data sets and storing them in formats conducive to data access and creating great visualizations. We will cover a number of common and more unique data sets and discuss specifically the uses, types of data, creators and consumers, and benefits or drawbacks to each data source.

WHAT DATA SETS ARE

Data sets are groups of information that may be stored in a number of formats in today's digital age. These formats can include lists of customers, products, sales records, or even logs from a server or computer system. These sets are then combined in a number of different ways to produce information that businesses can use to drive decisions.

WHY WE NEED THEM

We need these data sets to help us answer questions such as these:

- What are our customers buying?
- What products are the most profitable?
- What kinds of trends do we see in our sales over time?
- How do these trends affect the buying behavior or volume of sales?

> **"It is a capital mistake to theorize before one has data"**
>
> Sir Arthur Conan Doyle

These and other questions are important to any organization that is looking to get more insight into how it does business. Your business is often faced with these kinds of questions (and their more complex versions), and having data sets available to work with will enable folks (soon to be you) to gain the know-how to use them to provide answers.

HOW DATA SETS ARE CREATED

Data sets get created in a number of ways: automatically by some systems, by teams of people, and by organizations for publishing. In this chapter you learn to use a couple of the most common methods, including the following:

- Cut\copy and paste
- Import or export from a computer system
- Manually entering data that comes from offline sources

Any one of these methods might be easier for your particular situation, as you learn later in the chapter where each of these methods is discussed, but they are all focused on bringing different pieces of data (customer names, products purchased, registrations, and/or other important data points) together to paint a picture of activities and conditions that you want to analyze.

WHY DATA SETS ARE IMPORTANT

The data sets mentioned in the previous section are important since you need good source data to ultimately create great visualizations, and they are the reasons this book was written. These data sets, and the systems or processes that create them, become the basis for all the analysis you will do. Their capability to provide clean and accurate information, a consistent approach to organization of the data, and completeness of the included fields is directly proportional to the quality and quantity of analysis that those sets of data will support.

COMMON DATA SET ELEMENTS

Data sets share a number of elements or qualities that help you work with them and navigate their contents to reach the information you're looking for. This section dives deeper into those to help you understand what to pay attention to.

DATA QUALITY

You should spot check or, if possible, do a more in-depth analysis of the data you've accumulated to make sure it is accurate and free of miscellaneous characters and punctuation that might cause you a problem when writing expressions or formulas in your visualization platform. Being able to count on clean data is a great advantage for the visualization techniques you are learning in this book. This means if you are pulling this data from different sources or locations that may have been manually updated or altered, you need to pay special attention or go through a cleansing process where the data is reviewed for accuracy.

DATA RATINGS

When possible, it is good to triangulate between data sources. For instance, when working with data such as the national GDP, you may pull data from the Organisation for Economic Co-operation and Development as well as the CIA fact book. Internally, you may cross-reference data from your ERP, financial, and CRM systems. When doing so, it is often good to give your data a rating that can be surfaced in your reports—for instance, if all three systems agree, that's gold or 100%; if two systems agree, that's silver or 67%, etc. The percentages are useful when you look at many of these data points in aggregate. If you have only one or two data points with low confidence, you can trust your aggregated data.

METADATA

Hand in hand with clean data go descriptive column headers. If you do not have these in place, you will have to adjust them later in the data consumption cycle, which might impact the performance and methods you can take to visualize your data. See a good before and after example of descriptive column headers in Figure 4-1.

Metadata is important because many visualization tools will pull this information in to allow you to reference your data by its descriptive properties so you can navigate the data sets more easily.

CustomerIdentification	FirstName	LastName	BirthDate	MaritalStatus	Gender	EmailAddress
AW00011602	Larry	Gill	4/13/1977 12...	S	M	larry16@advent...
AW00011603	Geoffrey	Gonzalez	2/6/1977 12:...	S	M	geoffrey16@adv...
AW00011610	Blake	Collins	4/23/1975 12...	S	M	blake47@advent...
AW00012517	Alexa	Watson	8/25/1977 12...	S	F	alexa0@adventu...
AW00012518	Jacquelyn	Dominguez	9/27/1977 12...	S	F	jacquelyn13@ad...
AW00012519	Casey	Gutierrez	12/17/1977 1...	S	M	casey34@advent...
AW00012714	Colleen	Lu	7/17/1973 12...	S	F	colleen11@adve...
AW00012728	Jeremiah	Stewart	6/26/1979 12...	S	M	jeremiah44@ad...
AW00012871	Leah	Li	10/6/1976 12...	S	F	leah2@adventur...
AW00013671	Frank	Ramos	2/7/1974 12:...	S	M	frank25@advent...
AW00013826	Candice	He	11/25/1977 1...	S	F	candice2@adve...
AW00013830	Andrea	Cox	8/3/1977 12:...	S	F	andrea11@adve...
AW00013838	Jill	Rubio	6/27/1976 12...	S	F	jill29@adventur...
AW00014838	Darren	Alvarez	7/26/1977 12...	S	M	darren26@adve...
AW00014839	Natasha	Sanz	5/18/1977 12...	S	F	natasha20@adv...
AW00014840	Autumn	Zhu	10/23/1977 1...	S	F	autumn13@adv...
AW00014848	George	Louverdis	9/10/1975 12...	S	M	george5@adven...
AW00014849	Dwayne	Martin	10/12/1975 1...	S	M	dwayne0@adve...
AW00014991	Edwin	Zhao	2/26/1976 12...	S	M	edwin11@adven...

FIGURE 4-1 *Before and after descriptive column names*

FORMATTING

Data formatting is also important. If you have currency values, make sure they reflect the correct currency. If you have international data, make sure any nuances for handling other languages are in place, such as support for international font types, and so on. Problems with language-specific characters or alphabets is often not an issue if the data is coming from a modern computer system, but can be the case if it is manually entered. Other concerns for international data include special accents or punctuation formatting. Spreadsheets can shine here because data enhancement can be easily done by a business user or administrative professional and does not require IT interaction to change the data. See a good example of proper data formatting in Figure 4-2.

DATA VOLUME

The volume of data you're working with needs to be in the manageable range for the tools you're using. There are technologies better suited for greater volumes of data such as SQL tables; tabular models; and, of course, Hadoop for very large volumes. Excel will handle up to 100,000 to 200,000 rows and then will begin to experience some performance problems with scaling that many rows. There is also a hard limit at 1 million rows. Make sure you are aware of the types of problems you might run into. These types of sources will be covered more in depth in this and future chapters, but it's important to make sure you know that you can start with a smaller set of data and then begin working with larger sets once you're comfortable with the types of analysis that you're performing.

EmailAddress	EnglishEducation	SpanishEducation	FrenchEducation	EnglishOccupation	SpanishOccupation	FrenchOccupation
larry16@advent...	Partial College	Estudios universitari...	Baccalauréat	Clerical	Administrativo	Employé
geoffrey16@adv...	Partial College	Estudios universitari...	Baccalauréat	Clerical	Administrativo	Employé
blake47@advent...	Partial College	Estudios universitari...	Baccalauréat	Clerical	Administrativo	Employé
alexa0@adventu...	Partial College	Estudios universitari...	Baccalauréat	Clerical	Administrativo	Employé
jacquelyn13@ad...	Partial College	Estudios universitari...	Baccalauréat	Clerical	Administrativo	Employé
casey34@advent...	Partial College	Estudios universitari...	Baccalauréat	Clerical	Administrativo	Employé
colleen11@adve...	Partial College	Estudios universitari...	Baccalauréat	Clerical	Administrativo	Employé
jeremiah44@ad...	Partial College	Estudios universitari...	Baccalauréat	Clerical	Administrativo	Employé
leah2@adventur...	Partial College	Estudios universitari...	Baccalauréat	Clerical	Administrativo	Employé
frank25@advent...	Partial College	Estudios universitari...	Baccalauréat	Clerical	Administrativo	Employé
candice2@adve...	Partial College	Estudios universitari...	Baccalauréat	Clerical	Administrativo	Employé
andrea11@adve...	Partial College	Estudios universitari...	Baccalauréat	Clerical	Administrativo	Employé
jill29@adventur...	Partial College	Estudios universitari...	Baccalauréat	Clerical	Administrativo	Employé
darren26@adve...	Partial College	Estudios universitari...	Baccalauréat	Clerical	Administrativo	Employé
natasha20@adv...	Partial College	Estudios universitari...	Baccalauréat	Clerical	Administrativo	Employé
autumn13@adv...	Partial College	Estudios universitari...	Baccalauréat	Clerical	Administrativo	Employé
george5@adven...	Partial College	Estudios universitari...	Baccalauréat	Clerical	Administrativo	Employé
dwayne0@adve...	Partial College	Estudios universitari...	Baccalauréat	Clerical	Administrativo	Employé
edwin11@adven...	Partial College	Estudios universitari...	Baccalauréat	Clerical	Administrativo	Employé

FIGURE 4-2 *Proper data formatting*

AUTOMATED DATA

If you have calculated values in your data, you need to make sure those are identified. Spreadsheets and other data analysis tools can create powerful calculations, but they may have some limitations as you begin to use them for sourcing. For example, in some cases, drill-through functionality is limited based on the type of calculation and where it is in your data source. If it is coming from an OLAP cube, there will be limited functionality if it is being calculated in the OLAP layer and not in the spreadsheet. In addition, data that is autogenerated may have lots of repeated information that you don't need, and importing it would only make your analysis tasks more cumbersome.

TYPES OF DATA SETS AND SOURCES

There are many different types of data, from lists of people and products to financial documents and more. This section reviews some of the important sources you will see most often in projects like those in this book.

DATA IN THE INTERNET AGE

It's no secret that in today's enterprises many organizations are finding data in all sorts of new places. Departments are doing more of their own IT and analysis, and the concept of self-service reporting is no longer a myth; it is rapidly becoming the norm. Folks are using data from wherever they can access it to give them a leg up on doing better analysis and finding more insight from data they already have. This section covers some common data sources you will run into in an enterprise and when you may want to leverage them for storing your data as you collect it.

SPREADSHEETS

Spreadsheets, which are one of the most common data sources, are popular because they are so easily created and very accessible. Spreadsheets can store many different types of data, but typically store financial information and extracts from other systems, and function as a collection point for data consolidated from many other sources. A recent Gartner report said that more than 90% of all the reports in the world wind up in Excel to be manipulated. With that being the case, it is easy to see why Excel and spreadsheets became such a critical source for our data.

WHEN TO STORE DATA IN A SPREADSHEET

Spreadsheets are typically created by analysts and then consumed by analysts, sales professionals, and executives. Professionals in many departments are consumers of this data, and in many cases it is reviewed in a meeting either on a shared screen over the Internet or on a projection in a conference room. Spreadsheets are consumed in many ways, but the most important thing to remember about the simple spreadsheet is that it's not really simple at all. Spreadsheets can have complicated formulas and macros built into them.

These complications can cause challenges when using spreadsheets as a source and should be mitigated as part of your data processing or loading, depending on how the visualizations are being sourced. Some of these concerns can be mitigated by converting your spreadsheets to use PowerPivot or a tabular model (more on this later). These options give you more powerful capability to embed calculations that will perform better on larger volumes of data. Spreadsheets are an incredible, powerful source and will likely be used extensively in any visualization exercise, but remember that data may not need to be sourced directly from spreadsheets and to use the most appropriate source for the type of visualization desired.

Spreadsheets can provide an easy-to-use and easy to source (i.e., many tools connect to it directly) platform for data visualizations if your data size is relatively small and you have a need to easily combine data from multiple sources. If you can leverage the power of Excel's functions and features to help ensure that your data is high quality and formatted appropriately for consumption, this might be a great option for you. Next, let's talk about using data stored in a database for our source.

HOW DID WE GET TO EXCEL?

Spreadsheets (which are covered later in this chapter) form the foundation for organizing data in the digital age. In 1978, Harvard Business School students Daniel Bricklin and Bob Frankston came up with the idea to create an interactive calculating program called VisiCalc. This was one of the first programs that led to the functionality that we know as a spreadsheet program.

Spreadsheets are wide, flat pages with columns and rows that organize data about particular transactions for a business purpose. It spreads the information across a sheet for the business person to analyze, hence the name. VisiCalc came out of the original spreadsheet world developed by Professor Richard Mattessich in 1961. He used mainframe computers and a new programming language called LANPAR.

Lotus 1-2-3 came along in 1980 and was the first "modern" spreadsheet. Microsoft then countered with Excel (written originally for the 512K Apple Macintosh) in 1985. Microsoft acquired Lotus in 1995 and with the advent of DOS and then the Windows operating system, Excel has grown to be the most widely used spreadsheet application in personal use and by businesses around the world.

SQL TABLES

SQL tables are another common source, although they are typically accessed and leveraged differently. When the term *SQL table* is used, many times we are specifically speaking about a table that is in a relational database. This can be a data warehouse or data mart, CRM system, ERP solution, or simply a table in a Microsoft Access database that a user has created to do an individual analysis. This is a pretty common solution for many organizations that do not have a cohesive strategy for data management and reporting. Many users are taking the "I'll-find-it-myself" strategy and managing the extraction of data from a number of different places in the organization.

The types of data stored in tables are usually more organized physically than in spreadsheets or other locations, but this can be deceiving. Just because the data is organized well physically, stored in tables with relationships, and labeled in detail, doesn't mean that the application or user process that is populating them has the right amount of governance or access rights built in. That governance is critically important because when you are building data sources for visualization, data quality is so important. A key part of creating data visualizations is knowing the data well enough to help others understand and interpret it more effectively. Storing data in tables is normally a byproduct of that data coming from another source where it was worked with previously, then put in a table, and is now persisted that way. If you're going to keep the data, add to it, and continue to improve it, a table is often a better long-term location than a spreadsheet that could be easily deleted from the file system.

OLAP AND TABULAR MODELS

OLAP and tabular models are terms for systems that store data in a special format called multidimensional, or in the case of tabular, as a column store with a multidimensional interface. This means the data is designed and stored in a way that allows the end user to connect data across different business segments more easily. These models are usually set up by developers or power users and deployed to a server in your environment. This provides a trove of data for end users to navigate through and begin to explore and build visualizations. These are very common data sources and are made up of data from tables and other sources to consolidate the information in one place that other tools can connect to and analyze.

PowerPivot is an instance of a tabular model embedded inside Excel and can be published from PowerPivot to Analysis Services.

REPORTS AND DATA FEEDS

Reports and data feeds are also good sources of data. May tools these days can connect directly to reports and data "feeds," or online streams of data. These tools can pull this data in as if it were a spreadsheet or table and enable users to work with it in more creative ways. These sources are advantageous because many times the security and integrity of the data was already addressed upstream in the process. The risk is that using reports as data sources for other reports can lead to a long chain of reports pulling data from reports and lead to a scenario where the data has gotten polluted—that is, the figures coming through are wrong.

HADOOP AND OTHER NONRELATIONAL SOURCES

You may have heard the term *Big Data* around your organization or in the industry; it often means someone is referring to unstructured or loosely organized data that comes in large volumes. These sources come with their own tools to analyze the data and powerful results can be generated. Caution should be taken, however, because this data has not been cleansed or organized, is often quite raw, and should be used for exploratory purposes only before moving it to a more stable and organized framework for specific or in-depth analysis. This analysis can be done in Hadoop, but is not typically for beginners who are more familiar with visual tools.

Map-reduce, the algorithm underlying technologies such as Hadoop, is at its heart a mechanism to split a processing problem into parts (the *map* part of the name), distribute the data among nodes, do the processing (the *reduce* part of the name), and then recombine the data. A diagram of this process sourced from `http://code.google.com/p/mapreduce-framework/wiki/MapReduce` is shown in Figure 4-3.

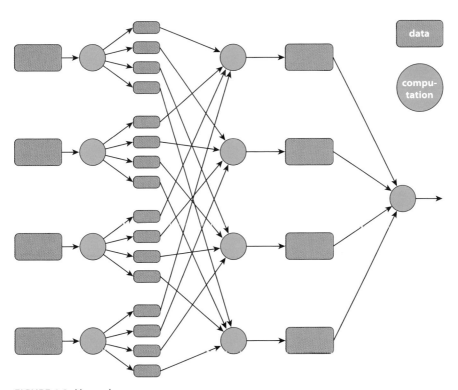

FIGURE 4-3 *Map-reduce*

CREATING DATA SETS FOR VISUALIZATION

When you create data sets specifically for visualization there are tasks and priorities you need to pay close attention to that make the process much smoother. Now is the time to learn them! Let's get started.

COPY AND PASTE

Many data sets are composed of data from other locations around the organization. Although this is part of the power of the spreadsheet, it is also dangerous. This data has now become portable and static in its current form, but being able to combine a text file containing customer and marketing mailing list data with geographic information can significantly enhance our ability to create great visual effects with our data while keeping its preparation time and effort manageable.

EXPORTING DATA FROM SYSTEMS

Users, developers, and administrators can export data from systems. The user can also get data from an automated feed or e-mail delivery. Although exporting data is a good way to get data in some cases because the format will be predictable, it may not be the most intuitive or flexible method. Review your options to see whether this is the best fit for a first data set. An example of this is a SAP user with the appropriate rights exporting data to a format such as CSV, which can be opened in Excel or imported into a database for analysis.

IMPORT TECHNIQUES AND TOOLS

Through Excel's built-in functionality, much of this data is imported from enterprise or departmental systems and then combined to create a unique, business-oriented view of a product, service, or internal data focus point. This importing is done easily by most end users and provides a quick and easy way to get data in while maintaining connections to those sources so data can be reimported at some point, if necessary. Tools such as Microsoft Access or SQL tables may be used as sources, so Excel can do some additional data preparation not easily performed in the source.

GETTING STARTED

In this chapter you create a representative data set like those you use throughout the book. So make sure you have all the sample files downloaded for the book to follow along as we move forward.

YOUR FIRST DATA SET

When creating your first data set, it is important to get advice from others in your organizations about an easy data set to begin working with. Alternatively, you can start with some of the samples included in this book or with other free data from sites such as Data.gov, infochimps.com, and others where free data is available for download. Working with data that is familiar is often a good exercise because it helps reduce confusion for folks new to these techniques.

Check with your developers, analysts, and administrators for data that you're allowed to access, or pair up with someone working on a data project and offer some "free" help to get some exposure to the processes used in your organization for this type of work. This exposure can be invaluable when learning how to better visualize data because you'll have additional perspective on what folks like and dislike when it comes to reviewing their information.

YOUR FIRST DATA SET

In this chapter you work with a simple and freely available database from Microsoft called AdventureWorks. You can download this database at `http://msftdbprodsamples.codeplex.com/`. The file you want is the SQL Server 2012 DW database. When it downloads you will need to attach the files to a SQL Server instance. If you have trouble with this please see your database administrator. This will work with all editions of SQL Server 2012.

Other chapters use data sets provided by the authors with the book, and obtained from the Organisation for Economic Co-operation, so be sure to review the sections in each chapter that cover installing and configuring those data sets along with the instructions provided in Chapter 3 for installing all the data sets at one time. Installing them all at once will provide the best overall experience as you move through the chapters' walkthroughs. The data sets were carefully crafted to support the walkthroughs and demos, and some chapters have data sets to make them more approachable while others have very specific sources of data to be able to showcase specific features in a product or approach.

GETTING DATA

The first step is getting some data, so open Excel and connect to your database, as explained in the following steps.

1. With Excel open, go to the Data tab and select Get External Data ➤ From Other Sources ➤ From SQL Server, as shown in Figure 4-4.

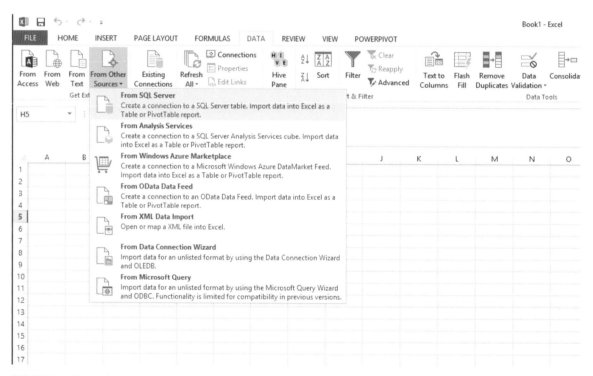

FIGURE 4-4 *Connecting to your data source*

2.   Select the tables you want to import, as shown in Figure 4-5, and click Next.

FIGURE 4-5 *Selecting tables to import*

3.   Choose the Table option, as shown in Figure 4-6.

CLEANING YOUR DATA

You can clean this data up by removing some columns you do not need. Then you are ready to begin analyzing the data using many of Excel's tools (more on this in future chapters).

Next you make some formatting changes to allow for better visualization.

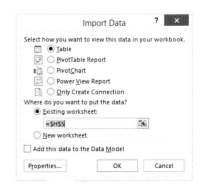

FIGURE 4-6 *Create a new table in Excel*

DATA CLEANSING

The process of data cleansing can often be messier than this: when pulling from sources such as those used for the book, data will often need to be pivoted (the rows and columns swapped) and headings repeated, and this will often be a manual process when working in tools such as Excel. Integration tools such as SQL Server Integration Services are commonly used when this needs to be automated.

MOVING YOUR DATA INTO A GOOD FORMAT FOR VISUALIZATION

Now that you have your data in a good clean layout, you can format it as a pivot table, which is a basic type of visualization but is very powerful within Excel. After you've formatted your data as a pivot table (as shown in Figure 4-7), you can begin to do some nice drag-and-drop analysis on the data, as shown in Figure 4-8.

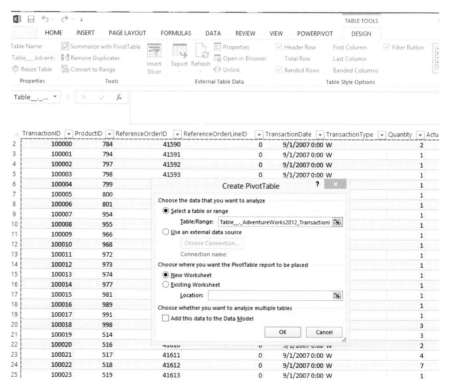

FIGURE 4-7 *Create a pivot table*

First things first: Highlight your entire table, go to the design tab, and select Summarize with pivot table (see Figure 4-7). This will convert your regular table into something you can use for the drag-and-drop (or slice and dice) type of analysis mentioned earlier.

Next, drag the column names you'd like to filter or sort to the field box in the PivotTable Fields list. You must click somewhere in the table for this to work. You will begin to see results like those shown in Figure 4-8.

FIGURE 4-8 *Sorted and organized pivot table*

VERIFYING YOUR DATA BY PROTOTYPING

The best way to tell if your data process is working is to do some basic visualizing or "playing around" to see whether the data is lining up as expected. In this instance, we'll build a simple report, as shown in Figure 4-9.

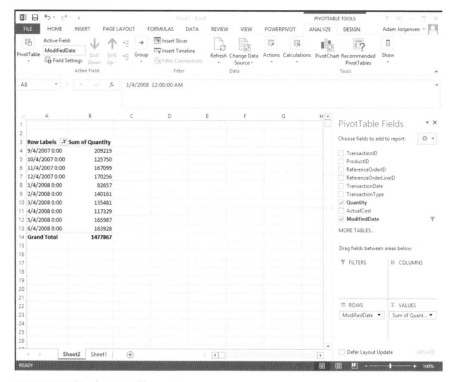

FIGURE 4-9 *Simple pivot table report*

Since the previous section got you comfortable with dragging and dropping, let's drag Modified Date into the Rows box and Quantity into the Values box in the PivotTable Fields list. This will create a simple report you can use to test your process.

This is the simplest possible Excel pivot—in Part 3 of this book you learn how to format your pivot tables.

SUMMARY

Many visualization techniques and technologies can make the most of different sources of data. In many cases, the sources described in this chapter are used together to align information for easier consumption and understanding by the users. This chapter provided an introduction to your first data set. Going forward, the next chapters will all be focused on how to imagine and build next–generation data visualizations on the next generation of tools. So buckle up and turn the page.

CHAPTER 5

Excel and PowerPivot

This chapter is about the two most frequently used tools in a power users' arsenal for working with and visualizing data. It will review Excel and PowerPivot and discuss important use cases for leveraging them in your quest to for visualizing your data. They are the best tools to gather data and then begin visualizing and analyzing data quickly. This is the foundation for many of the types of visualizations you'll be doing in the rest of the book, so it's important to be familiar with them.

WHAT ARE EXCEL AND POWERPIVOT?

Excel and PowerPivot are easy-to-use, very intuitive programs that work together to create a powerful set of tools and capabilities for the end user. Excel came first in the 1990s, with PowerPivot following as part of SQL Server 2008 R2's release cycle to deliver powerful data volume enhancements through a column store engine.

Calling Excel a spreadsheet application seems so 1990s because it has grown so much, but its foundation is still the top data analysis tool in the world. More on this in the "What Does Excel Do for Me?" section later in this chapter. PowerPivot is a free add-in for Excel that provides capabilities far beyond what traditional Excel could even deliver, including more Analysis Services–style functionality (online analytical processing (OLAP)) tools directly in Excel and accessible by the end user.

POWERPIVOT

PowerPivot is available as an add-in for all editions of Excel 2010. As of the writing of this book, while PowerPivot is built into Excel 2013, the advanced edit functionality was only included in Excel 2013 Professional Plus (not to be confused with Excel 2013 Professional).

POWERPIVOT VERSUS BISM VERSUS ANALYSIS SERVICES

When you work with PowerPivot, you will notice that there are several names for this technology as new editions of the software it is part of with are released. In addition to PowerPivot, you will hear names such as the following:

- **BI Semantic Model (BISM):** new in SQL Server 2012
- **BISM tabular:** new server version of PowerPivot

Each of these is accurate in its own way. So let's explore them before we move forward.

PowerPivot

PowerPivot is the correct name for the client-side tools. This functionality is installed from a free add-in that you can find at `http://www.powerpivot.com`. Choose your add-in version (32- or 64-bit) and install. The installation is very simple with no options, and the functionality is then added to Excel. You will know you succeeded when you see the POWERPIVOT tab and its options shown in Figure 5.1.

FIGURE 5-1 *The POWERPIVOT tab in the Ribbon*

BI Semantic Model (BISM)

BI Semantic Model (BISM) is the name Microsoft gave to its OLAP suite in the new SQL Server 2012 release. The tools, features, and applications were all enhanced to align them with modeling the way a business needs to see data, adding flexibility and functionality to support it. PowerPivot is a part of this new feature set, but it is not all of it. BISM tabular is another feature, and so are other enhancements such as Power View, which you learn more about in Chapter 6. Figure 5-2 shows the BISM architecture.

BISM Tabular

BISM tabular is the new server version of Analysis Services that supports models created in PowerPivot. Now that PowerPivot has been available for a while, we can upload these models to a production Analysis Services Server and share them across the company, taking advantage of the extra memory on a server to process and collaborate on larger, more intensive models. Figure 5-3 shows some of what this new interface looks like.

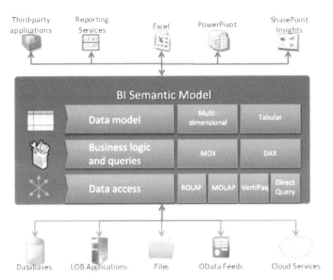

FIGURE 5-2 *BISM architecture view*

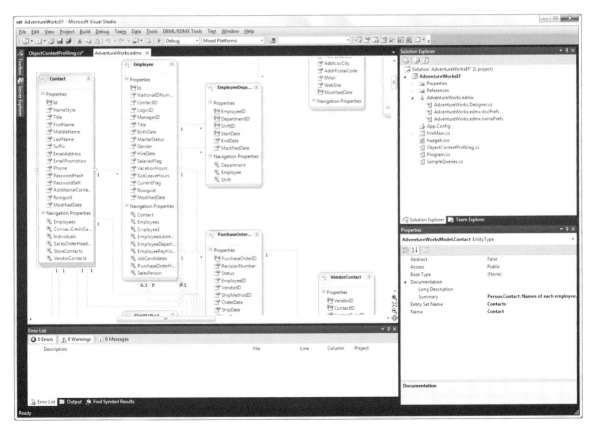

FIGURE 5-3 *SQL Server Data Tools*

Use Cases

Excel is often used by a variety of professionals to collect, sift through, and analyze data in an organized and predictable fashion. The users' activities include pivoting data to be able to see how numbers or information look when different filters, parameters, and criteria are applied. The functionality and design of Excel makes this process very straightforward and painless.

PowerPivot is often used by the same folks who want to work with a much larger amount of data and need to *persist* the model. In other words, they want to keep their creations around and continually enhance then with features like partitioned data, automated data refresh, hierarchies for easier browsing, and course, much more data than Excel can handle natively. Analysis of tens of millions of rows of data is possible in PowerPivot, while Excel struggles above 60K rows in a native Excel table. This is because of the new *column store* features in PowerPivot that deliver significantly increased compression and performance when iterating over the data.

These persisted models are then shared and made available for collaboration by publishing them to SharePoint either through Excel Services or BISM tabular integrated with SharePoint to enable browsing and collaboration across the organizations. A typical workflow looks like this:

Create Workbook ➢ Enhance in PowerPivot ➢ Publish to SharePoint ➢ Collaborate

This workflow is illustrated in Figure 5-4.

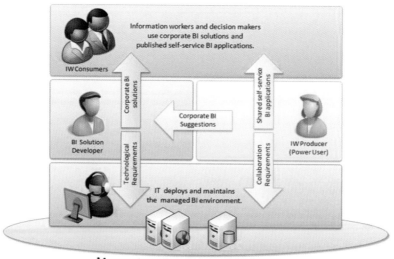

Managed BI Collaboration Environment

FIGURE 5-4 *A self-service BI model*

How Do These Models Fit into Your Organization?

Think through your organization and the types of people and roles who are always working with data, asking for more data, and needing more memory on their machines or access to data sources. Some examples include:

- Accounting and finance teams
- Marketing analysts
- Retail, manufacturing, and logistics analysts
- Executives
- Reporting analysts

Many of these people will already be familiar with these tools but will love the additional assistance professionals can give them with all the new things you're learning in this text.

COLUMN STORES

The term *column store* has been mentioned several times in this chapter already with only a basic explanation. This section highlights the importance and building blocks of this powerful technology. The technology is not new, although it's very new to client tools such as PowerPivot.

SQL Server's traditional index structure is based on a B-Tree model. B-Tree models are great for finding data that match a particular condition in a query. They are also pretty fast when you need to scan all the data in a table. There are a couple of main reasons we need the column store, however.

Compression is critical to getting increased performance out of the same data on the same disks. Most of the time, data is stored in rows as shown in Figure 5-5.

With a column store, the data is reorganized into a column-wise fashion similar to Figure 5-6.

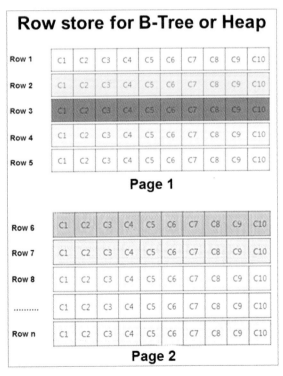

FIGURE 5-5 *Row store versus column store*

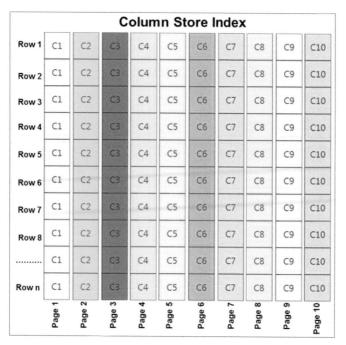

FIGURE 5-6 *Column store index*

When you put that together it looks something like Figure 5-7.

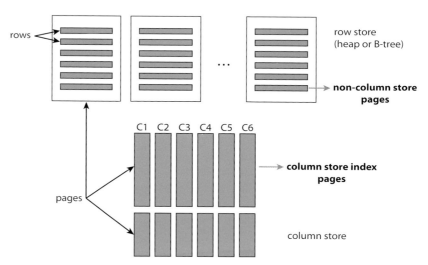

FIGURE 5-7 *Selecting from a column-store index*

If this seems complicated, that's okay. You don't need to know all the internal details, but if you'd like to know more, use your favorite search engine to search for "Columnstore Indexes" and go to the page for "Columnstore Indexes: A New Feature in SQL Server known as Project 'Apollo'" on `blogs.technet.com`.

MULTIDIMENSIONAL VERSUS IN MEMORY MODELS

PowerPivot represents a new shift in enhancing the capabilities around in-memory models. This differs from the traditional multidimensional model in that now we don't need to build out a traditional OLAP cube to be able to do much of the OLAP-type analysis. Not that we might not want to build it out, but sometimes that is more work than we have time for. Typically, you would want to use a multidimensional model when size or complexity overruns the PowerPivot or BISM tabular toolset.

For size, this would be data that would be too much for a server memory foot-print or perhaps require complicated MDX scripting. PowerPivot can do much of this scripting as well, however, so don't discount the power of its DAX language.

CREATING YOUR FIRST POWERPIVOT MODEL

Let's move forward by creating our first PowerPivot model. This model will be based on a sample data set in the `Chapter05.zip` from this book's download files. First, you want to have the PowerPivot add-in installed; or if you are already running Office 2013, you just need to enable it.

To enable the add-in in Excel 2013, go to File ➢ Options ➢ Add-ins ➢ Com Add-ins ➢ GO. After the add-in is enabled, you should see a dialog like the one shown in Figure 5-8.

FIGURE 5-8 *Add-ins in Excel*

Make sure the "Microsoft Office PowerPivot for Excel 2013" check box is selected. Now you'll see the PowerPivot tab in the top of the Ribbon and you can get to work!

STEP 1: UNDERSTAND YOUR DATA

The `VI_UNData.bak` database contains tables based on United Nations data collected for a number of countries around the globe. It contains a number of statistics and facts by country that we'll be using throughout the book. For this first example, we'll take a couple of tables and build a simple model.

Open a new workbook in Excel, go to the PowerPivot tab, and click the Manage icon, as shown to the left in Figure 5-9.

FIGURE 5-9   *The PowerPivot Ribbon in Excel 2010*

STEP 2: CREATE YOUR FIRST MODEL

Now that we have the right add-in configured, let's create our model. There are a number of ways to do this, but the primary way is to import data from one or many data sources. For this example, we are going to use the United Nations data sample from the book's downloadable files.

Make sure you have the database restored to an accessible server and then select your PowerPivot tab and click the Manage icon. Then click "Get External Data" and choose SQL Server database. In this case, the database is the database backup file you downloaded for this chapter that you should have restored and made accessible somewhere in your environment. The next several sections will highlight the steps to load data into your model.

Step 2a: Select Your Data Source and Data to Load into Your Model

The UN data sample is a SQL database, but remember that the "power" in PowerPivot comes from the ability to use virtually any source of data and then combine it with data from other sources. See the following figures for the process to get your data.

First, you connect to your data source. Click the manage icon in the Ribbon to open the PowerPivot window. This window is where you do most of your work with PowerPivot. Next, locate the section in the Home tab for getting data. Click the From Database button, then select From SQL Server, as shown in Figure 5-10.

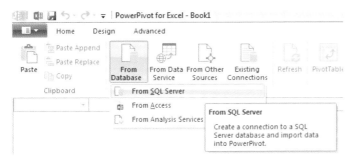

FIGURE 5-10　*Creating a SQL data source*

Enter the server and connection credentials for the data source you're connecting too, then choose the VI_UNData database as shown in Figure 5-11.

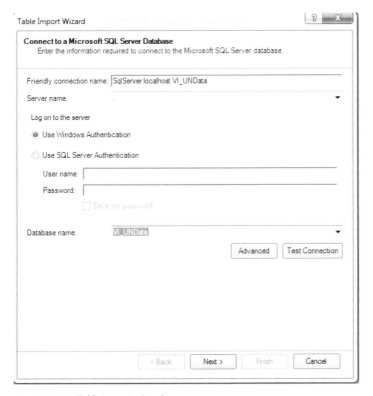

FIGURE 5-11　*Table import wizard*

Figure 5-12 shows the check boxes next to each table. You can also give the tables friendlier names, which you use in this model. This is important to make the model more readable and usable down the road. You could filter your data here as well, but you don't need to do that in this case. Click finish to complete the import.

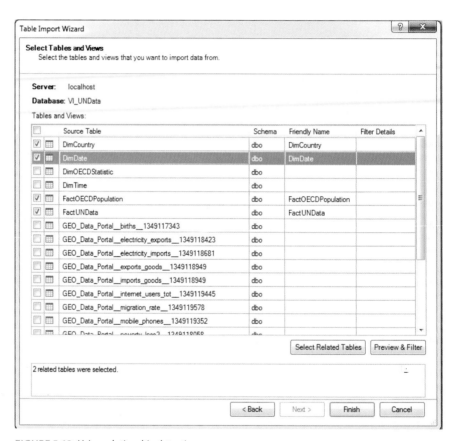

FIGURE 5-12 *Using relationship detection*

Figure 5-13 shows the import running successfully! Great work!

Step 2b: Build and Check Relationships

If there are existing physical keys or relationships in the underlying data, they will be imported into PowerPivot if you clicked "Import Related Tables." However, the goal is to combine data and begin visualizing it, so you can create additional relationships in your model based on how the data lines up. You just drag and drop the column names onto each other and the relationship is created! Simple! See the before and after in the figures that follow.

To build your relationships, switch to the diagram view in your PowerPivot window using the icon at the lower right, as shown in Figure 5-14.

FIGURE 5-13 *Import screen*

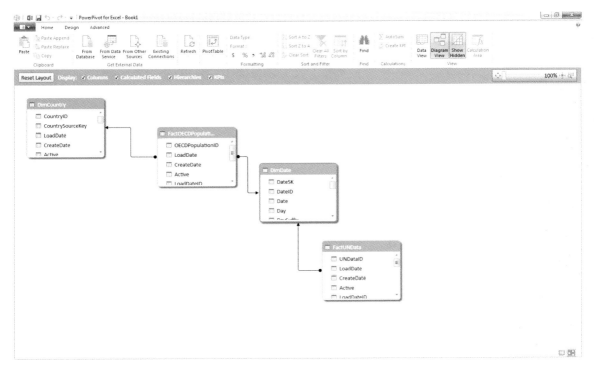

FIGURE 5-14 *The diagram view*

Find the columns in your tables that relate to each other and drag them from one table and drop them on the column name that matches in the related table. For this example, FACTOECDPopulation.CountryID was dropped on DimCountry.CountryID. Continue this for the remainder of your tables. Often you'll drag the column from the fact table and drop it on your dimension table.

Step 2c: Clean-Up Work

The last thing to do before verifying your model is clean it up. Inevitably, you will bring in columns you thought you needed but wind up not using, or columns whose names don't really match or mean anything semantically valuable to you or your end users. See how in the following figures.

Highlight the columns that you're not using (you can pick columns with little or no data or that don't seem to be as useful). Right-click in the header of the column and select Delete. The columns with empty rows near the top right in this Figure 5-15 are the columns we chose to delete.

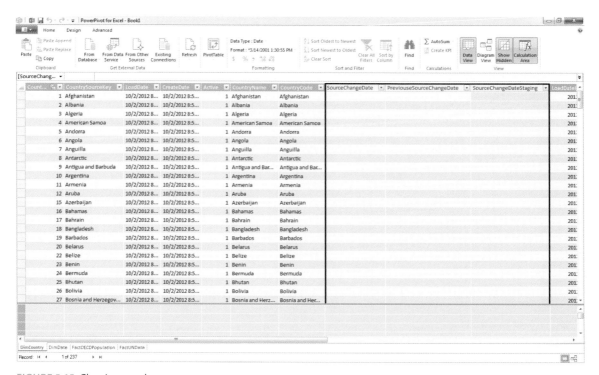

FIGURE 5-15 *Cleaning up columns*

Figure 5-16 shows the second clean-up step where you rename your columns to something more usable. You can right click on the column header and select Rename. This will then edit the model right there and persist the change. You can see this renaming in Figure 5-16.

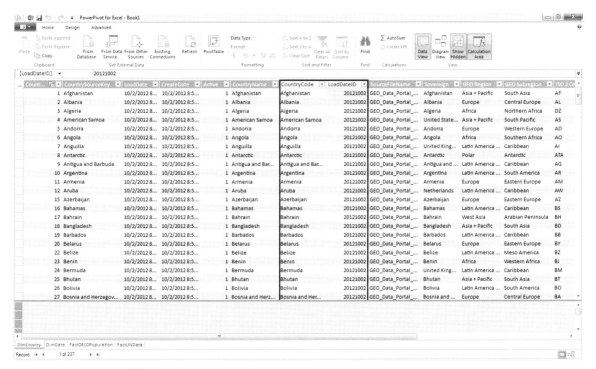

FIGURE 5-16 *Renaming columns*

STEP 3: DOES YOUR MODEL WORK?

To test your model, let's explore it in Excel. Click the PivotTable button on the Home tab in the Ribbon, as shown in Figure 5-17.

Now that we know we can use our model, let's take a look at some things that Excel can do for us. The next section will build some tables and visualization on top of this foundation.

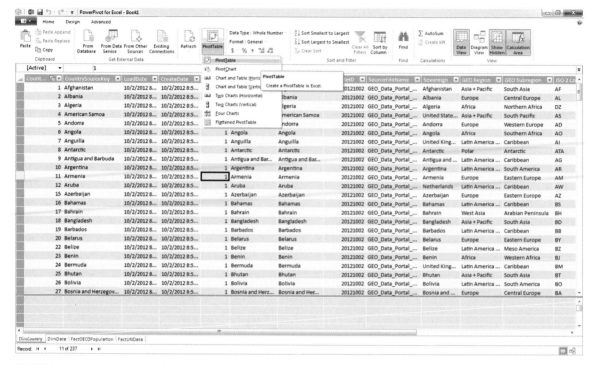

FIGURE 5-17 *Creating a pivot table*

WHAT DOES EXCEL DO FOR ME?

If you're still asking this question, you haven't been paying attention! Kidding, but only a little. Excel is very powerful. Even without PowerPivot, Excel gives us some great functionality for analyzing our data. In fact, without Excel's pivoting, charting, and analysis tools, PowerPivot would not be as functional either because we often explore our models right in Excel.

PIVOT CHARTS AND TABLES

Using pivot charts and tables is an incredibly powerful and easy way to begin simple visualizations that provide some great self-service capabilities for end users. They allow for dynamic work on charts and tables by using drag-and-drop functionality and easy-to-learn formulas and techniques for more advanced users.

Intro to Pivots in Excel

Let's explore our model and see some examples of pivots. Pivots enable us to change the axis alignment of our data to show, or "pivot," it differently. This is a big key to a lot of Excel's power. See examples of us building and using pivots in Excel. We do this by changing where we drag the columns in the grid on the right. See the difference in where the columns are placed in the grid and how that affects the pivot report's axes.

In your model in PowerPivot, click the Explore in Excel icon to get an empty Excel pivot table. Then you drag some of the values into the boxes in the Field Well on the bottom right to begin to see the report take shape. Notice that we've put the year as the column, the country in the rows, and population as a simple value. Figure 5-18 shows how this looks.

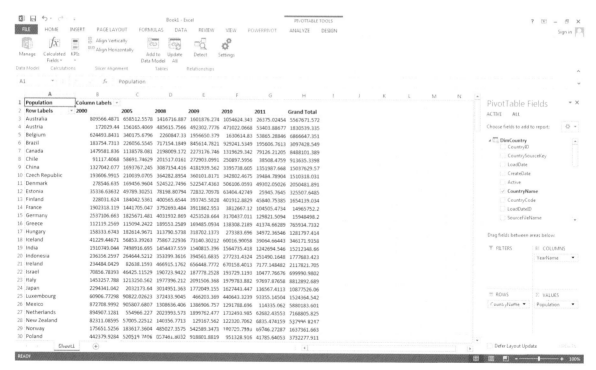

FIGURE 5-18 *The layout of a pivot table*

Filters versus Slicers

We can add extra functionality by going to the Ribbon, as shown in Figure 5-19, and inserting a *slicer* (a visual filter), or we can use the built-in Excel filters (see Figure 5-20). Inserting a filter is as easy as dragging the column you want to filter by into the filter area in the Field well (where you just dragged the other columns).

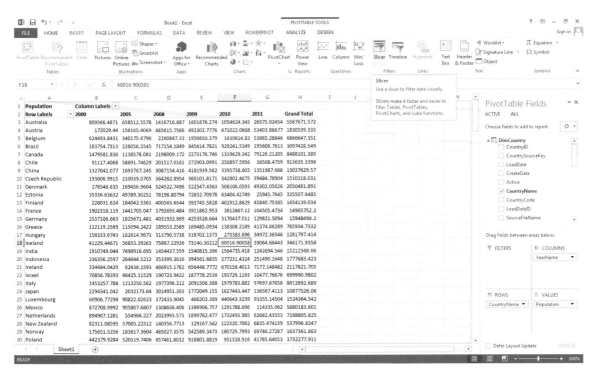

FIGURE 5-19 *Inserting a slicer from the Ribbon*

Inserting a slicer is one extra step. You need to click on your pivot table some-where and select Insert ➢ Slicer. Then you can choose the fields you'd like to slice by. These function as live filters on the canvas as opposed to in a drop-down list, so they are better for common filters that users would combine. They are also sometimes more visually preferable to regular filters. The slicers we chose are shown in Figure 5-20.

See how easy that was? Now we can format and sort our report using some of the cool functionality in Excel.

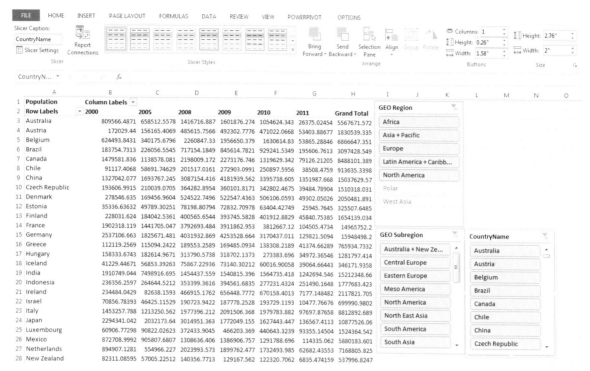

FIGURE 5-20 *Slicers on a worksheet*

Formatting and Sorting Pivots

All the formatting is right at your fingertips. We have so many options to play with here to dial in how we want this to work. Let's see the following few figures, in which we can choose options and see the results of our formatting capabilities in Excel.

The best way to experiment with formatting is to right click on columns in your pivot table and select Format Cells. This will allow you to choose all kinds of formatting options including currency, date formatting and other customer formats like phone numbers, internal codes, etc. These options will be covered throughout Part III of this book in the Excel implementation examples in each chapter.

You also have the option to do custom filtering on a pivot. Figure 5-21 shows an option to filter by value.

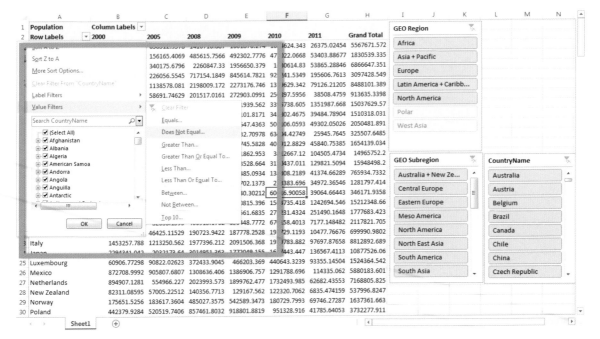

FIGURE 5-21 *A value filter*

SUMMARY

This chapter covered some great ways to begin assembling data for analysis. We covered the different ways we can use Excel and PowerPivot to build simple models and tables to begin using them as baselines for visualizing our data on top of them. You can now build a model, improve it and clean it up, and begin visualizing it in Excel. In Chapter 6 you learn about bigger and better models and visualizations using Power View.

Power View

This chapter focuses on building a solution in Power View so you can continue your data visualization efforts. It covers what Power View is, what the requirements are to create Power View reports, how to create a report, data modeling tips, and also how to deploy and share the reports.

WHAT IS POWER VIEW?

Power View is a new reporting feature that was added in Reporting Services 2012. Power View was created to provide web-based self-service reporting capabilities to end users. It is designed for rapid data exploration and mash-ups of data from a tabular BI Semantic Model (BISM). The tabular data model can either be created using PowerPivot or Tabular Analysis Services. Users can very quickly create highly visual and interactive reports with Power View and the experience is greatly simplified. Report developers no longer have to deal with setting properties on objects included in the design, worry about relationships in the data, how a particular visualization will look, or how to connect items together for filtering.

With Power View the property settings are not present like they are with the other Reporting Services development tools such as Report Builder and Report Designer. The modeler of the data has already taken care of the relationships in the data. Power View provides you a WYSIWYG (What-You-See-Is-What-You-Get) experience, so there's no flipping back and forth between design and preview anymore to see what your report will look like. Items within Power View reports are also connected to each other based on how the data is related, so clicking on an item in a chart legend can automatically filter related data in a table.

Power View is also a new feature in Excel 2013, so now this new functionality is available either as an add-in that you can easily enable in Excel 2013 or through Reporting Services in SharePoint integration mode. Figures 6-1, 6-2, and 6-3 show some of the types of visualizations you can do with Power View.

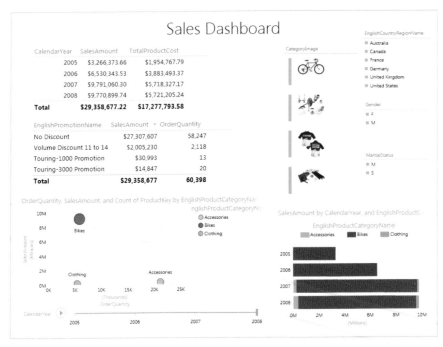

FIGURE 6-1 *Sales Dashboard Power View report*

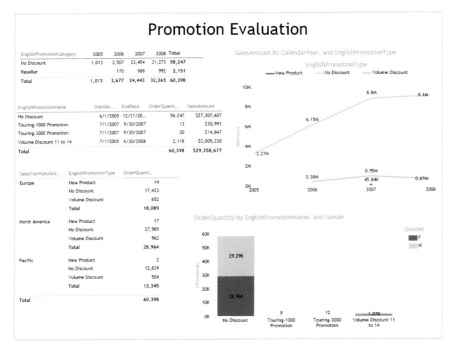

FIGURE 6-2 *Promotion Evaluation Power View report*

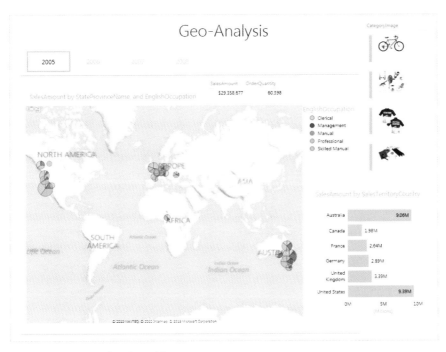

FIGURE 6-3 *Geo-Analysis Power View report*

POWER VIEW MULTIDIMENSIONAL MODEL SUPPORT

As of this writing, only tabular models are supported with Power View. In November 2012 Microsoft released a CTP of SQL Server 2012 that provides support for Analysis Services multidimensional models to work with Power View. This new capability could very well be released by the time this book is released. For exercises in this chapter, just the tabular data models were used.

Table 6-1 outlines the different visualizations that are available in Power View.

TABLE 6-1 Power View Visualization Options

VISUALIZATION	ADDITIONAL INFORMATION
Table	Regular table or matrix style, which can include row and column groups. Tables can also include totals for the values, which can be turned on or off.
Bar chart	Bar charts also include options for clustered, stacked, and 100% stacked. Data labels can be included as well.

VISUALIZATION	ADDITIONAL INFORMATION
Column chart	Similar to the bar charts, they include options for clustered, stacked, and 100% stacked. Data labels can be included as well.
Line chart	Line charts can support multiple values or can be broken out by a particular dimension attribute. Data labels can be included as well.
Pie chart	Pie charts can be broken out by a particular dimension attribute. Data labels cannot be included.
Small multiples	Also known as trellis charts; can turn a single chart into smaller repeating charts based on groupings and can be organized either horizontally or vertically. This option is available in the Field Well when a chart is selected.
Scatter chart	Also known as a bubble chart. Provides ability to analyze three metrics simultaneously and also provides a play button feature to enable viewing how data changes over time. You can view the history of a particular bubble by clicking it to see the trail over time (assuming time was set up in the chart).
Map	The map uses the Bing map service to provide geocoding to plot the data elements using geographical data elements such as text or latitude and longitude.
Card	The card provides an index style layout for dimension members, which can include images as well as text and data values.

BISM: THE FIRST REQUIREMENT FOR POWER VIEW

As mentioned previously, a BISM tabular model is the foundation for the Power View reports in Reporting Services. If you are using Excel 2013, which now has native support for data models, you will be able to create a Power View report from any data formatted as a table in addition to using tabular data models. The native data model capabilities in Excel 2013 are limited, and an advanced BISM tabular model will provide you much more functionality. Also, it is a good idea to build a BISM tabular model with Analysis Services to centralize your data and enhancements (such as calculated values or images, etc.). That is functionality you can't get if you just import data into Excel and then create a Power View report.

CREATING A POWER VIEW REPORT

In this section you create a Power View report from scratch. This process involves connecting to a deployed BISM tabular model and using that data and functionality to drive the Power View experience.

CREATING A DATA SOURCE

Be sure to install the data samples for this chapter before beginning this section. For more information, see the "Installing the Power View Samples" section later in this chapter. The data sample files will be used to perform the exercises in this chapter.

First, you need to create the data source. You can do this in one of several ways. You can connect to your data model through Excel 2013 and import the data into an Excel worksheet. Although this process will limit the amount of data and functionality you can leverage, it is great for simple tasks. You can use PowerPivot to import the data and then create tables in Excel to analyze or you can connect to a PowerPivot data model that is published in SharePoint. Right now, your data model is published to an Analysis Services server somewhere, and that is the type of solution we're focusing on. For now, let's jump into Excel.

CREATING A NEW POWER VIEW REPORT IN EXCEL

To create your new report, open Excel 2013 and select the Data tab. Then select From Other Sources in the top-left third of the Ribbon. See Figure 6-4.

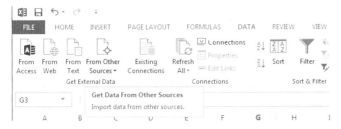

FIGURE 6-4 *Getting external data from other sources*

FIGURE 6-5 *Choosing to view data in a Power View report*

Next, select From Analysis Services, enter your connection information, and click Next. Now select the Chapter 6 - BISM Model from the database dropdown and click Finish.

From the Import Data dialog box choose Power View Report, as shown in Figure 6-5, and click OK. If you do not see the Power View Report option, that means that the add-in has not been enabled yet, so click Cancel and follow the steps in the "Enabling the Power View Add-in" sidebar—then you will be able to complete these steps.

ENABLING THE POWER VIEW ADD-IN

In order to enable the Power View add-in click on File in the Ribbon, and then Options ➤ Add-Ins, and then select COM Add-ins from the Manage drop-down list and click Go. Now check the box next to Power View and click OK.

After the Import Data dialog box closes you should see a screen like that shown in Figure 6-6.

FIGURE 6-6 *Clean Power View report canvas*

When you see the Power View interface for the first time, you'll notice how uncluttered it looks. Let's review the sections of this interface and see where to go for certain types of actions.

- **Canvas:** The center section dominated by the watermark is called the canvas, which is where your different visualizations will show up. You can build tables, slicers, charts, and other elements to create an interactive experience.

- **Field List:** The upper right of the screen should look familiar if you've used Excel's pivot table functionality in the past. It is where the tables from the data model show up for you to work with.

- **Field Well:** The Field Well, found in the bottom right, is where you drag and drop fields to enable them in different elements on the canvas. We can change some settings here as well to help them show up the way we want.

- **Filters Area:** The Filters Area restricts the amount of data displayed in your canvas elements. We could, for example, restrict to showing just a particular year or a city/state combination for more detailed viewing of our data. If it gets in the way, you can toggle it using the "<" icon at the top of the Filters Area or remove it completely with the Filters Area option in the Ribbon.

- **View area:** The View Area is available when using the SharePoint Power View option and allows for tracking different states and/or views of the data in the same report file to provide capabilities to analyze data at different points in time and/or in different ways.

- **Ribbon:** This is the familiar interface introduced with Office 2007 in which many of your other common tasks such as saving, design, and data connectivity are grouped together.

Now we can begin creating our first report, but before we do let's review the steps at a high level and then we'll complete an exercise:

1. First, you can give your report a title such as Reseller Performance by clicking on the item on the Power View canvas labeled Click here to add a title.

2. Next, you select the data you want to analyze and explore by dragging it onto the canvas. You can rearrange the fields in the Field Well to make the report look more appealing. Remember that you don't need to do any relationship building here. If the relationships exist in the model,

they will be surfaced here. As you see here, the fields have created a table on the canvas, which is the starting point for any item added.

3. Now you can change the initial table into a different visualization such as a column chart by switching over to the Design tab in the Ribbon.

4. You can then drag other fields into the Filter pane to the right of the canvas, as shown in Figure 6-6, which provides additional context-sensitive filters on the report.

5. Additional fields you add to the canvas that you want as slicers can be enabled by selecting them and then clicking slicer in the Ribbon. Simple!

Creating Your First Simple Power View Report

Now you dive deeper and build a financial-style report step by step. Because financials are not always eye-grabbing, you can add some visualizations to it to spice it up.

1. Open Excel 2013, if it isn't open already, and go to the Data tab. Make sure you are in a worksheet in the Excel workbook, because if you are in a Power View report the items will be greyed out. Select Existing Connections, and then select the connection file that you created previously in this chapter in the section "Creating a Data Source," and refer to that section if you still need to create the data source connection. This will display the Data Import dialog box where you will then want to select the Power View Report option, and click OK, as shown in Figure 6-5.

2. Now you create your first table in Power View. In the Power View Fields list, select InternetSales ➢ OrderQuantity and SalesAmount. In the Field Well click on the drop-down arrow next to OrderQuantity and select Sum. Also select Geography ➢ EnglishCountryRegionName and StateProvinceName. This process creates your first table on the canvas. Figure 6-7 shows an example.

3. Using filters is easy in this new interface. Between the main part of the canvas and the field list is the Filters Area. Drag fields from the list into the Filters pane such as SalesTerritory ➢ SalesTerritoryGroup and Date ➢ CalendarYear. Make selections from these two fields in the Filters pane and watch as the data changes in the table. Experiment with dates, numeric values, and regular text columns to see the different types of sliding filters and check box lists you can get.

FIGURE 6-7 *Your first table in a Power View report*

4. Click in the corners of the table and drag them to make the table more readable. Get used to resizing these visualizations because you'll be moving things around a lot to fit everything on the canvas.

5. Now we can make this report even better by changing it to use tiles. Click in the table and then go to the Design tab in the Ribbon. Click the Tiles button and select Convert to use tiles. Now the report is tiled by the region name, and you can click through the tiles in a visually appealing manner. Your final report should look similar to that shown in Figure 6-8.

FIGURE 6-8 *A Power View report with filters and tiles*

Enhancing Your Power View Reports

Now that you've created your first simple report, let's add some pizzazz to your reports by adding images.

1. Create a new Power View Report in Excel connecting to the data model provided with this chapter. If you need any help refer to the first step in the previous exercise.

   Let's add some images to a new version of the report we created in the previous exercise. In the next couple of steps, you build a report with even more interaction.

2. Create a table on the report using Geography ➢ StateProvinceName and InternetSales ➢ OrderQuantity and SalesAmount from the field list. Make sure to select Sum from the drop-down arrow next to OrderQuantity in the Field Well just like in the previous exercise. Then Select ProductCategory ➢ CategoryImage and drag it into the Tile By section in the Field Well, as shown in Figure 6-9. When you add CategoryImage to the Field Well you will probably receive a Security Warning message above the worksheet. You will need to click the Enable Content button to allow for the images to be displayed. The images are referencing URL locations on the Internet, so you will also need an Internet connection for these to display properly.

FIGURE 6-9 *The Field Well showing Tile By CategoryImage*

3. Next, drag the following fields onto the canvas to use as slicers:

   ▪ Geography ➢ EnglishCountryRegionName

   ▪ Date ➢ CalendarYear

   ▪ SalesTerritory ➢ SalesTerritoryRegion

   ▪ Customer ➢ EnglishEducation

   ▪ Customer ➢ EnglishOccupation

   For the CalendarYear table you may need to change the setting in the Field Well to Do Not Summarize (if it is set to Sum) so that you will be able to change this to a slicer.

4. Click each one of the fields you just added on the report, select the Design tab in the Ribbon, and then click Slicer. This will turn each of these fields (tables) into a live filter with no additional work on your part to hook them up or build relationships to the other items on the report. Figure 6-10 shows the finished example after the items have been rearranged, sized, and with selections made in the slicers.

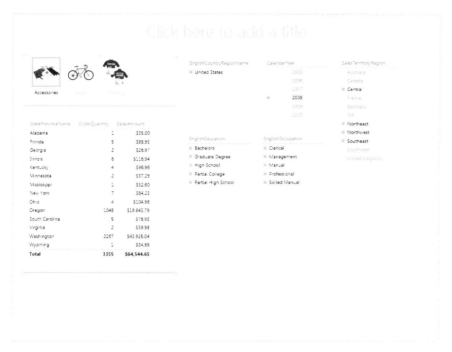

FIGURE 6-10 *Power View report with images and slicers*

ENHANCING DATA MODELS FOR POWER VIEW

Before you make your data model available to end users to create reports against, there are a few enhancements that should be done to improve the usability and adoption of the model. These enhancements include cleaning up the data model as well as setting some additional settings within the model that Power View can then leverage when you're creating reports. Now let's take a look at what is involved with these enhancements.

CLEANING UP YOUR DATA MODEL

There are a number of things you can do to clean up your data model and make it more valuable for your efforts or for your end users' needs. Let's explore some of them here:

- **Remove unnecessary columns.** Many times we import a lot more columns than we need into our data models. Now is the time to go about cleaning them out. Just remove them; or if you feel they must be there, you can right-click the column header and select Hide From Client Tools.

- **Make sure column names are clear and understandable.** Go through your data model and make sure the names are clear and legible. Now is the time to make this easily understandable for your end users. These names can be edited by either changing the properties of a column in the properties pane of SQL Server Data Tools, or by right-clicking the column header and selecting Rename.

- **Review formatting of data and ensure the data is clean.** You should always spend some time reviewing the data in your model to make sure it fits the profile you believe to be correct. Sometimes you won't know and that's okay, but check for simple things such as ensuring that the Description column does not contain Prices and other things like that.

- **Add any images you might need for building cards or more-advanced visualizations.** Review the previous section on Enhancing Your Power View Report to see how to add images and other impressive interactivity to your model so you can consume them in Power View.

ADDING METADATA FOR POWER VIEW

After the data model has been cleaned up, there are some additional items that can be looked at to further enhance it when used with Power View. These items include the default field set, table behavior settings, and categorizing the data in your columns within your tables accordingly. This section discusses these and provides an example from a Tabular Analysis Services project. In a PowerPivot data model, these items are found in the Reporting Properties section of the Advanced tab in the PowerPivot window.

Default Field Set

First there is the default field set. This setting on a table in your data model provides you the ability to select one or more columns from your table (including measures) and allows you to order them as you see fit. Now when a user clicks on the table in the Power View Fields, all of the columns that were defined in the default field set will be added to the canvas. This provides a quick way to add multiple columns that are typically used for a particular table in a report. Figure 6-11 shows an example of what the Default Field Set dialog boxes looks like.

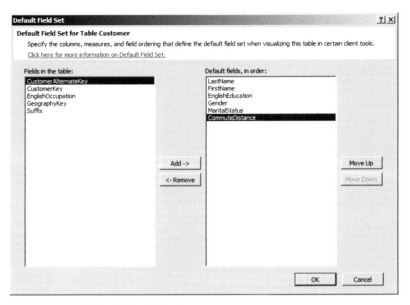

FIGURE 6-11 *Default Field Set dialog box*

Table Behavior

The table behavior properties can be used to set the following properties for a particular table: Row Identifier, Keep Unique Rows, Default Label, and Default Image. The Row Identifier allows you to designate the column in the table that is the unique identifier (primary key) for that table. The Keep Unique Rows setting allows you to establish which column(s) in the table will be used to determine unique rows when reporting. So, for instance, in the Chapter 6 – BISM Model, if the Row Identifier is set to CustomerKey, the Keep Unique Rows could be set to CustomerAlternateKey or possibly FirstName and LastName. That way if a customer is in the table multiple times you can report on them as a single customer instead of multiple customers and avoid sending them multiple offerings.

The Default Label and Default Image do exactly what you would think—they allow you to define the label and image for each unique row in the table. So for the ProductCategory table you would select EnglishProductCategoryName for the Default Label and CategoryImage for the Default Image. The Default Image can reference either binary data-type columns or text columns that are designated as URL references to image files. See Figure 6-12 for an example of the table behavior dialog box.

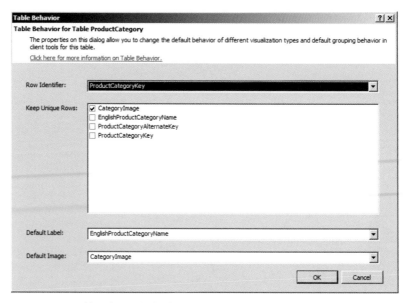

FIGURE 6-12 *Table Behavior dialog box*

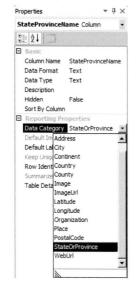

FIGURE 6-13 *Data Category column property*

Data Category

Data category is a property setting that is available on a column within your data model. Some of the values for this property are address, city, continent, image, imageURL, place, etc. Once this property is set on the column, Power View can interpret that information and use it so that it knows that the text is a URL reference to an image or that the text represents a country name. This can then be used to display images and map the data depending on the type of visualization used in the report. Figure 6-13 shows an example of this property setting in a Tabular Analysis Services project for the StateProvinceName column in the Geography table.

SHARING POWER VIEW REPORTS

Now that you have learned how to create these highly interactive Power View reports, the next step is to share them with others. There are a few options for this—one is that you can publish them to a SharePoint portal and another option is to use the export to PowerPoint capability. Let's look at these two options a little further.

PUBLISH IN SHAREPOINT

It is especially useful to be able to share not only your Power View creations, but also your PowerPivot data models. This section explores doing that and shows some of the value it provides.

Deploying Your Data Model to SharePoint

When you want to share your data model with co-workers or a team, you can save it to a SharePoint library, enabling them to create new Power View reports right from the SharePoint interface. Here are the steps that you can use to deploy the PowerPivot Excel file to SharePoint.

1. Open the PowerPivot Excel file (in this example this is an Excel 2013 file).

2. Select the File tab in the Ribbon.

3. Now click Save As and then Browse, enter the location, as shown in Figure 6-14, and click Save (in Excel 2010 this is done as Save & Send, then Save to SharePoint, and Browse).

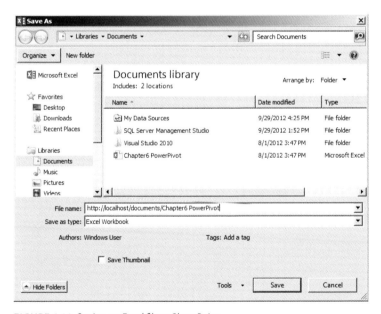

FIGURE 6-14 *Saving an Excel file to SharePoint*

4. Now the file will be uploaded to SharePoint in the document library that you specified.

Alternatively, you can share your own reports and people can view them if given the right access. These Power View reports could have potentially been included in the Excel file with the PowerPivot data model already, they could be in a separate Excel file like the one we created in the exercises in this chapter against the Tabular Analysis Services model, or they could be created and saved directly in SharePoint. If they are included in the Excel file, you can follow the steps just listed to save them to SharePoint.

Now that the file is in SharePoint, users have the ability to connect to that file from their desktops in a new Excel file and create reports from it. In addition, users could also create connection files in SharePoint that could in turn be used to develop Power View reports from directly in SharePoint, or even use them as sources for PerformancePoint dashboards.

Saving Your Power View Reports in SharePoint

If you are creating the Power View reports directly in SharePoint instead of Excel, you can quickly save and share the reports directly in a document library. Once the files are in the document library or possibly a PowerPivot Gallery, then you can provide access to these reports for others to reference and explore. The following are the steps that you can use to save a Power View report directly in SharePoint.

1. After you have created your Power View report in SharePoint, select the File tab in the Ribbon.

2. Then click Save (or Save As; since this is your first time saving the report those options will act the same) and enter a file name for the report file, which has a file extension of RDLX, as shown in Figure 6-15.

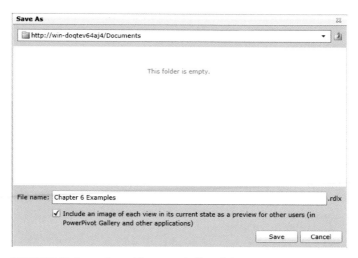

FIGURE 6-15 *Save a Power View report in SharePoint*

You see in Figure 6-15 that there is an option to have images of the views with the report file as well. These images can then be used to display in, say, the PowerPivot Gallery if you choose to save your reports in that type of a library. If you do then you will get to see a preview of the views that are included in your report file.

3. Now you can browse to a new location if the current location is not where you want to store the report file. When you are ready, you can click Save.

EXPORTING TO POWERPOINT

Power View reports created in SharePoint (not the ones created by using Excel) have another great feature: they can be exported to PowerPoint. This makes these reports more mobile, and full interactivity is possible as long as the person has connectivity to the data source. To export your Power View reports to PowerPoint, simply press the button shown in Figure 6-16 while you are viewing the report in SharePoint.

In addition to being able to make these reports more mobile and being able to incorporate them into a presentation, this also provides a nice way to be able to print all of the reports at the same time. If you tried to print them from SharePoint you would only be able to print one view within a report file at a time, so if you have multiple pages, using the Export to PowerPoint option works nicely. In addition to that, you are also able to save them to a PDF format once they are exported.

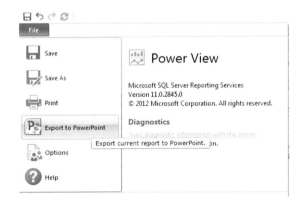

FIGURE 6-16 *Power View Export to PowerPoint option*

INSTALLING THE POWER VIEW SAMPLES

The samples are simple to install. You need an instance of SQL Server 2012 SP1, SQL Server Data Tools, a tabular instance of Analysis Services running in your environment, and a SharePoint installation with PowerPivot and Reporting Services integration. Follow these steps:

1. Restore the `CH6db.bak` file to your SQL Server 2012 SP1 database instance.

2. Open the project file in the `Chapter 6 - BISM Model` directory.

3. Check the `Model.bim` Workspace Server property. Make sure that this points to the right server for your environment. The server setting will default to `localhost`.

4. Check the model's existing connection server setting. Open the `Model.bim` file and, from the File menu under Model, you can open the existing connections and edit the SQL Server data source with the project so that it points to the right server for your environment. The server setting will default to `localhost`.

5. Check the properties for the project and make sure it points to the right server for your environment. The server setting will default to localhost.

6. Deploy the model to your tabular instance of Analysis Services.

You're now ready to connect to it with Excel 2013 and start building reports!

SUMMARY

In this chapter, you created models to explore your data and then created some simple visualizations using Microsoft Power View. Power View, like many of the tools in this book, is bigger than we can cover completely in one chapter. We hope this introduction has inspired you to test it out more thoroughly in your environment!

CHAPTER 7

PerformancePoint

PerformancePoint provides a very powerful toolset dedicated to designing scorecards and dashboards. PerformancePoint, being introduced in 2007, is one of the newest Microsoft business intelligence (BI) tools.

Compared with other Microsoft BI tools, PerformancePoint offers the designer the most useful functionality. As a key benefit for rapidly designing content, most of the useful functionality need not require planning and specific implementation because the features are common options associated with the various scorecard elements. Balancing this functionality is less control over visual elements, and rather limited print and export options. This chapter will provide an introduction to key PerformancePoint functionality used to develop visualizations.

TABULAR VERSUS MULTIDIMENSIONAL SOURCES

The key foundational element used with a PerformancePoint solution is a data source. The data source supplies data for use by key performance indicators (KPIs), analytic charts, grids, dashboard filters, and other PerformancePoint objects. The types of data sources supported for use with PerformancePoint include tabular and multidimensional sources. It is important to note that PerformancePoint will treat both tabular and multidimensional sources the same way for the purpose of design activities.

Tabular data sources include Excel spreadsheets, Excel Services spreadsheets, SharePoint lists, and relational database tables. These tabular-type

Analysis Services in Tabular mode is treated as a multidimensional source in PerformancePoint, and its tables are treated as dimensions.

data sources work best with PerformancePoint when organized in a way that distinguishes columns as either dimension data or fact (measure) data by the PerformancePoint Dashboard Designer during data import. One example of this organization is that a column within a spreadsheet that should contain fact (measure) data must contain only numeric values in order to be classified as a fact source by the Dashboard Designer.

Multidimensional data sources are those that include dimensions, measures (facts), and support—either the MDX or DMX language. PerformancePoint multidimensional data sources presently include Analysis Services and PowerPivot workbooks.

Key usage differences exist among the tabular and multidimensional data source capabilities within PerformancePoint. A key limitation found when using a tabular data source is that data is flattened, so it cannot represent parent/child relationships nor can it model hierarchies between dimensional values. Additionally, tabular sources cannot be used by analytic charts and grids. The data exploration feature, Decomposition Trees, is also not supported for tabular data sources.

REQUIREMENTS FOR RUNNING PERFORMANCEPOINT

This section discusses the various hardware and software requirements for running PerformancePoint and the Dashboard Designer.

The Dashboard Designer, used to create and organize PerformancePoint objects into dashboards, requires a computer having a dual core, 32-bit processor with 2GB of memory and 2GB of disk space. Additionally, a SharePoint-supported browser is required (details are provided in the "SharePoint Requirements" section that follows.

Analysis Services 2000 is no longer being supported as a data source and, along with SharePoint, PerformancePoint requires 64-bit server architecture.

SHAREPOINT REQUIREMENTS

To install, configure, and run SharePoint web servers and application servers, the host server must have a 4 core 64-bit processor with 8GB of memory and

80GB of disk space. Additionally, the database server that stores the SharePoint data requires a 4–8 core 64-bit processor with 8–16GB of memory and 80GB of disk space. This database server requires a 64-bit edition of Microsoft SQL Server from the following versions:

- Microsoft SQL Server 2012 (requires SharePoint Server 2010 SP1 or later)
- Microsoft SQL Server 2008 R2
- Microsoft SQL Server 2008 SP1 with Cumulative Update 2 for SP1
- Microsoft SQL Server 2005 SP3 with Cumulative Update 3 for SP3

A 64-bit version of Window Server 2008 with SP2 or Windows Server 2008 R2 or later is required for SharePoint installation, and the SharePoint preparation tool will install any of the following if they are missing from the server:

- Web Server (IIS) role
- Application Server role
- Microsoft .NET Framework version 3.5 SP1
- Microsoft Sync Framework Runtime v1.0 (x64)
- Microsoft Filter Pack 2.0
- Microsoft Chart Controls for the Microsoft .NET Framework 3.5
- Windows PowerShell 2.0
- SQL Server 2008 Native Client
- Microsoft SQL Server 2008 Analysis Services ADOMD.NET
- ADO.NET Data Services Update for .NET Framework 3.5 SP1
- A hotfix for the .NET Framework 3.5 SP1 that provides a method to support token authentication without transport security or message encryption in Windows Communication Foundation (WCF)
- Windows Identity Foundation (WIF)

SharePoint requires a supported Internet browser in order to successfully view and interact with content. Support for Internet browsers is categorized into supported, supported with limitations, and not supported (as follows):

TABLE 7-1 SharePoint 2010 Supported Browsers

BROWSER	SUPPORTED	SUPPORT WITH LIMITATIONS	NOT SUPPORTED
Internet Explorer 10	32-bit	64-bit	
Internet Explorer 9	32-bit	64-bit	
Internet Explorer 8	32-bit	64-bit	
Internet Explorer 7 (no longer supported in 2013)	32-bit	64-bit	
Internet Explorer 6			X
Google Chrome	X		
Mozilla Firefox	X		
Apple Safari		X	

The first step in installing PerformancePoint Services is ensuring that the Enterprise Features are installed. To do this, go to Upgrade and Migration in the Central Administration site, and click Enable Enterprise Features. This is only necessary once for any Enterprise Feature. After you have done this, enable these features by clicking Enable features on existing sites. This will enable the Enterprise Features across all existing sites—you can do this manually if you want to enable the features on only some sites. The next step is to run the configuration wizard—make sure to choose PerformancePoint and the Secure Store service!

AUTHENTICATION ISSUES WHEN USING SECURE STORE SERVICE

To successfully use PerformancePoint a Secure Store Service (SSS) is required to be configured. When an SSS is not properly configured, the Dashboard Designer will have errors when trying to create new data sources that are resolved by ensuring that the SSS is running, it has a correctly generated encryption key, and an unattended service account is set for PerformancePoint.

SSS may already have been configured for another application, but if it has not, it will need to be set up. The steps to be taken are:

1. Install SSS

2. Create a key for encryption

3. Create a new Secure Store Application

4. Assign credentials to the new application

KERBEROS

SSS is not required when Kerberos is being used—Kerberos is required for role-based security in SharePoint 2013, and is outside the scope of this book.

Kerberos allows users to connect to an Analysis Services data source under their own credentials, whereas SSS will store a single credential for accessing the data source.

Configure a Secure Store by registering a managed (domain) account in SharePoint (via Central Administration ➢ Security ➢ General Security) to run the Secure Store application pool, start the SSS (via Central Admin ➢ Application Management ➢ Service Applications ➢ Manage Services on Server) on the application server in the SharePoint farm, and create an SSS application (also via Central Admin ➢ Application Management ➢ Service Applications ➢ Manage service applications).

From Central Admin, choose the Manage Service Applications option under Application Management, then click the Secure Store Service and you will see a screen like Figure 7-1.

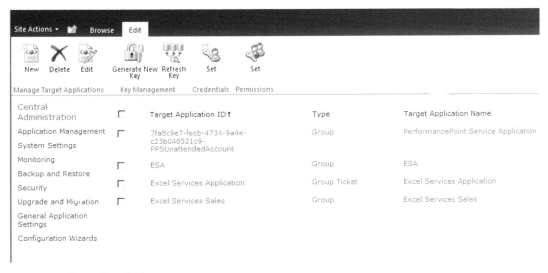

FIGURE 7-1 *Secure Store Service*

If there are no applications listed, you will need to start by generating a new key—this is the key that will be used to encrypt the credentials stored in the Secure Store Service, so ensure that you save the passphrase in a secure location.

Now that you have created a key to encrypt the usernames, you will set up the account that PerformancePoint will use.

Set an unattended service account using SharePoint Central Administration by selecting Manage Service Applications and then clicking the PerformancePoint Service Application. Select PerformancePoint Service Application Settings and set the username and password for the Unattended Service Account.

KPIS, SCORECARDS, FILTERS, REPORTS, AND DASHBOARDS

This section gives you a tour of the various component objects within PerformancePoint along with an overview of how each contributes to the design of a data presentation solution. In order to create any of these components, a site collection using the BI Center template is required. You create a new site collection in Central Admin ➢ Manage Applications ➢ Create site collection and choosing the Business Intelligence Center under the Enterprise tab.

CREATING A DATA SOURCE

To connect PerformancePoint to the data, a data source is required. SharePoint further requires that all data connections be stored in a trusted data connection library. When PerformancePoint Services is configured, it automatically trusts all SharePoint libraries—this can be overridden to allow only certain libraries to contain PPS data sources.

All PerformancePoint design occurs within a tool named Dashboard Designer. There are several ways to start the Dashboard Designer. If not previously installed, from web browser, open the Business Intelligence Center, select a section from Monitor Key Performance, Build and Share Reports, or Create Dashboards, and click the Start using PerformancePoint Services link. On the PerformancePoint site, click the Run Dashboard Designer button. You can also open the Dashboard Designer by opening the Business Intelligence Center or the PerformancePoint site, right clicking on any PerformancePoint content listed and selecting the Edit in Dashboard Designer. After Dashboard Designer has been opened previously, you can launch it from the Start menu (via Start ➢ All Programs ➢ SharePoint ➢ PerformancePoint Dashboard Designer).Within PerformancePoint, as shown in Figure 7-2, the data source can be created by selecting the Data Source menu option located on the Create Menu of Dashboard Designer or from within a SharePoint Data Connections library by selecting New Document from the Documents view. The server name will need to be inserted next. Often, "." can be used if you are working from a local machine, else the server name will be required. Sometimes an instance name in the format "*servername\instancename*" will be needed. Then you should be able to choose the appropriate database from the drop-down, and then the cube from the drop-down.

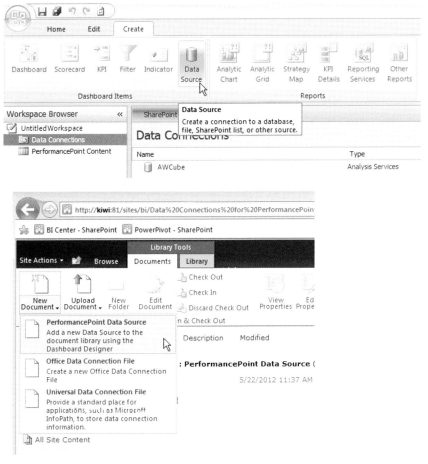

FIGURE 7-2 *Methods of creating new PerformancePoint data sources*

MAPPING THE TIME DIMENSION

PerformancePoint has a Time Intelligence feature to support a rich variety of common time selections such as Last Quarter, Current Financial Year, or Last 3 Quarters. This Time Intelligence feature associates a common time label with a specific filter period that is defined using the Simple Time Period Specification (STPS) language.

Configuration of Time Intelligence is performed on the data source using the Time tab. This is covered in the "Installing the PerformancePoint Samples" section at the end of the chapter, specifically for the samples used in the book. After starting by selecting a dimension in the data source that stores calendar dates, a reference date to begin a year for the dimension is provided.

Next, the hierarchy level of the date provided is selected. In the case of a date of January 1, 2005, the hierarchy level may be set to Day. A reference date that is equal to the period specified by the hierarchy level is entered and then each member level has its appropriate time aggregation set to the dimension level corresponding with a given member level (e.g., Calendar Year member level is mapped to Year time aggregation level). A sample Time Intelligence Reference Data Mapping is demonstrated in Figure 7-3.

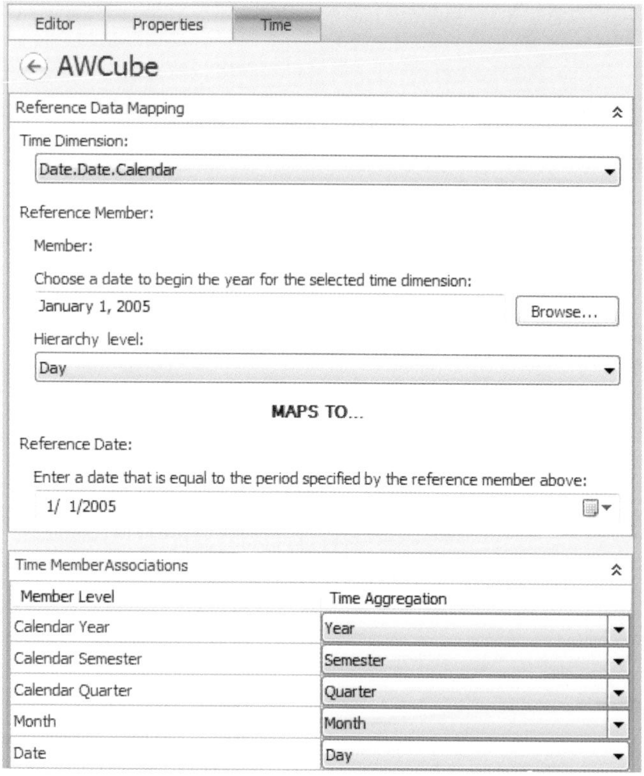

FIGURE 7-3 Configuring PerformancePoint data sources with Time Intelligence

With the Time Intelligence properly configured for a PerformancePoint data source, the Time Intelligence formulas can be used within a filter created by selecting the Time Intelligence template when creating a new filter. Figure 7-4 shows the selection of a Time Intelligence filter from the Select a Filter Template dialog box that appears when creating a new filter within PerformancePoint.

The resulting Time Intelligence filter can be added to PerformancePoint dashboards in order to permit users selecting these common Time Intelligence date values.

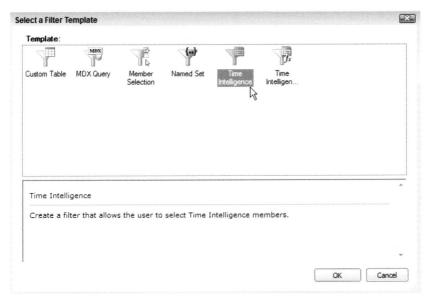

FIGURE 7-4 *Creating a PerformancePoint filter that uses Time Intelligence*

Quick Samples

Formula structure: `[(]<Period>[Offset>[()][ <Function>[<Offset>]]]`

TABLE 7-2 Example Formulas

TO DISPLAY	FORMULA	RESULT
Yesterday	`day-1`	The previous day relative to the current date.
Tomorrow	`day+1`	The next day relative to the current date.
The current quarter and today	`quarter, day`	A set of time periods consisting of the current day and current quarter.
Last 10 days	`day:day-9`	A 10-day range including today.
Last 10 days (excluding today)	`day-1:day-10`	A 10-day range NOT including today.
Same day last year	`(year-1).day`	Current date (month and day) for last year. For example, if the current date were December 10, 2010, then `(year-1).day` would show information for December 10, 2009.

TO DISPLAY	FORMULA	RESULT
Same month last year	`(year-1).month`	Current month for last year. For example, if the current month were December, 2010, then `(year-1).month` would show information for December, 2009.
Same range of a period of six months last year	`(year-1).(month-5): (year-1).(month)`	From 18 months ago to one year ago. For example, if the current month were December 2010, then `(year-1).(month-5): (year-1).month` would show information for the time period ranging from June, 2009 to December, 2009.
Same range of months to date for last year	`(year-1).firstmonth: (year-1).month`	From the first month of last year up to and including the month parallel to the current month this year.
Year to date	`yeartodate`	A single time period representing the aggregation of values from the beginning of the year up to and including the last completed period. The period corresponds to the most specific time period defined for the data source.
Year to date (by month)	`yeartodate .fullmonth`	A single time period representing the aggregation of values from the beginning of the year up to and including the last completed month.
Year to date (by day)	`yeartodate .fullday`	A single time period representing the aggregation of values from the beginning of the year up to and including the last completed day.
Parallel year to date	`yeartodate-1`	The aggregation of the same set of default time periods completed in the current year except for the prior year.
Parallel year to date (by month)	`(yeartodate-1) .fullMonth`	The aggregation of time periods last year that is equal to year to date periods for the current year.

General conventions

- When no offset is specified, the current period is assumed.

- Using a time period with an offset along with a function requires the use of parentheses.

- Casing of formulas does not impact formula evaluation or meaning.

- White-space does not impact formula evaluation or meaning.

- Time period including "to date" permits the use of offsets.

- Formulas should use singular nouns rather than plural nouns (e.g., year not years)

Syntax Elements

Operators (Table 7-3), time periods (Table 7-4), and functions (Table 7-5) are used to create TI formulas.

TABLE 7-3 Operators

OPERATOR	USE
.	The period or "dot" operator delimits time periods from functions. The string in front of the dot always corresponds to the time period. The string following the dot always corresponds to the time period function. Example: `year.firstMonth`
+ or −	The plus (+) and minus (−) operators are used to determine the offset relative to the current date. Use the minus sign (−) to specify time periods in the past. Use the plus sign (+) to specify time periods in the future. Example: `day-1`
()	Parentheses are used to group a time period and its offset when you use them together with a function. Required. Example: `(year-1).firstMonth:(year-1).month`
,	Commas are used to delimit multiple time periods in the same formula. Example: `year, Quarter, Month, day`
:	The colon operator (:) specifies a range of time periods. Example: `day:day-4`

Standard Time Periods

Table 7-4 shows standard time periods used within TI formulas.

TABLE 7-4 Standard Time Periods

PERIOD	EXAMPLE
Year	Year-1, year+2
Quarter	quarter, Quarter-4
Month	Month-2
Week	Week-51
Day	Day-9, day+2
Hour	Hour-12
Minute	minute-30
Second	second+5

Standard Time Period Functions

TI formulas can use the time period functions provided in Table 7-5 to modify any standard time period via usage of the dot operator (.).

TABLE 7-5 Standard Time Period Functions

FUNCTION	USE
FirstQuarter	Specifies the first quarter in a year.
LastQuarter	Specifies the last quarter in a year.
FirstMonth	Specifies the first month in a year or quarter.
LastMonth	Specifies the last month in a year or quarter.
FirstWeek	Specifies the first week in a year, quarter, or month.
LastWeek	Specifies the last week in a year, quarter, or month.
FirstDay	Specifies the first day in a week, month, or larger time period.
LastDay	Specifies the last day in a week, month, or larger time period.
FirstHour	Specifies the first hour in a day, week, or larger time period.
LastHour	Specifies the last hour in a day, week, or larger time period.

FUNCTION	USE
FirstMinute	Specifies the first minute in an hour, day, or larger time period.
LastMinute	Specifies the last minute in an hour, day, or larger time period.
FirstSecond	Specifies the first minute in a minute, hour, or larger time period.
LastSecond	Specifies the last minute in a minute, hour, or larger time period.

Period-to-Date Formulas

PerformancePoint 2010 introduced period-to-date formulas in order to provide a way to aggregate data up to the last completed period requested. These formulas will exclude incomplete time periods and use the lowest time precision supported by the underlying data source. The period-to-date periods shown in Table 7-6 may be used within TI formulas.

TABLE 7-6 Period-to-Date Formulas

PERIOD	USE
YearToDate	Specifies a time period from the beginning of the year to the current period.
QuarterToDate	Specifies a time period from the beginning of the quarter to the current period.
MonthToDate	Specifies a time period from the beginning of the month to the current period.
WeekToDate	Specifies a time period from the beginning of the week to the current period.
DayToDate	Specifies a time period from the beginning of the day to the current period.
HourToDate	Specifies a time period from the beginning of the hour to the current period.
MinuteToDate	Specifies a time period from the beginning of the minute to the current period.

Period-to-Date Functions

Formulas needing to specify periods may use the period-to-date functions including those provided in Table 7-7.

TABLE 7-7 Period-to-Date Functions

FUNCTION	EFFECT
FullQuarter	Specifies that the period to date should include up to the last full quarter.
FullMonth	Specifies that the period to date should include up to the last full month.
FullWeek	Specifies that the period to date should include up to the last full week.
FullDay	Specifies that the period to date should include up to the last full day.
FullHour	Specifies that the period to date should include up to the last full hour.
FullMinute	Specifies that the period to date should include up to the last full minute.
FullSecond	Specifies that the period to date should include up to the last full second.

Parallel Period-to-Date

Formulas often require the ability to compare and contrast values across similar periods during the current and prior years. Time Intelligence formulas support including an offset value to the to-date period needed as shown.

```
YearToDate-1
```

The formulas support any to-date time period including those using a full period function.

```
(YearToDate-1).FullMonth
```

KPIs

A critical component used to measure and track performance is a *key performance indicator* (KPI). Within PerformancePoint, a KPI represents a measurement of a particular business process, including the actual value from a data source, a desired target achievement level, the visual indicators used when reporting the result of comparing the target with actual values, and a scoring pattern that represents the method used when scoring the resulting comparison value.

To create a KPI, open the Dashboard Designer and select the KPI dashboard item from the Create menu. On the KPI Template dialog box, the Blank KPI option is selected, and the KPI editor is then used to map the KPI to data sources. Figure 7-5 illustrates a sample KPI being created by the KPI editor.

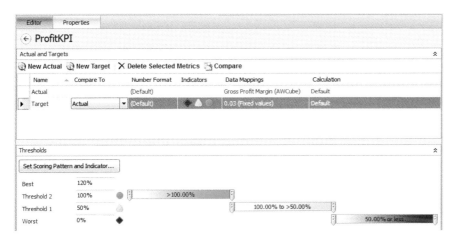

FIGURE 7-5 *Creating a PerformancePoint KPI using the KPI editor*

Configure the data sources for both actual and target rows within the KPI editor by clicking the 1 (Fixed Values) link that is located within the Data Mappings column. Note that the actual and target data mappings are configured separately, so support is mapped to different sources. Multiple actual and target values per KPI is available. This supports, as an example, the ability to provide multiple period, actual and target evaluation of the KPI (e.g., Now, This Month, This Year).

Selecting the proper scoring pattern and indicators involves editing a target row within the KPI editor and setting the scoring pattern, banding method, desired indicators, and worst value expected. Figure 7-6 demonstrates information provided by the Edit Banding Settings editor within PerformancePoint.

The scoring patterns define whether a resulting value is considered a good or bad score and include the following options:

- Increasing Is Better: No upper limit on what is considered good and larger values are desired

- Decreasing Is Better: No lower limit on what is considered good and smaller values are desired

- Closer To Target Is Better

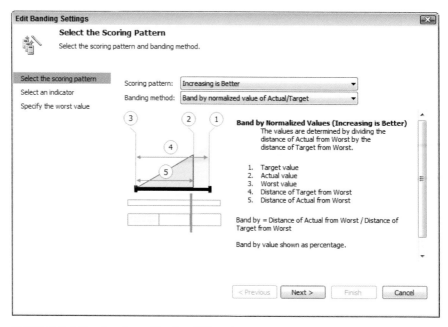

FIGURE 7-6 *Editing banding setting for a KPI target*

The banding method defines how values are compared in order to generate a status value and includes the following options:

▦ Band By Normalized Value Of Actual/Target: Enables comparison of scores that would otherwise be incompatible (e.g., percentages and dollar amount values) by converting the raw KPI values to a common scale and then averaging the converted scores

▦ Band By Numeric Value Of Actual: Uses exact values for thresholds that divide the status levels

▦ Band By Stated Score (Advanced): Specifically ignores the calculation of a score and uses a defined value from the data source

SCORECARDS

Some of the most useful and powerful objects within PerformancePoint, scorecards are used to display snapshots of business' performance by displaying key performance indicators (KPIs). The scorecard is organized into groupings of related goals referred to as objectives and their component metrics. Figure 7-7 shows an example of a PerformancePoint scorecard with a Profit KPI being measured across Sales Territories.

A scorecard, ultimately, is a special PerformancePoint report that can include the following features:

	Actual		Target	
⊟ ProfitKPI			◆	
⊟ All Sales Territories	0.58%	1 ◆	-99%	
Australia	-6.82%	1 ◆	-107%	
Canada	1.24%	1 ◆	-99%	
France	-0.81%	1 ◆	-101%	
Germany	-5.61%	1 ◆	-106%	
NA		1 ◇		
United Kingdom	0.15%	1 ◆	-100%	
United States	1.01%	1 ◆	-99%	

FIGURE 7-7 *PerformancePoint scorecard*

- Status indicators showing a summary of the current actual performance versus a targeted value

- Trend indicators showing how values have performed versus a prior time period

- KPIs that measure performance comparing actual values with desired target values

- Drill-down/drill-up navigation in order to see different levels of detail by expanding or collapsing rows or columns

- Time Intelligence for displaying dynamic time period values (e.g., Last Two Quarters)

- Analysis of individual member contributions via a Decomposition Tree

- Filtering of other reports on the dashboard based upon the current selection within the scorecard

- Special filtering of top/bottom values

- Export to PowerPoint or Excel

- View information about a given KPI using a KPI details report

FILTERS

Enabling end users to target the data in which they want to analyze within a dashboard is accomplish by designing PerformancePoint filters. Filters can be classified as one of two types: dashboard filters and object filters. The dashboard filters are separate PerformancePoint objects designed for use in a single dashboard or across multiple dashboards. Object filters are found within analytic reports and scorecards. It is important to note that a scorecard can also be used as a filter for other dashboard objects on the scorecard.

Several types of dashboard filters are available, as follows:

- Member Selection: Uses Analysis Services or tabular dimension members

- MDX Query: Uses Analysis Services to form an expression

- Named Set: Uses Analysis Services items defined as a named set

- Time Intelligence: Enables specific preconfigured time filters specified using Simple Time Period Specification (STPS) syntax

- Time Intelligence Connection Formula: Similar to the Time Intelligence filter, but uses a calendar to permit date selection

- Custom Table: Enables using a data table created within an application such as Excel

Connecting filters to various other PerformancePoint objects is described later in this chapter. Note that depending on the type of dashboard filter, different items should be selected to configure the source value sent from the filter as shown in Table 7-8.

TABLE 7-8 Filter Connections Table

CONNECT TO OBJECT	SOURCE VALUE	NOTES
Dimension Values	Member Unique Name	Replaces rows or columns with the selections made within the filter
Axis, Page, Row, Column Hierarchies	Display Value	Captions from object's data source displayed when matching filter selections
Time Intelligence Formula	Formula	Filters scorecards to the period of time selected
Current Date-Time	Current date-time	Filters scorecards to the current date
Time Dimension	Data source	Filters analytic charts and grids with the specified period supplied by the Time Intelligence formula

ANALYTIC REPORTS

Reporting on data with PerformancePoint often involves the creation of analytic reports that include analytic grids and analytic charts. The Analytic components require Analysis Services. Both are designed by dragging and dropping available objects from the Details pane on the right side of the Dashboard Designer into the Rows/Series, Columns/Bottom Axis, or Background designer panes located below the report design. The analytic report requires that the Rows/Series and Columns/Bottom Axis contain items while placing items in the Background is optional. An example analytic report in design within Dashboard Designer is shown in Figure 7-8.

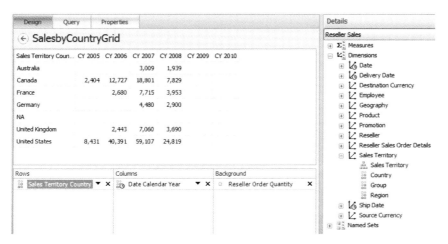

FIGURE 7-8 *Adding PerformancePoint Objects to an analytic report*

The analytic reports are highly interactive; supporting many powerful capabilities, including the following:

- Pivoting the data displayed
- Using Analysis Services actions
- Sorting values
- Sorting chart legend values
- Filtering: Removing empty values, selecting particular value, removing a value
- Drilling up/drilling down to view different levels of detail
- Exporting to PowerPoint or Excel
- Applying top or bottom filtering
- Viewing contributions of members using a Decomposition Tree
- Changing to a chart

DASHBOARDS

PerformancePoint combines various different objects represented as web parts into a dashboard or web part page. As a result, the dashboard is the central visual organizing component, responsible for determining what content appears and where it is located on the web page. Dashboards are divided into zones that can host the various forms of PerformancePoint content, including the following:

- Scorecards
- Reports (analytic charts and analytic grids)
- Filters
- Non-PerformancePoint content (e.g., Excel Services, Reporting Services reports)

The dashboard is designed by dragging and dropping available objects (e.g., scorecards, reports encompassing analytic charts and analytic grids, and filters) from the Details pane on the right side of the Dashboard Designer into a dashboard zone located in the Dashboard Content section of the Editor window. Figure 7-9 shows the design of a new dashboard having a header zone spanning the width of the dashboard with left and right column zones directly beneath the header.

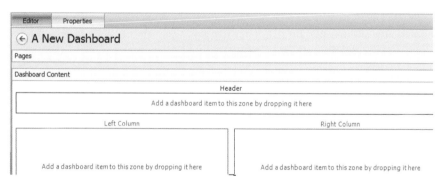

FIGURE 7-9 *Dashboard content zones*

Once the dashboard design is completed, it is published to a designated SharePoint site that has been previously configured to work with PerformancePoint.

COMBINING VISUALIZATIONS IN PERFORMANCEPOINT

This section introduces some of the non-PerformancePoint content that may be included within the PerformancePoint dashboard. Examples include Reporting Services reports and Excel spreadsheet reports.

EMBEDDING AN SSRS REPORT

Reporting Services offers a great deal of flexibility in how it renders data while also offering additional chart types that are not found within PerformancePoint. Furthermore, many existing reports contain key information desired for inclusion within a PerformancePoint dashboard. Lastly, scorecards that are used within the dashboard can filter the reports.

Adding Reporting Services reports to PerformancePoint is done by navigating to the PerformancePoint content library within SharePoint, selecting a new report, and then selecting the Reporting Services report template. Next, specific reporting settings are configured as needed, including these:

- Server mode (SharePoint Integrated or Native)
- Report Server URL
- Report URL
- Display Options (show toolbar, parameters, and docmap)
- Zoom (percent of actual rendered report size to display in a web part)
- Format (e.g., HTML 4.0)
- Section (to limit just part of a report to be included)
- Report parameters

Once the report has been added to the PerformancePoint content library, it can then be added to a dashboard as other PerformancePoint objects. Additionally, the report can be configured to work with PerformancePoint connections permitting, for example, filtering by passing values to report parameters.

EMBEDDING EXCEL REPORTS

Excel files often contain very useful and important business information that is desired for inclusion in a PerformancePoint dashboard. SharePoint allows Excel files to be used directly on SharePoint sites when Excel Services is configured. Once Excel Services is enabled and Excel workbooks are stored within the SharePoint site, support for these files is provided within PerformancePoint by the Excel Services type of report.

To create an Excel Services report, open Dashboard Designer, and from the Create menu and Reports menu group, select Other Reports. Figure 7-10 shows the selection of Other Reports from within the Report Ribbon group within Dashboard Designer.

FIGURE 7-10 *Creating other reports in Dashboard Designer*

Within the Report Template dialog box, select an Excel Services report. Finally, configure the Editor properties with the following:

- SharePoint site: The SharePoint site hosting the Excel file
- Document library: The specific SharePoint library hosting the Excel file
- Excel workbook: The name of the Excel file
- Item name: The specific named item to display from the Excel file

Once the Excel Services report has been added to the PerformancePoint content library it can then be added to a dashboard as other PerformancePoint objects. Additionally, the report can be configured to work with PerformancePoint connections—permitting, for example, filtering by passing values to report parameters.

CREATING WEB PART PAGES IN SHAREPOINT

SharePoint uses web part pages that contain web parts displaying various types of content. Site owners, site members, and others having the necessary permissions can create and modify web part pages, adding or removing web parts to arrange the content of the pages. Likewise, PerformancePoint dashboards are created by selecting a template that has zones, putting PerformancePoint objects together in the zones and establishing connections between the objects so they can pass values for filtering or other actions. Figure 7-11 shows the templates available for designing the dashboard zones, columns, and rows.

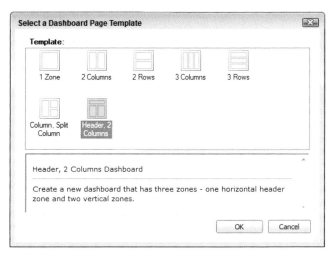

FIGURE 7-11 *Selecting a Dashboard page template*

ADDING WEB PARTS

Within Dashboard Designer, adding content to the page is accomplished by dragging PerformancePoint content (e.g., scorecards, reports, and filters) from the Details pane to the Dashboard Content section. The content is then placed into the desired zone (e.g., Left Column, Right Column, or Header—when using the Header, 2 Columns dashboard page template). Figure 7-12 shows what Dashboard Designer displays while dragging a scorecard into the dashboard's Left Column zone.

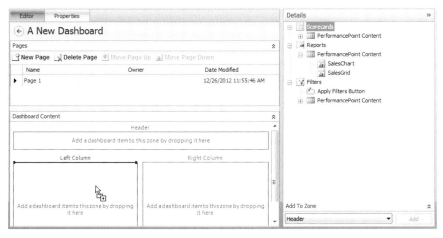

PerformancePoint creates SharePoint web part pages that can be edited in SharePoint's editor. PPS web parts can also be mixed in with other SharePoint web parts on native SharePoint pages.

FIGURE 7-12 *Dragging Items onto Dashboard Zones*

PERFORMANCEPOINT CONNECTIONS

A key advantage of using PerformancePoint is the ease in which dashboard connections and filters can be designed and configured. PerformancePoint objects that support providing or receiving connections use the Connections dialog box to configure the connection. Complex filtering can be performed by refining connections by using connection formulas (e.g., a Dimension value filter can show just those values selected while the connection formula could further refine the selection to include the top five).

In order to connect a filter to an existing PerformancePoint object, open the Dashboard Designer. Within the Details pane located on the right side, expand the Filters section and the PerformancePoint Content section. Simply drag the desired filter to a dashboard zone in the middle pane. Once the filter is located in the dashboard zone, click the down arrow on the right side of the filter name and select Create Connection. Figure 7-13 demonstrates the option of using a PerformancePoint object's action option menu to create a connection.

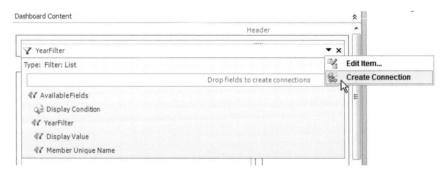

FIGURE 7-13 *Using the Create Connection menu option*

The Connection dialog box will display; on the Items tab set the Send Values To drop-down list to the PerformancePoint object that will receive the values from the filter. On the Values tab of the Connection dialog, set the Connect To value to the target field that will get filtered, and set the Source Value to the appropriate value based upon the source being used (e.g., Member Unique Name is commonly used with Analysis Services filter sources). Figures 7-14 and 7-15 illustrate the connection dialog steps to connect a filter to another dashboard object and also what the target object looks like after the connection has been successfully implemented.

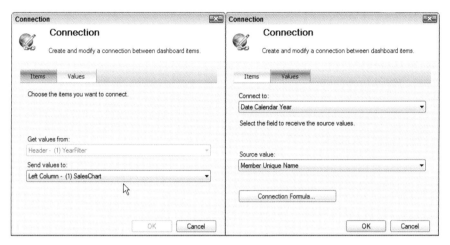

FIGURE 7-14 *Connection dialog items and values tabs*

The result is a fully functional filtering of a PerformancePoint object using a PerformancePoint filter. Other comparable connections are configured in a similar fashion, and all support the capability to pass values to and from different dashboard objects in order to support advanced capabilities.

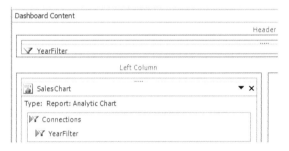

FIGURE 7-15 *Analytic chart with year filter connection*

Time Intelligence expressions and MDX queries can be used as expressions within connection formulas. When using Time Intelligence expressions, the Simple Time Period Specification (STPS) syntax is required for defining the expression. STPS syntax and examples were provided earlier within this chapter's "Mapping the Time Dimension" section. MDX queries used as expression will include monikers included within double angled brackets. The following MDX expression example uses the MDX nonempty values function combined with the Sourcevalue moniker to map to the value being passed by a source using the connection:

```
NONEMPTY(EXISTS([Dimension].[Hierarchy - Dimension].[Level number].
members,<<SourceValue>>,'Measure Group'))
```

INSTALLING THE PERFORMANCEPOINT SAMPLES

Each chapter with a PerformancePoint sample has a ZIP file with the PerformancePoint files, which have an `.DDWX` extension. Start by unzipping this file. To use the samples, open Dashboard Designer, then click Import items on the home screen and browse to the `.DDWX` file, then click OK. That will bring up a screen like Figure 7-16.

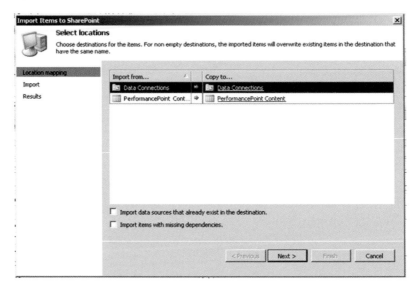

FIGURE 7-16 *Importing PerformancePoint components*

Click Next to import, then click Finish to finalize the import.

You will need to modify the data source to point to your local Analysis Services instance—do this by clicking on dsOECD, and editing the server name to your server, and then choosing the appropriate database and cube. This should be OECD_Data and Model, as shown in Figure 7-17, but your server name will likely be ".".

Next, you need to map the time source. The first step is to choose the hierarchy with the dates from the model—in this case it is `DimDate.YMD`. Next, choose a date to map. The date is important, as year calculations are all based on that day being the first day of the year, so you'll choose the 1st of January. You do this clicking browse, then choosing the date. You'll choose "Day" as the date to map, and then you will choose what date this entry in the dimension maps to in live dates. You can use this to map "Today" to an equivalent date in the past, and with the Adventure Works data you will almost always do this: in production data you will always choose the same date. Finally, you need to set the Time Member Associations: YearName to Year, MonthName to Month, and Date to Day. You should then see a screen like Figure 7-18. Finish by saving your data source.

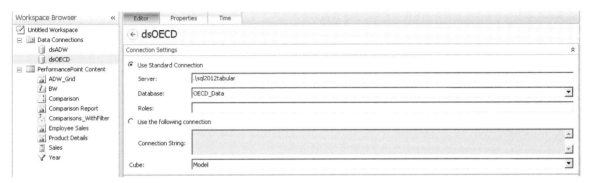

FIGURE 7-17 *Setting up a data source*

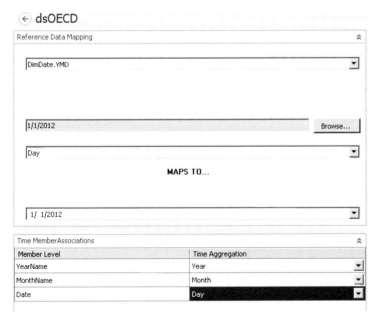

FIGURE 7-18 *Setting up a data source*

SUMMARY

This chapter introduced PerformancePoint and its key features. First, a comparison and contrast of tabular and multidimensional data sources was provided, followed by a review of requirements for running SharePoint and PerformancePoint. Next, some considerations for authenticating with data sources using the Secure Store Service (SSS) were outlined. A tour of the key PerformancePoint components, including data sources, Time Intelligence mapping, key performance indicators (KPIs), scorecards, filters, analytic reports, and dashboards was provided. Finally, combining visualizations in dashboards as well as constructing PerformancePoint dashboard pages was detailed.

CHAPTER 8

Reporting Services

Reporting Services has an engine dedicated to the marrying of data to a predeveloped visual design, which makes it a very useful tool for displaying information. Reporting in general has seen a great deal of expansion in its capabilities, and in many instances it now has overlapping use cases with other tools. For example, in the past, other tools such as PerformancePoint would have been considered a much more appropriate choice for producing scorecards, but Reporting Services has expanded its capabilities and is able to generate scorecard-type content depicting very graphical summarized information.

Compared with all the other Microsoft business intelligence tools, Reporting Services offers the designer the most control over visual elements, formatting within the reports, and rendering options such as PDF or Excel output. Although this control is very useful, the trade-off is that every piece of layout and interactivity must be planned and implemented while you're designing reports. Offsetting this effort are the greater visualization capabilities in Reporting Services, such as charts, gauges, indicators, trendlines, and mapping. This chapter is an introduction to developing visualizations using Reporting Services.

NATIVE VERSUS INTEGRATED MODE

Reporting Services offers two supported modes of installation and operation: Reporting Services Native mode and SharePoint Integrated mode. No one operating mode is best suited to all the various reporting and use scenarios that the consumer may require. Therefore, it's important to understand just what each mode can offer a reporting architecture.

REPORTING SERVICES SERVER SUPPORTS MULTIPLE INSTANCES

It is important to understand that a given Reporting Services report server, like the database engine, can support multiple instances. You can configure each instance of Reporting Services in either native or SharePoint Integrated Mode, but after you select the mode it is very difficult to change it (for details on how to switch server modes, please see the Microsoft MSDN article "Switch Server Modes" at `http://msdn.microsoft.com/en-us/library/bb326407.aspx`).

To support multiple Reporting Services instances you need to create a new database, and only one instance can be associated with SharePoint. In the SQL Server 2012 release, more than one Reporting Services instance can be associated with SharePoint.

NATIVE MODE

Reporting Services has a Native mode that enables both users and administrators to access reports using a Report Manager web application. The Native mode provides a report server that is a standalone application providing report viewing, management, administration, processing, and delivery. The Native mode provides a complete self-service approach to report browsing and access, but it's not without its limitations.

The original Report Manager web application was intended to be used as a sample application to aid in the design and development of custom web applications that would use the Reporting Services application programming interfaces (APIs) demonstrated within Report Manger. Many people feel that Report Manager provides a quick solution for handling basic reporting needs, but that it offers very little opportunity to customize the management and delivery of reporting.

When configured in Native mode, you can view reports on SharePoint websites using SharePoint web parts, but there are no management capabilities provided via these web parts and they cannot be connected to other SharePoint web parts.

SHAREPOINT INTEGRATED MODE

SharePoint Integrated Mode enables users and administrators to access the Reporting Service report server using the SharePoint server. This mode offers three levels of integration within SharePoint, including sharing storage, security, and site access of other business applications and data. SharePoint centrally stores all application and user content data in SQL Server databases while also providing a robust web application security system that is responsible for managing access to content and data hosted on SharePoint sites. Additionally, the SharePoint web application platform hosts business applications that permit user collaboration and centralized document management for reports and other types of content such as Word documents and Excel spreadsheets. As a result, one of the primary benefits of selecting SharePoint Integrated Mode is that it provides a unified portal presenting, managing, and securing business documents and information in one place. Because reports can be managed as just another form of content, applying the same security and administration model as other SharePoint content, this integration is very attractive to most IT departments as SharePoint administrators may assume reporting administration duties, thereby reducing administrative overhead.

Figure 8-1 illustrates the connectivity between Reporting Services, configured in SharePoint Integrated Mode, and the SharePoint farm via the Reporting Services Add-in.

One significant change to make note of is that as of SQL Server 2012, Reporting Services SharePoint Integrated Mode is now implemented as a SharePoint 2010 shared service, which involves tighter administrative integration with SharePoint. As a result, Reporting Services may be configured within SharePoint Central Administration rather than having to use a separate tool as previous versions of Reporting Services required.

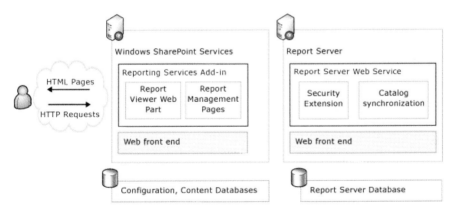

FIGURE 8-1 *SharePoint Integrated Mode using the Reporting Services Add-in*

The SharePoint Integrated Mode of deploying Reporting Services includes some loss of the functionality found with Native mode. Notably, the following features are not supported with SharePoint Integrated Mode:

- Linked Reports
- Custom Security

■ Report Scripting Host (`rss.exe`)

■ Report Manager (website replaced by SharePoint sites)

Some of the key strategic advantages of the SharePoint Integrated Mode of deploying Services include the following:

■ Reports and the libraries in which they are deployed use SharePoint centralized security (permissions and authentication providers).

■ SharePoint libraries may be used for subscription delivery (using a SQL Server 2012 SharePoint delivery extension).

■ Reports and the libraries in which they are deployed use SharePoint document administration, security, and collaboration (for example, alerts).

■ Report Server File Sync permitting report files stored within SharePoint document libraries are synchronized with the report server when changes are made via the document library.

■ SharePoint scale-out applies to Reporting Services applications.

■ SharePoint Shared Service Application pool host the Reporting Services shared service.

■ SharePoint cross-farm support may be used for viewing reports.

■ SharePoint backup and recovery also covers reporting applications.

■ SharePoint claims-based authentication may be used by Reporting Services applications.

> **SharePoint backup and restore does not back up the Reporting Services encryption keys. Use the SharePoint Central Administration Manage Reporting Services Application Key Management page to perform a backup of Reporting Services encryption keys prior to performing a SharePoint backup.**

SHARED AND EMBEDDED DATA SOURCES

Another point of consideration for report design using Reporting Services involves determining whether data sources will be shared among many other reports or embedded within a given report. Data sources are used within Reporting Services to provide a connection to external data; as such they contain connection strings and credentials for authorizing access to the data. You can also configure the connection itself to be a dynamic connection string that is provided through the use of an expression that enables a user to specify which source is to be used when the report is run.

The primary difference between a shared and an embedded data source is that the shared data source is stored and managed on the report server, whereas the embedded data source is stored and managed within the report. The net result of this difference is that embedded data sources are independent of one another and require separate maintenance. More specifically, they require modification of a report in order to apply changes. The shared data source is stored as a separate object on a report server, which allows this type of source to be used by many reports, models, and subscriptions. By centralizing the data source within one object, the maintenance and administration is also greatly simplified, permitting modifications without having to edit and redeploy many reports.

FREQUENTLY CHANGING DATA SOURCE: CONSIDER SHARED DATA SOURCES

You should strongly consider shared rather than embedded data sources when the data source might frequently change, especially when the particular connection that is part of the data source is used by many reports. This has an impact on maintainability, and also aids in deployments between environments, as only a single data source needs to be updated.

AUTHENTICATION: A BETTER SOLUTION

Managing access to reports and the data that reports display is a key to planning a successful Reporting Services architecture. To deliver well-targeted report content, often user credentials need to be sent to the data source in order to permit appropriate filtering of information. Reporting Services offers many different ways to address authentication and authorization of users as well as permitting passing user credentials to the data sources.

Authentication is used by Reporting Services to determine the identity of the entity (person, computer, service account) requesting access. With authentication the report server simply identifies who is accessing Reporting Services and does not determine if permissions are granted to the entity accessing the report server. The determination as to whether an entity has permission to access the report server is handled by authorization.

THE DOUBLE HOP PROBLEM

The network environment in which Reporting Services is deployed determines the supported types of connections used when supporting access to data sources. With Kerberos enabled, delegation and impersonation features available in Windows Authentication to support connections across multiple servers may be used to pass user credentials to remote data sources. Without having Kerberos enabled, Windows connections are only able to pass user credentials to one server prior to expiration. In this case, users are only able to connect and pass their user credentials from their computer to the report server. After this first connection, the user credentials are not subsequently permitted to be passed from the report server to a remote server containing the data source for the reporting.

To successfully pass user credentials from the user's computer through the report server to the data source servers, Reporting Services has the following options:

- Set reports to use stored or prompted credentials when querying data sources

- Configure Kerberos authentication protocol and enable impersonation and delegation in order to permit credentials to be delegated to other computers without limits

Configuration of Kerberos authentication is outside of the scope of this book. The next section discusses the option to use stored or prompted credentials allowing the end user's credentials to be passed without having Kerberos configured.

SET EXECUTION CONTEXT: REQUIREMENTS AND SETUP

To permit the end user's credentials to be successfully passed to the data source without configuring Kerberos, the data source must be set to use stored credentials and use both the Use as Windows Credentials When Connecting to the Data Source and Impersonate the Authenticated User After a Connection Has Been Made to the Data Source options. Figures 8-2 and 8-3 show the specific configuration of the data source during report design and server configuration.

Name: Your Data Source Name

Description:

☐ Hide in list view

☑ Enable this data source

Data Source Type: Microsoft SQL Server Analysis Services ▾

Connection string: Data Source=SSAS;Initial
Catalog=YourDB

Connect using:

○ Credentials supplied by the user running the report

     Display the following text to prompt user for a user name and password:

     Type or enter a user name and password to access the data sou

     ☐ Use as Windows credentials when connecting to the data source

⦿ Credentials stored securely in the report server

     User name: domain\SSASAdminUser

     Password: ••••••••

     ☑ Use as Windows credentials when connecting to the data source

     ☑ Impersonate the authenticated user after a connection has been made to the data source

○ Windows integrated security

FIGURE 8-2 *Reporting Services Data Source configuration on the Report Server without Kerberos*

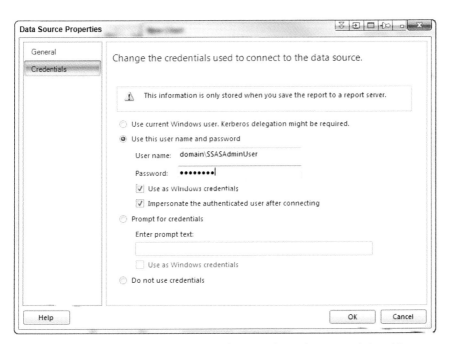

FIGURE 8-3 *Reporting Services Data Source configuration during data source design without Kerberos*

For Analysis Services data sources, setting these options causes Reporting Services to add the `EffectiveUserName` property into the connection string and populate it with the user that is running the report. The key requirement for using the `EffectiveUserName` property with an Analysis Services connection is that the stored credential account must be an Analysis Services administrator.

In some cases when SharePoint uses a distributed architecture separating the front-end web server from an application server hosting Reporting Services, additional configuration of the Analysis Services server to support this capability including creating an SPN (Service Principal Name) for the Analysis Services service account as well as enabling the account's delegation setting within Active Directory may be required.

For SQL Server data sources, setting these options sets the `SETUSER` function to be used to impersonate the user to run the data source query. The key requirement for using `SETUSER` to impersonate another user within SQL Server with a SQL Server connection is that the stored credential account must be a member of the SQL Server `sysadmin` fixed server role or be a `db_owner` fixed database role. Additionally, when using SQL Server authentication and the username and password are database credentials, do not select Use as Windows credentials when connecting to the data source.

EXPRESSIONS IN REPORTING SERVICES

Reporting Services supports the use of expressions (Visual Basic code) to control aspects of report content, design, and interactivity. These expressions include constants, operators, and references to report values (fields, functions, and collections) or external (custom) code.

You can achieve advanced report designs primarily by successfully using expressions to control the report content and appearance of report objects. You may also use expressions to create formulas that evaluate data values in order to determine what type or format of indicator should be displayed. This use of report expressions is very useful when creating key performance indicators (KPIs) within a Reporting Services report. Displaying the current status of a KPI value an expression can determine if a value was in a desired range and, if so, to render a stoplight graphic with a green light illuminated.

Another common reporting design involves highlighting information by conditionally appending graphics beside the data values. The following example expression, implemented in a column of a report, returns the name of an indicator graphic to display when the current account balance is less than 75 percent of the prior period's balance:

```
=IIF(Sum(Fields!AccountBalance.Value) /
     Sum(Fields!AccountBalanceLastPeriod.Value) <
     .75, "indicator_small", "nothing")
```

Similarly, you can use report expressions to alter the color or other text box appearance attributes in order to draw attention to the values under given conditions. The following example expression changes the color of the `AccountBalance` field when the value is a negative amount:

```
=IIF(Fields!AccountBalance.Value < 0, "Red","Black")
```

Ultimately, Reporting Services expressions enable many dynamic and interactive report design features that can aid in effectively communicating the data stories found within the data.

BUSINESS INTELLIGENCE DEVELOPMENT STUDIO AND VISUAL STUDIO VERSUS REPORT BUILDER

Understanding what tools are available to design and publish reports is an essential part of working with Reporting Services. In this section two primary tools are contrasted, Report Builder and Business Intelligence Development Studio (BIDS).

BIDS has been the defacto report design and publishing tool of Reporting Services since the product's inception. The base of Business Intelligence Development Studio (BIDS) is a core subset of Microsoft's Visual Studio development environment which is successfully used to develop other forms of software and as a result has significant investments in usability and key development tools such as source code control.

Report Builder has been, at best, a confusing product that was originally introduced as a tool to provide end users with a report design experience. The confusion surrounding this product centers on the abandonment of the

The report code developed when using either Report Builder or Business Intelligence Developer Studio (BIDS) is identical, and as a result, reports authored in either tool are fully compatible with both report design tools.

original Report Builder (version 1.0) in favor of a completely different tool in the SQL Server 2008 release. Ultimately, Report Builder in the current version is a solid tool for report design, and, in many cases, it offers additional value-added features not found within BIDS.

Report Builder offers a more guided path for developing certain reporting features through the use of wizards. For example, when starting a new report in Report Builder, a sophisticated getting started wizard, shown in Figure 8-4, immediately assists in getting the report design started.

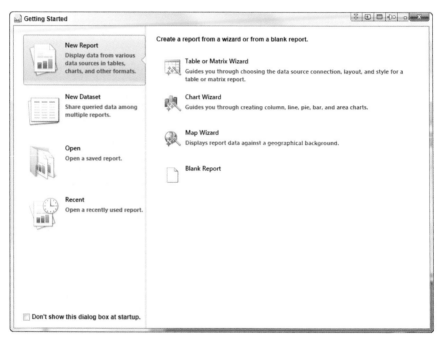

FIGURE 8-4 *Report Builder Getting Started Wizard*

One of the key differences is that Report Builder creates report datasets through the use of a query designer (wizard), as shown in Figure 8-5, that is reminiscent of those in Microsoft Access, thus affording the report designer a much more managed path to complete this common report design activity.

Of the more frustrating differences, Report Builder does not offer intelligence built into the expression editor. As a result Report Builder does not offer assistance in completing the expressions by showing prompts indicating the parts of the expression required for completion.

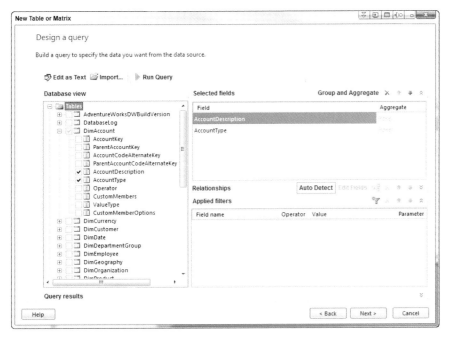

FIGURE 8-5 *Report Builder Design a Query*

Another common report designer productivity feature missing from Report Builder is the ability to quickly switch report items by changing the properties windows drop-down. While Report Builder does have a properties window that can be activated in the Ribbon, items can only be selected by clicking on them. Figure 8-6 shows the properties windows drop-down expanded to permit navigation to other report objects.

Some of the key innovations found within Report Builder do not exist within BIDS. Most significantly absent is the ability to jump start a report design by using Report Parts. Report Parts encapsulate report objects such as the connection, datasets, and visual elements (for example, a chart or matrix) for use in many reports and may only be used via Report Builder.

Working with subreport parameters is a bit more difficult using BIDS because it does not have a drop-down list prepopulated with the parameters found within the subreport, which is a feature offered within Report Builder.

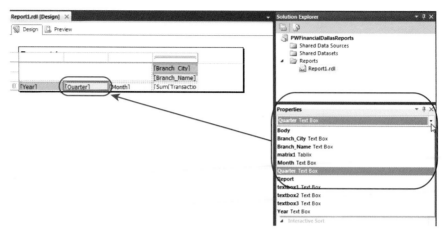

FIGURE 8-6 *BIDS report properties navigation*

Report building is shown in Figure 8-7.

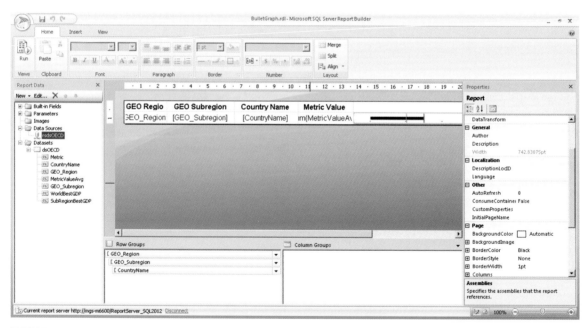

FIGURE 8-7 *Report Builder*

INSTALLING THE REPORTING SERVICES SAMPLES

The chapters that include Reporting Services samples include files with an .RDL extension in the ZIP. Despite the guidance given in this chapter for the general best practice of using shared data sources, these .RDL files will all contain an embedded data source, which you will need to edit to point to your restored databases.

To do that, open Report Builder 3 (available for download at www .microsoft.com/en-us/download/details.aspx?id=6116), and then select File ➤ Open, browse to the .RDL file you extracted. Next, right click on the data source and click Data Source Properties as shown in Figure 8-8.

Finish by changing the server name to the machine you are working on—often, if you have a default instance, you can simply use "." to access your local server. The data source screen is shown in Figure 8-9.

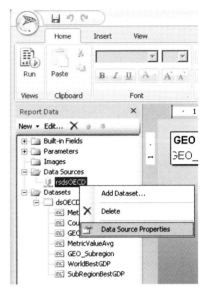

FIGURE 8-8 *Changing a data source*

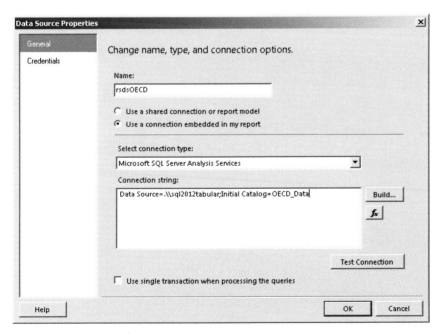

FIGURE 8-9 *Changing a data source*

SUMMARY

This chapter introduced Reporting Services and its key features. First, a brief overview of both native and integrated modes for configuring Reporting Services was provided. Next, shared and embedded data sources were reviewed. Special attention was given to accessing reports including providing a method often does not require the complex configuration of Kerberos. A discussion of the value of report expressions followed. Lastly, this chapter contrasted the two report design tools, Report Builder and Business Intelligence Developer Studio.

CHAPTER 9

Custom Code

Most of the visualizations used in this book are based upon the standard Microsoft toolset, but for some types of visualization, those tools just don't have enough capabilities. Missing visualizations include column charts that are both clustered and stacked (allowing for another dimension of data), color wheels, as covered in Chapter 14, heatmaps (although you can build them in Excel by using cells), network graphs of various types, and tree graphs (although the Decomposition Tree is available in PerformancePoint).

When a tool doesn't have the visualization you need, it's time to write your own in a language such as C#. There are various ways of using code to create a visualization, and this chapter explains the different methods.

AUDIENCE

This chapter sets the groundwork for the HTML5 examples covered in Chapters 11, 12, and 15: each chapter contains only one HTML5 example. While this chapter and the examples can theoretically be done by someone with no HTML5, Javascript, or C# background, experience in some form of coding (such as VBA) will be advantageous. The rest of the book can be read without this chapter.

SILVERLIGHT, WPF, XAML, AND HTML5

Prior to the release of Windows 8, and indeed prior to the broad success of the non-Microsoft computer in the form of the iPad and the Android tablet, the toolset choice for visually rich applications was simple: Windows Presentation Foundation (WPF) on the desktop and Silverlight (a web-based subset of

WPF) for the web. The tool of choice for developing these applications was Expression Blend, and the world was a happy place for developers. The key for development was creating markup for the design of the application using a language called XAML (eXtensible Application Markup Language), separating the design from the functional code.

WORLDWIDE TELESCOPE (WWT) BUILT IN SILVERLIGHT

As seen in Figure 9-1, Silverlight (and to an even greater extent WPF) allows for full customization of the graphics within an application. This kind of visualization extends far beyond the traditional BI visualizations.

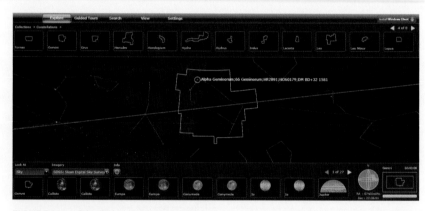

FIGURE 9-1 *A Silverlight astronomy visual tool*

App is a shortening of the word application and is typically used in the context of smartphones where apps are available from "app stores." This use has spread to Windows and Office with the launch of app stores for the Microsoft platform.

The broad success of the iPhone and the iPad changed everything. Suddenly, cross-platform support became a much bigger issue than it had been, and the myriad of business intelligence (BI) apps released for the iPad became competition for the Microsoft tools, although some worked with the Microsoft platform as a whole (RoamBI is one example; you can find it at www.roambi.com/). The challenges of developing for the Apple iTunes store are mostly political in nature, as evidenced by the dispute between Amazon.com and Apple around the Kindle app. Amazon.com had to remove a link to its online store in the app, and users had to buy content through Apple—with 30 percent of the purchase price going to Apple.

Amazon.com's response was to build an HTML5 application that didn't go through the Apple store. This approach is simpler when you consider the wider (and growing) world of non-iOS tablets—Android as well as WinRT.

In the visualization world, HTML5 is thus the best approach to creating a visualization. Visualizations that you create using HTML5 can easily work on multiple platforms. In addition, as you create a visualization, it's essential that you consider the tablet form factor and the user's ability to consume and interact with a visualization on the go, such as in a board meeting. One of the limitations is that tablets are not useful for authoring content, and advanced BI customizations, including self-service BI, simply don't work as well on a tablet.

HTML5 AND ASSOCIATED TECHNOLOGIES

When you read "HTML5," it is not just HTML5 that is being discussed. The term is used broadly to include a number of technologies, such as CSS 3 (Cascading Style Sheets) and JavaScript.

What is so special about HTML5 over HTML 4 that makes it so much better for visualization? Aside from anything else that it provides, the *canvas element* is the key: The canvas element allows for the direct manipulation of graphical elements such as arcs and lines. However, just using the canvas, you would still need to write an extensive amount of code to generate stunning visualizations, so you will want to use some of the existing libraries. There are several libraries that are worth looking at:

- Flotr2: `http://www.humblesoftware.com/flotr2/index`
- Raphael: `http://raphaeljs.com/` (technically SVG rather than HTML5)
- D3 (used to be Protovis): `http://d3js.org/` and `http://nvd3.org/`
- JavaScript InfoVis Toolkit: `http://philogb.github.com/jit`

You can find more examples at `http://socialcompare.com/en/comparison/javascript-graphs-and-charts-libraries`.

These libraries each have different capabilities and intents. Flotr2 is a generic HTML5 charting library; Raphael and D3 are aimed at aiding graphical manipulation on a webpage; and InfoVis provides a diverse set of visualizations. As the goal is to create visualizations that are not present in the Microsoft toolkit, rather than design interactive websites, this book uses InfoVis for most custom visualizations. A selection of the visualizations available is shown in Figure 9-2.

The other great aspect of using HTML5/JavaScript is that Excel 2013 can natively embed this code to run in the client. You can read more on doing this at `http://msdn.microsoft.com/en-us/library/office/apps/jj220038`.

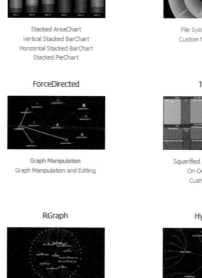
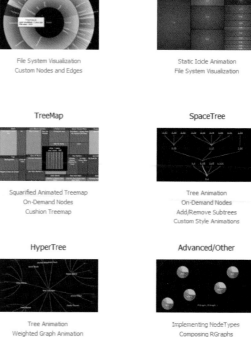

Area, Bar and Pie Charts

Stacked AreaChart
Vertical Stacked BarChart
Horizontal Stacked BarChart
Stacked PieChart

Sunburst

File System Visualization
Custom Nodes and Edges

Icicle

Static Icicle Animation
File System Visualization

ForceDirected

Graph Manipulation
Graph Manipulation and Editing

TreeMap

Squarified Animated Treemap
On-Demand Nodes
Cushion Treemap

SpaceTree

Tree Animation
On-Demand Nodes
Add/Remove Subtrees
Custom Style Animations

RGraph

Tree Animation
Weighted Graph Animation
Graph Operations
Drag and Drop Nodes

HyperTree

Tree Animation
Weighted Graph Animation
Graph Operations

Advanced/Other

Implementing NodeTypes
Composing RGraphs
Combinig SpaceTrees and RGraphs

copyright © 2012 SenchaLabs - Author: Nicolas Garcia Belmonte

FIGURE 9-2 *A selection of charts from the InfoVis library*

THE FUTURE OF SILVERLIGHT

Silverlight itself is a dying product. The latest release—Silverlight 5—will most likely be the last release. However, the fundamental development paradigm of both Silverlight and WPF is declarative development using XAML, and this approach is deeply embedded into Windows 8.

PERFORMANCEPOINT AND POWERVIEW

Both PerformancePoint's Decomposition Tree and PowerView use Silverlight—the intent to move PowerView from Silverlight has been expressed by Microsoft, but no roadmap was available at the time of writing. Nothing is known about the future of Silverlight for the Decomposition Tree either.

The concept is that a combination of XAML and a language of your choice (C#, Visual Basic, C++, and even JavaScript) are used to develop Windows Store applications (these were originally called Metro apps, but this name was changed) that are aimed at being touch-enabled and using a different user interface (UI) experience. A key feature of Windows Store application is the tile UI, in which applications update their "live tiles." The technology stack is shown in Figure 9-3.

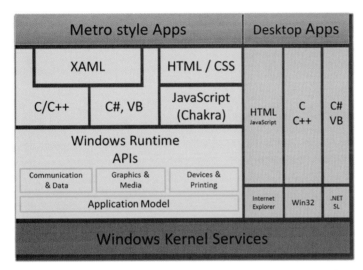

FIGURE 9-3 *The Windows 8 development stack (note that Metro style has been replaced with Windows Store)*

ACCESSING DATA FROM HTML5

You can access data from HTML/JavaScript in many ways. The simplest, of course, is to have server-side code generate the page with the data embedded. This requires a page refresh for any data changes, but it can often be a good method.

Alternative methods involve having a web service called from JavaScript, which returns the data required. The earliest approaches used a technique called AJAX, for Asynchronous JavaScript and XML. More recently, this has been mostly replaced by using JSON (JavaScript Object Notation) instead of XML to reduce the amount of data flowing from the server to the browser. Libraries such as jQuery make this approach easy, with an object call: `jQuery.getJSON`.

A code sample of using jQuery (from the jQuery API page at `http://api.jquery.com/jQuery.getJSON/`) is included here:

```
<html>
<head>
<style>img{ height: 100px; float: left; }</style>
<script src="http://code.jquery.com/jquery-latest.js"></script>
</head>
<body>
<div id="images">

</div>
<script>
$.getJSON("http://api.flickr.com/services/feeds/
  photos_public.gne?jsoncallback=?",
{
tags: "mount rainier",
tagmode: "any",
format: "json"
},
function(data) {
$.each(data.items, function(i,item){
$("<img/>").attr("src", item.media.m).appendTo("#images");
if ( i == 3 ) return false;
});
});</script>

</body>
</html>
```

The `getJSON` function takes three parameters: The first parameter is the URL to be accessed, the second parameter is the list of parameters to be passed to the URL, and the third parameter is the function that will process the data when it is received.

INSTALLING THE HTML5 SAMPLES

Running most of the HTML5 samples is as easy as double-clicking the .HTML file and accepting the security warning. However, when working with web service calls, for security reasons the JavaScript calling the web service and the web service itself should be on the same website.

All the samples are available in the download files for this book at `www.wiley.com/go/visualintelligence`.

Start by opening IIS from Administrative tools ➢ IIS Manager in the Windows menu.

SUPPORTED OPERATING SYSTEMS

You need Windows Server or Windows 7, or 8 Enterprise or Premium to do this. The home editions do not support IIS. You may need to install the IIS role as well; check here to install it: `www.iis.net/learn/install/installing-iis-7/installing-iis-on-windows-vista-and-windows-7`.

You will do this from Turn Windows features on or off in Windows 7 and 8, and Add roles to server in Server Manager for Windows Server.

You should see a screen like Figure 9-4 on opening IIS Manager.

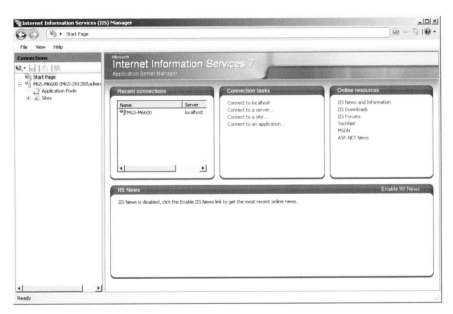

FIGURE 9-4 *IIS Manager*

Expand the web server, right-click Application Pools, and add a new application pool. Make sure to set it to .NET 4 as shown in Figure 9-5. Click OK.

Right-click Sites and choose Add Web Site. Set up the site as shown in Figure 9-6. Make sure to select the application pool you just created. You will need to click on the ellipsis next to the Physical Path to create your new folder. Also set your port to 5555. The Host name of "localhost" means that this website will be hosted on the local machine.

FIGURE 9-5 *A new app pool in IIS*

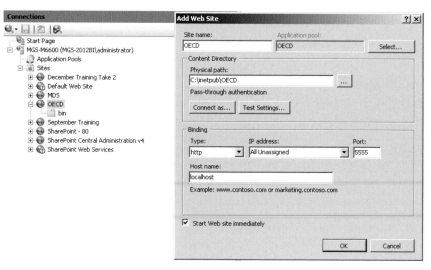

FIGURE 9-6 *A new IIS site*

Now, browse to the `C:\inetpub\OECD` folder that you created in the previous screen and copy the samples in treemap.zip to this folder. Make sure to remove the files from the zip into the root of this folder. At this point, you can open the samples by going to `http://localhost:5555/treemap.html`. Depending on your security settings, you may need to click Allow blocked content to see it.

A WEB SERVICE SAMPLE IN C#

As you learned earlier, visualizations are nothing without the data to feed them, and JSON is the format of data typically used in HTML5 applications. JSON stands for JavaScript Object Notation. In order to create JSON with data in it, you will need to write server-side code that creates it, and that is where C# comes in.

EARLIER VERSIONS OF .NET

If you are using .NET 2.0, you are not able to use the built-in JSON serializer. Instead, you can download one from `http://json.codeplex.com/`. You also need to create a basic web service rather than use a WCF service.

This web service has one objective: retrieve data from SQL Server, Analysis Services or any other data source, and publish it as JSON that the JavaScript can consume. .NET 4 provides a convenient JSON serialization method that converts a C# class to JSON. Of course, to do that, you need a C# class, and there is a wonderful utility at `http://json2csharp.com/` that enables you to paste in JSON to generate a C# class. More details on how you will accomplish this after you have created the solution.

In this section you will be creating a new C# web service, enabling it for use by JavaScript, using the converter to create a C# class that generates JSON, and adding code to put data in that new class.

Open up Visual Studio and create a new project. Go to File and select New project➤Visual C#, then WCF in the left-hand panel, and WCF Service Application on the main screen.

> You will need Visual Studio to do this work. The content in this book was developed using Visual Studio 2010 Professional, but both Visual Studio 2012 Professional and the free version (Visual Studio Express for Web, available at `http://msdn.microsoft.com/en-us/library/dd537667.aspx`) should also work.

WINDOWS COMMUNICATION FOUNDATION (WCF)

Windows Communication Foundation (WCF) is Microsoft's programming model for using managed code to build unified web services and other distributed systems that can talk to each other. It replaces the earlier "ASMX" web services that were provided in .NET.

You can see the new project screen in Figure 9-7.

FIGURE 9-7 *New Project screen*

Rename your project from the default to OECDWebSvc, then click OK.

In Solution Explorer, Right-click the `IService1.cs` file and delete it; then right-click `Service1.svc` and rename it to `OECD.svc`.

You can see what the project should look like in Figure 9-8.

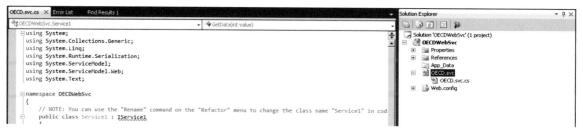

FIGURE 9-8 *Solution overview*

Replace the content of `OECD.svc` with the following code:

```
using System;
using System.Collections.Generic;
using System.Linq;
using System.Runtime.Serialization;
using System.ServiceModel;
using System.ServiceModel.Web;
using System.Text;
using System.ServiceModel.Activation;

namespace OECDWebSvc
{

    [ServiceContract(Namespace = "OECDSvc")]
    [AspNetCompatibilityRequirements(RequirementsMode =
    AspNetCompatibilityRequirementsMode.Allowed)]
    public class OECD
    {
        [DataContract(Namespace = "OECDSvc")]
        public class Response
        {
            [DataMember]
            public string tmString { get; set; }

        }
        [OperationContract]
        [WebInvoke(BodyStyle = WebMessageBodyStyle.Wrapped,
    RequestFormat = WebMessageFormat.Json, ResponseFormat =
    WebMessageFormat.Json)]
        public Response POSTTreemapByRegions(String sRegions)
        {
```

```
            return (new Response() { tmString = "basic Response" });
        }
    }
}
```

The class attributes `ServiceContract` on line 13 and `AspNetCompatibility Requirements` on line 14 define what this class can do. The `DataContract` attribute on the response class on line 17 defines what this web service is going to return—in this case, just a string. The reason you have to return a string and not a pure JSON object is the naming convention of `$area` and `$color`, which you have to fix. C# does not support $ or a space in a name in class, whereas the InfoVis library requires them. You'll get to that a little later in this section. Finally, the method attributes `OperationContract` on line 24 and `WebInvoke` on line 25 tell the web service that this is a `POST` service—this is the method that the web page will use to communicate to the web service, as opposed to the other type of service, the `GET` service.

Next, open the `web.config` file—it is located in your solution explorer in Visual Studio directly underneath the `OECD.svc` file you have been working on. Replace the contents with the following:

```xml
<?xml version="1.0"?>
<configuration>

  <system.web>
    <compilation debug="true" targetFramework="4.0" />
  </system.web>
  <system.serviceModel>
    <behaviors>
      <endpointBehaviors>
        <behavior name="OECDSvc.OECD">
          <webHttp />
          <enableWebScript  />
        </behavior>
      </endpointBehaviors>
      <serviceBehaviors>
        <behavior>
          <!-- To avoid disclosing metadata information, set the
           value below to false and remove the metadata endpoint
           above before deployment -->
          <serviceMetadata httpGetEnabled="true"/>
          <!-- To receive exception details in faults for debugging
           purposes, set the value below to true.  Set to false
           before deployment to avoid disclosing exception
           information -->
          <serviceDebug includeExceptionDetailInFaults="true"/>
        </behavior>
      </serviceBehaviors>
    </behaviors>
```

```
    <serviceHostingEnvironment multipleSiteBindingsEnabled="true" />

    <services>
      <service name="OECDSvc">
        <endpoint address="http://localhost:5555/OECD,svc"
         behaviorConfiguration="OECDSvc.OECD
         binding="webHttpBinding" contract="OECDSvc.OECD" />
      </service>
    </services>
  </system.serviceModel>
  <system.webServer>
    <modules runAllManagedModulesForAllRequests="true"/>
  </system.webServer>
</configuration>
```

The default example has used port 5555. Note that you need to replace `http://localhost:5555/` with the website you're using on your machine if you changed this—this is located in the endpoint tag eight lines from the end. Go ahead and create a new empty website in Internet Information Services (IIS) now if you don't have one (this was covered in "Installing the HTML5 Samples" earlier in the chapter, and if you followed that section you should have a website setup—you should use that one.)

The final piece of the basic website setup is changing the service markup. Go to `OECD.svc`, right-click, choose View Markup, and then replace the content with the following code:

```
<%@ ServiceHost Language="C#" Debug="true" Service="OECDWebSvc.OECD"
 CodeBehind="OECD.svc.cs" Factory="System.ServiceModel.
 Activation.WebServiceHostFactory"%>
```

This can be seen in Figure 9-9.

Next, you need to return some data. In this example, the data is hardcoded. In the download samples for the chapter (available at `www.wiley.com/go/visualintelligence`), it is pulled from a database. This data needs to be returned in JSON, based on the format that InfoVis requires.

JSON TO C# TO JSON

You may be wondering why you are going through this process. You need to deliver JSON (which will be dynamically generated) in a very particular structure to our visualization, and you will be using C# to generate that JSON. While you could code this yourself, instead you are going to use a converter tool that looks at a sample of the correctly structured JSON and outputs an appropriate C# class.

FIGURE 9-9 *The new markup for OECD.svc*

So take the JSON from `Treemap.js` (`Treemap.js` is part of the code downloads for this chapter, available at `www.wiley.com/go/visualintelligence`),
where it says `var json = {xxxxx};` and take everything including the two
braces but excluding the equal sign and semi-colon, and paste it into the
converter. You can see what to copy in Figure 9-10. Make sure to copy all
the JSON before the line that has ends with //, but excluding the semi-colon.
Note that Figure 9-10 has been edited, and you need all the content from
the brace on line 31 to the brace on line 290.

TEXT EDITORS

While Notepad or Wordpad that are included with Windows could be
used for this, a free editor such as Notepad++ (available from `http://
notepad-plus-plus.org/`) will be much easier to use, as it includes syntax
highlighting and line numbers. You will set the syntax highlight by going
to Language ➤ J ➤ Javascript in the menu.

Create a new class called `Treemap.cs` by right-clicking on your solution file
and clicking Add ➤ Class, as in Figure 9-11.

```
29    function init(){
30        //init data
31        var json = {
32            "children": [ {
33                "children": [{
34                    "children": [],
35                    "data": {
36                        "GDP Per Capita": "56",
37                        "$color": "#FDAE61",
38                        "image": "",
39                        "$area": 56
40                    },
41                    "id": "Austria",
42                    "name": "Austria"
43                },{
44                    "children": [],
45                    "data": {
46                        "GDP Per Capita": "88",
47                        "$color": "#FDAE61",
48                        "image": "",
49                        "$area": 88
50                    },
51                    "id": "Belgium",
52                    "name": "Belgium"
53                },{
54                    "children": [],
55                    "data": {
56                        "GDP Per Capita": "195",
57                        "$color": "#D73027",
58                        "image": "",
59                        "$area": 195
60                    },
61                    "id": "Czech Republic",
```
■ ■
```
286        } ],
287        "data": {},
288        "id": "root",
289        "name": "Regions by National Reserve and GDP per capita"
290    };
291
292    //end
293    //init TreeMap
```

FIGURE 9-10   *The JSON that is the data for the visualization*

The JS library we're using has a challenge when working with C#, in that it uses $ symbols in the names of variables in the JSON definition, and in C#, $ is reserved. The JSON library generator cleans this up for us by replacing $ with __invalid_name__$. For your purposes, your end product must have these exactly the same, so for now you will replace that invalid name with a placeholder, and immediately prior to returning the JSON, replace the place-holder with $.

Paste the code that you got for the JSON class over the class (make sure to leave the lines starting with USING at the top, as well as the line starting with namespace, and the final brace that closes the namespace. The class contents are contained within the braces following the name of the class). You will need to make some amendments to make this code work correctly however.

Replace __invalid_name__$ with DOLLAR (you do a reverse replace later).

Spaces are also illegal, so do a replace for __invalid_name__GDP Per Capita with GDP_Per_Capita.

You can see the class in Figure 9-12.

FIGURE 9-11 *Adding a class*

FIGURE 9-12 *C# code*

You now need to finish changing the class to work with the rest of your code. Change the namespace to OECD.JSONSerialization. Change the class name that says "RootObject" to Treemap. It should appear as in Figure 9-13 below. You can test if the code is correct by building the project—pressing Ctrl-Shift-B will do so.

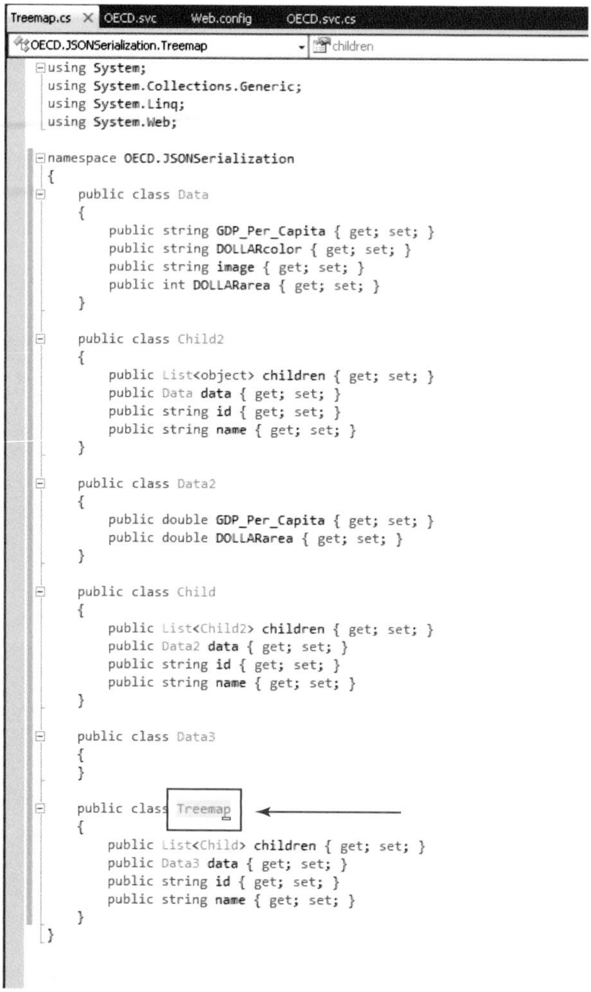
Treemap.cs
OECD.svc
Web.config
OECD.svc.cs
OECD.JSONSerialization.Treemap
children
using System;
using System.Collections.Generic;
using System.Linq;
using System.Web;
namespace OECD.JSONSerialization
{
public class Data
{
public string GDP_Per_Capita { get; set; }
public string DOLLARcolor { get; set; }
public string image { get; set; }
public int DOLLARarea { get; set; }
}
public class Child2
{
public List<object> children { get; set; }
public Data data { get; set; }
public string id { get; set; }
public string name { get; set; }
}
public class Data2
{
public double GDP_Per_Capita { get; set; }
public double DOLLARarea { get; set; }
}
public class Child
{
public List<Child2> children { get; set; }
public Data2 data { get; set; }
public string id { get; set; }
public string name { get; set; }
}
public class Data3
{
}
public class Treemap
{
public List<Child> children { get; set; }
public Data3 data { get; set; }
public string id { get; set; }
public string name { get; set; }
}
}

FIGURE 9-13 *Treemap class*

Next, create a new class—`Serial.cs`—in the same manner you created the new `Treemap.cs` and paste the following code (overwrite everything on the page in this instance, as all the requirements are included in the following code.)

```csharp
using System;
using System.Collections.Generic;
using System.Linq;
using System.Text;
using System.Web.Script.Serialization;

namespace OECD.JSONSerialization
{
    public class Serial
    {
        public Treemap tmJSON;
        public Serial()
        {
            tmJSON = new Treemap();
            tmJSON.id = "root";
            tmJSON.name = "root";
            Child allChild = new Child();

            allChild.id = "region_Europe";
            allChild.name = "Europe";
            allChild.data = new Data2();

            allChild.children = new List<Child2>();

            Child2 grandChild = new Child2();
            grandChild.children = new List<object>();
            grandChild.id = "country-France";
            grandChild.name = "France";
            grandChild.data = new Data();
            grandChild.data.DOLLARarea = 35133;
            grandChild.data.GDP_Per_Capita = "35133";
            grandChild.data.DOLLARcolor = "#E66101";
            grandChild.data.image = "";


            Child2 grandChild2 = new Child2();
            grandChild2.children = new List<object>();
            grandChild2.id = "country-Greece";
            grandChild2.name = "Greece";
            grandChild2.data = new Data();
            grandChild2.data.DOLLARarea = 26934;
            grandChild2.data.GDP_Per_Capita = "26934";
            grandChild2.data.DOLLARcolor = "#FDB863";
            grandChild2.data.image = "";

            Child2 grandChild3 = new Child2();
            grandChild3.children = new List<object>();
            grandChild3.id = "country-Germany";
            grandChild3.name = "Germany";
            grandChild3.data = new Data();
            grandChild3.data.DOLLARarea = 39518;
            grandChild3.data.GDP_Per_Capita = "39518";
```

```
            grandChild3.data.DOLLARcolor = "#B2ABD2";
            grandChild3.data.image = "";


            allChild.children.Add(grandChild);
            allChild.children.Add(grandChild2);
            allChild.children.Add(grandChild3);
            tmJSON.children = new List<Child>();
            tmJSON.children.Add(allChild);
            tmJSON.data = new Data3();
        }
        public string serialize()
        {
            JavaScriptSerializer js = new JavaScriptSerializer();
            return js.Serialize(tmJSON);
        }
    }
}
```

This code hard codes the values for the treemap—in the samples for this chapter, a data-driven layer that returns the same data is provided. Finally, go back to OECD.svc (you created this at the beginning of the example; just double-click to open it). Add the following using statement at the top:

```
using OECD.JSONSerialization;
```

then replace:

```
return (new Response() { tmString = "basic Response" });
```

with:

```
            Serial s = new Serial();
            string sTM = s.serialize().Replace("DOLLAR", "$");
            return (new Response() { tmString = sTM });
```

This will call the class you just created to retrieve the data, and replace the placeholders with the $ symbols. Press Ctrl-Shift-B to rebuild.

Finally, right-click the project OECDWebSvc and choose Publish. You see the screen shown in Figure 9-14. You may need to create a new profile if Profile 1 does not appear in your drop-down—do this simply by entering a name in the text box, and then entering the settings

Set the URL to the website you created earlier, set the Site/Application to OECD, tick the Mark as IIS application on destination check box and click the publish button.

FIGURE 9-14 *Publishing your web service*

All of the changes thus far have been done in Visual Studio as part of the web service. The next set of changes will be done in Notepad++ once more.

Next, you need to make the JavaScript changes. Open `Treemap.js` in Notepad++. You need to change the `init` function to look like the following:

```
function init(){
 var json;
  $.ajax
  (
   {
    type: 'POST',
    url: 'http://localhost:5555/Service1.svc/POSTTreemapByRegions',
    dataType: 'json',
    contentType: 'application/json; charset=utf-8',
    data: '{ "sRegions": "All" }',
    success: function (response, type, xhr)
    {
     json = response.POSTTreemapByRegionsResult.tmString;
     CreateVisual(json);
    },
    error: function (xhr)
    {
```

```
        window.alert('error: ' + xhr.statusText);
      }
    }
  );
}
```

Note that this replaces the same code that you copied for conversion, but this time it is all the content from line 29 to the end of the file

This is an asynchronous call to the C# web service (which is specified in the line beginning with URL), and replaces the hardcoded data that was in this file originally. As an asynchronous call, you have to have another function that creates the visualization to allow it to only execute after data is returned. This function is called CreateVisual and is specified in the success result of the AJAX call.

Then, place the code below code directly below the code you have pasted above.

```
function CreateVisual(jsontext) {
  var json = eval('(' + jsontext + ')');
  var tm = new $jit.TM.Squarified({
    //where to inject the visualization
    injectInto: 'infovis',
    //parent box title heights
    titleHeight: 15,
    //enable animations
    animate: animate,
    //box offsets
    offset: 1,
    //Attach left and right click events
    Events: {
      enable: true,
      onClick: function(node) {
        if(node) tm.enter(node);
      },
      onRightClick: function() {
        tm.out();
      }
    },
    duration: 1000,
    //Enable tips
    Tips: {
      enable: true,
      //add positioning offsets
      offsetX: 20,
      offsetY: 20,
      //implement the onShow method to
      //add content to the tooltip when a node
      //is hovered
```

```
    onShow: function(tip, node, isLeaf, domElement) {
      var html = "<div class=\"tip-title\">" + node.name
        + "</div><div class=\"tip-text\">";
      var data = node.data;
      if(data.GDP_Per_Capita) {
        html += " GDP_Per_Capita: " + data. GDP_Per_Capita;
      }
      if(data.image) {
        html += "<img src=\""+ data.image +"\" class=\"album\" />";
      }
      tip.innerHTML =  html;
    }
  },
  //Add the name of the node in the correponding label
  //This method is called once, on label creation.
  onCreateLabel: function(domElement, node){
      domElement.innerHTML = node.name;
      var style = domElement.style;
      style.display = '';
      style.border = '1px solid transparent';
      domElement.onmouseover = function() {
        style.border = '1px solid #9FD4FF';
      };
      domElement.onmouseout = function() {
        style.border = '1px solid transparent';
      };
  }
});
tm.loadJSON(json);
tm.refresh();
}
```

That's really it. The rest of the sample's layout stays the same. Now open your browser and go to `http://localhost:5555/treemap.html`.

SUMMARY

In this chapter you learned the basics of using C# and HTML5/Javascript to create your own visualizations. These make using libraries such as InfoVis and others for the front end and writing your own web service to supply data to extend the visualization capabilities available from Microsoft much easier.

PART III

VISUAL ANALYTICS IN PRACTICE

In this part

CHAPTER 10

Scorecards and Indicators

A scorecard can be thought of as the business version of a school report card: it's a summary of how the business has performed over the last period, shown as numbers for key performance areas (KPAs), which are aggregated from key performance indicators (KPIs). A KPI is loosely similar to the subjects on a school report card, but generally a scorecard's KPIs have graphical indicators and interactive capabilities (unlike a school report card).

Scorecards have been popularized in recent years through the widespread adoption of Performance Management. Starting in the management consultancy McKinsey & Company in the 1930s, Performance Management as a discipline advocates building a measurable strategy to grow a business and identifying key performance indicators to measure various aspects of the business. Key performance indicators, roll up into key performance areas, and these are put together in a visual way in a scorecard, typically using "robot" indicators of red, yellow, and green to indicate whether targets are being met. On the Microsoft platform, Business Scorecard Manager evolved into PerformancePoint as the tool of choice for displaying these scorecards and other visualizations together in dashboards.

This chapter discusses how these tools can be used both for Performance Management and for business intelligence (BI) in general.

ACRONYM SOUP

Business Performance Management, Corporate Performance Management and Enterprise Performance Management really are all the same thing, leading to a confusion of acronyms—BPM, CPM, and EPM.

Differentiating from Business Process Management (BPM) and Enterprise Project Management (EPM) is important, leaving CPM as the easiest acronym.

A QUICK UNDERSTANDING: GLANCE AND GO

The main reason for implementing a scorecard system is to enable quick analysis of key metrics—the ability to view a metric (be it a KPI, an operational metric, or indeed any metric in your business) and either move on when values are within predefined bands, or start an investigation when the values are out of band. This definition often sits outside the traditional scorecard and dashboards arena, but is a very important and growing area for these tools.

Some key design features to enable this are vital—the details vary from tool to tool, but the basics are the same:

- A filter area to change the data displayed
- A scorecard area, with drill-down capabilities and indicators, to highlight where investigation is needed
- A further details area—either drill across or drill through

KPIs

KPIs are the heart and soul of scorecards. In its simplest form, a KPI is an actual value, measured against a target, and assigned to a band by the distance from the target. The reality of choosing KPIs for an organization's strategy is that the process is long, complicated and fraught with difficulties—for instance, measuring customer service representatives by how long they spend on the phone with customers (what appears to be an easy way to drive down costs) can have grave effects.

In this book, it's assumed that you've gotten all of that perfect, and you need to master using the technology.

The other piece of this puzzle is that technologies allow you to do much more than simply assign an actual, a target, and bands to a KPI. For instance, in PerformancePoint you can add both dimension and time filters, and have multiple actuals and targets—for example, actuals of Today, Month-to-Date, Year-to-Date, with targets of This-Day-Last-Year, Last-Month-to-Date, and Last-Year-to-Date. The bands are the range of values that are considered good, acceptable and poor. For instance, 120 percent and above against the previous year would be good, anything above 100 percent of the previous year would be acceptable, and anything lower than the previous year would be poor. In addition, the drilling functionality that comes out of the box adds a lot of depth to the scorecards.

Ease of Development

REPORTING TOOL	PREDEFINED CHART TYPE	EASE OF DEVELOPMENT
Excel	Yes	●
PerformancePoint	Yes	●
Power View	Yes	●
Reporting Services	Yes	●
Silverlight/HTML5	N/A	●

DRILL DOWN

Drill down is the process of starting analysis at a high level, with aggregated data, and narrowing the focus to show detail data. This is typically done using a list of higher-level dimension items with a drill-down plus sign next to each and inserting the more detailed items between the drilled member and the next member. Lower levels are indented to distinguish them. A minus sign allowing you to drill up is usually included as well. For instance, in a retail environment, the aggregated levels may be states or regions, showing sales figures, and drilling down allows you to view individual stores.

Ease of Development

REPORTING TOOL	PREDEFINED CHART TYPE	EASE OF EVELOPMENT
Excel	Yes	●
PerformancePoint	Yes	●
Power View	Yes	●
Reporting Services	Yes	●
Silverlight/HTML5	N/A	●

DRILL THROUGH

Drill through, although it has a similar function to drill down, is usually implemented as a double-click, or a click on a link, that takes you to a different report or worksheet to get more details about the KPI. Drill through is very often used to go to view the individual transactions that make up the values on a scorecard.

Ease of Development

REPORTING TOOL	PREDEFINED CHART TYPE	EASE OF DEVELOPMENT
Excel	Yes	●
PerformancePoint	Yes	●
Power View	No	●
Reporting Services	Yes	●
Silverlight/HTML5	N/A	●

DRILL ACROSS

Drill across is aimed at obtaining additional information about the dimension member. For example, when viewing the sales figures in a scorecard that has a store drill-down hierarchy, you may want to see the breakdown by product category and include a profit margin.

You accomplish this by linking the scorecard to another item on the same page—a chart or a table of values—and filtering this item by the dimension value that's been clicked in the scorecard.

Ease of Development

REPORTING TOOL	PREDEFINED CHART TYPE	EASE OF DEVELOPMENT
Excel	No	●
PerformancePoint	Yes	●
Power View	Yes	●
Reporting Services	No	●
Silverlight/HTML5	N/A	●

TOOL CHOICES, WITH EXAMPLES

Scorecards can be built with all of the Microsoft tools. PerformancePoint is designed around scorecards, but with SQL Server 2008 R2, scorecard functionality was added to Reporting Services. Excel has always been able to build scorecards and indicators, but has had this functionality natively since Excel 2010. In the following sections you learn in detail about the capabilities of each tool.

PERFORMANCEPOINT

PerformancePoint excels at scorecards, as it is aimed squarely at this segment of BI. A key point, however, is that PerformancePoint works immensely better when combined with Analysis Services or PowerPivot Services—the functionality around analytic charts, hierarchies for drill down in scorecards—which are all based upon having the semantic layer already built.

PerformancePoint dashboards can scale from the simplest—a single traffic light visualization (red/yellow/green) used on an operational page, as shown in Figure 10-1—to a completely interactive dashboard that has multiple pages, several filters, a scorecard driving an analytic chart and another scorecard, as shown in Figures 10-2, 10-3, and 10-4.

Store Metrics

	Yesterday	Yesterday (LY)		Company	Rank (YD)	District
⊞ Sales Amount	$3,072	$4,092	● -25%	●	245	●
DSW Sales	$255	$325	● -22%	●	88	●
⊞ Fab Finds Sales Amount	$249	$90	● 178%	●	214	●
⊞ Clearance Sales Amount	$528	$257	● 105%	●	152	●

FIGURE 10-1 *A scorecard showing rollups of store scores*

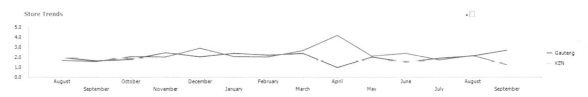

FIGURE 10-2 *The same dashboard but with the righthand scorecard switched for a chart*

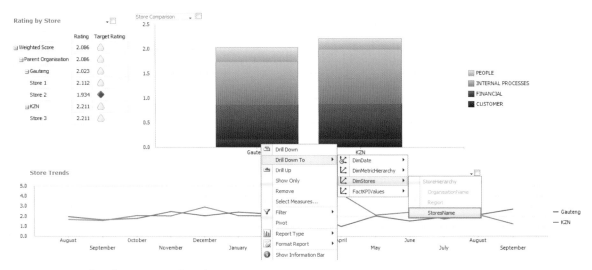

FIGURE 10-3 *Drilling down on an analytic chart*

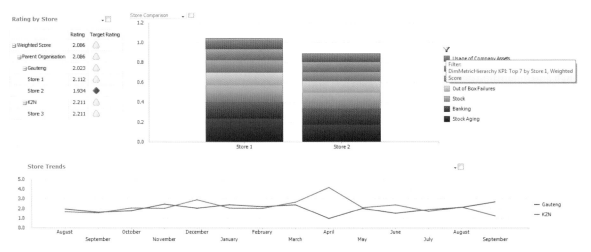

FIGURE 10-4 *Drilling down in an analytic chart*

The true power of PerformancePoint is that the connections between these components are completely developer driven—having some filters only affect a selection of components on the page is a great tool to have in your arsenal. Another useful advantage is that the filters remember the selection of each user—allowing them to seamlessly move from page to page and continue analyzing the same selections.

The following is a list of some key design guidelines to work with in PerformancePoint:

- Keep filters along the top of the page.

- Keep a scorecard that controls other components on the left.

- Add additional items on the right side and at the bottom linked to the scorecard.

Figure 10-5 shows an example of these.

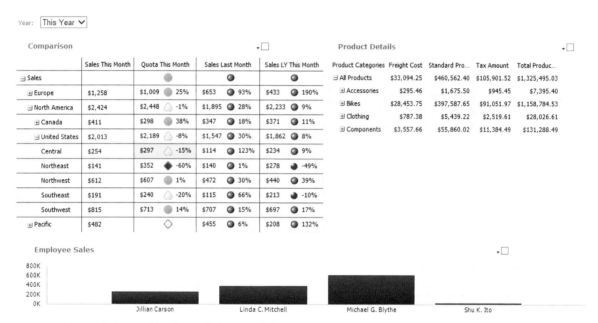

FIGURE 10-5 *Key design considerations in PerformancePoint*

EXCEL

Excel in Office 2013 has become a very powerful dashboard tool. Although it has some limitations compared to the power of PerformancePoint in terms of the control over the connections, Excel still has a very simple and intuitive interface.

Excel includes KPIs, with the sole limitation that you must use the built-in icons. PerformancePoint enables you to import your own indicators.

Excel is much more customizable than PerformancePoint when it comes to appearance. You can fairly extensively customize a basic pivot table, as you can see in Figure 10-6. When further customization is required, you can use cube functions, which allow for total control, as you can see in Figure 10-7.

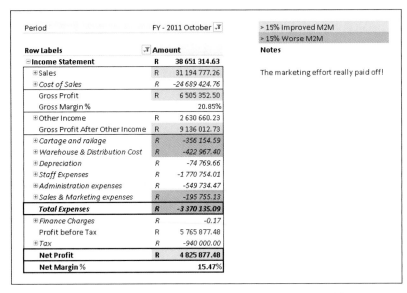

FIGURE 10-6 *A pivot table showing an Income statement, with conditional formatting*

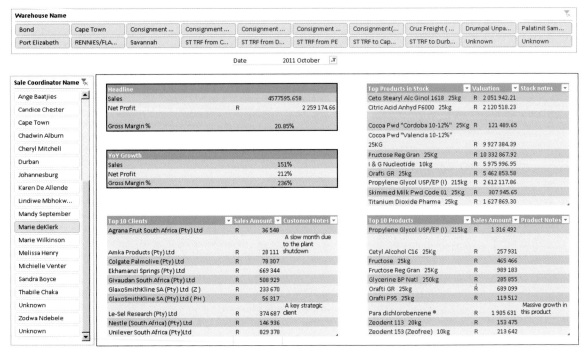

FIGURE 10-7 *An excel sheet customized to include notes fields*

The design principles for Excel are a little different, due to the limitation on filters that a standard filter can only be along the top of the screen, and the fact that slicers are inherently larger than the filters. The guidelines are the following:

- Keep filters along the top of the page.

- Keep data on one sheet visible to the user without scrolling when possible.

- Use slicers below the data on the sheet that are linked to all data points.

- Use slicers to the right of the sheet that are only linked to data on that sheet.

Slicers were introduced in Excel 2010, and give visual feedback about which of the available entries in the slicer have data in the associated pivot tables or charts. In addition, a slicer can be connected to multiple tables and charts, unlike the older filters. Figure 10-6 shows a slicer next to the tables it is connected to.

IMPLEMENTATION EXAMPLES

In this section you learn how to implement a scorecard in Excel (using PowerPivot) and in PerformancePoint. You also learn how to implement indicators in PerformancePoint using your own images in place of the standard ones.

To follow along with the samples, you will need to install the samples, which are available on this book's web site on Wrox.com. (See Chapter 4 for guidance with installing the database samples.)

IMPLEMENTING A SCORECARD IN EXCEL

After you have set up a data model for Excel, it is remarkably easy to create something quite good looking in a fairly short amount of time. Luckily, setting up this model is also fairly easy in the latest version of Excel. To do so, open a new Excel workbook, and, on the PowerPivot tab, click the Manage button. (See Chapter 5 for enabling PowerPivot if the tab is not visible). Click the From Database button, choose SQL Server, and enter the location of your SQL Server. Choose the VI_UNData database from the drop-down and click Next. Choose Select from a List of Tables and then select the DimDate, DimCountry, DimOECDStatistic, FactOECDPopulation, and FactUNData tables, and click Finish. Your screen should look like Figure 10-8.

In order to use indicators, you first need to have a target, and you also need to have a calculated measure on both the actual and the target.

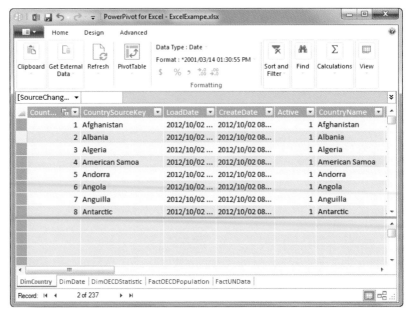

FIGURE 10-8 *A PowerPivot data set*

For the target, you are going to compare each country against the best of its peers. To do that, you are going to create a Data Analysis Expression (DAX) calculation as a calculated column on FactOECDPopulation. The DAX code to put into the column is:

```
=CALCULATE(
MAX(FactOECDPopulation[Value])
, FILTER (ALL(FactOECDPopulation), FactOECDPopulation
[DimOECDStatisticID]  = EARLIER(FactOECDPopulation
[DimOECDStatisticID])
)
)
```

After this, create a SUM rollup on both the new column and on the actual, which you will do by clicking the Sigma (sideways M) symbol on the Ribbon while you have those columns highlighted.

Then click the measure you just created on the actual column, and click Create KPI on the Home tab of the Ribbon. The pop-up box in Figure 10-9 appears. Configure it to use your new measure as a target by selecting your new measure from the drop-down and set the red band to 40%, set yellow from 40% to 80%, and set green above 120%.

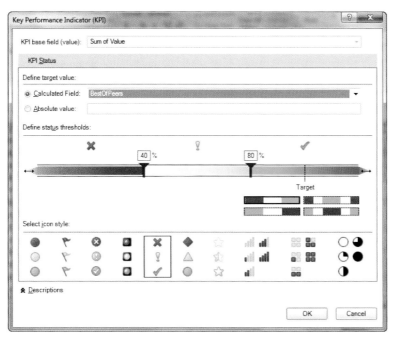

FIGURE 10-9 *Setting KPI values in Excel*

When you're done, create a new pivot table. Add the Sum of Value and Status measures to the pivot table, and drag the country column of the DimCountry table from the list of fields to the rows. You need to add a filter and choose a single metric to get a meaningful number. See Figure 10-10 for an example.

Metric	Partner countries and regions of African merchandise imports		
Row Labels		**Value**	**Status**
Belgium		2.80	●
Brazil		2.10	●
Canada		0.80	●
China		8.81	○
France		11.57	○
Germany		7.75	○
India		2.85	●
Italy		6.59	○
Japan		3.47	○
Netherlands		3.13	●
Portugal		1.01	●
Russian Federation		1.20	●
South Africa		3.20	●
Turkey		1.91	●
Grand Total		**4.08**	○

FIGURE 10-10 *A pivot table with indicators*

Of course, the ability to accidentally leave off a filter and get meaningless values is quite dangerous. With a slight tweak to your calculated measures, you can fix that up. Change your two measures (Sum of Value and Status) to the following DAX to show a value only when the DimOECDStatistics table has only one value:

```
Sum of Value:=IF(
HASONEVALUE(DimOECDStatistic[Metric]),
 SUM([Value]),
Blank()
)

BestOfPeers:=IF (HASONEFILTER(DimOECDStatistic[Metric]),
 SUM([MaxOfPeers]),
Blank()
)
```

PERFORMANCEPOINT SERVICES (PPS) SCORECARD: TRAFFIC LIGHTS

In this section, you are going to create a scorecard using the standard PerformancePoint indicator images for the KPIs. The data source you will be using is from the Organization for Economic Development.

Start by setting up the data connection and mapping the date dimension as described in Chapter 7. You are connecting to the OECD_Data tabular mode cube.

To make the connection, right-click the PerformancePoint content list and choose New ➢ KPI. Select Blank KPI in the screen that follows. You will see a screen like the one shown in Figure 10-11.

You need to map the KPI metrics to data points because they default to a fixed value. Click 1 (Fixed Values) under Data Mappings on the same line with the title Actual to start editing. In the screen that displays, click Change Source and then double-click the data connection you created. In Figure 10-12, the data connection is called dsOECD.

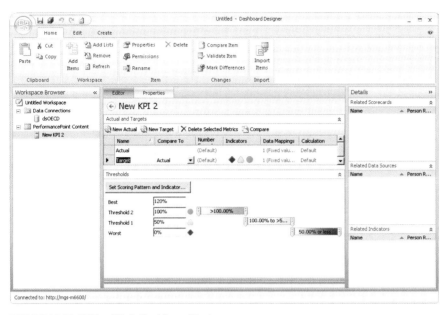

FIGURE 10-11   *Editing KPIs in Dashboard Designer*

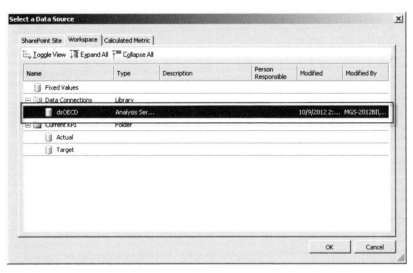

FIGURE 10-12   *The Select a Data Source dialog*

Choose MetricValueAvg in the Select a Measure drop-down field, as shown
in Figure 10-13, then click OK to close the window. Click the (Default) link
underneath Number Format and then choose Number. Click OK.

Be careful using the Average of Children rollup. It may lead to a miscalculation when you're doing averages of averages.

To finish setting up the Actual, click the Default link under Calculation, choose Average of Children, and then click OK.

Now, map the Target metric in exactly the same manner, but use MetricValueMax for the measure and Max of Children for the calculation. Your screen should look like the one shown in Figure 10-14.

Finish by naming your KPI Metric Value and then saving it by right-clicking on the KPI and clicking save.

FIGURE 10-13 *Selecting a data source*

Name	⌄	Compare	Number Format	Indicators	Data Mappings	Calculation
Actual			1,234,568		MetricValueAvg (dsOECD)	Average of children
▶ Target		Actual ▾	1,234,568	◆ △ ●	MetricValueMax (dsOECD)	Max of children

FIGURE 10-14 *A fully setup indicator*

It's now time to create a scorecard: Right-click the PerformancePoint content list and choose New ➢ Scorecard. Choose a Blank Scorecard from the Standard Scorecards category. Drag the KPI from the Details tab onto the left-hand column labeled Drag KPI Items Here. Click the Update button on the Edit tab of the Ribbon, and the scorecard displays as shown in Figure 10-15.

In the example in Figure 10-15, no values show because of the rollup up we chose; as there are no children, and neither average nor max will work. Drag the Regions hierarchy onto the Metric Value KPI so that the tooltip shows Last Child, as shown in Figure 10-16. Release the mouse button.

Right-click the All member select Autoselect Members ➢ Select Children, and then click OK. Click the Update button in the Edit tab to see the result.

The current result showing on the scorecard is meaningless because it is a rollup of all the indicators for all time. You are going to fix this by adding two filters for year and statistic. Begin by renaming the scorecard as **Metric Scorecard** and then saving it.

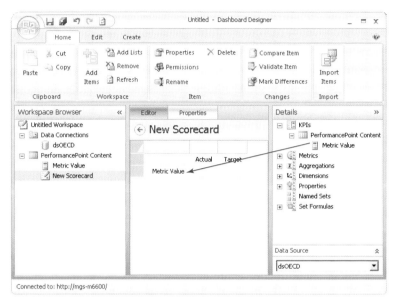

FIGURE 10-15 *Adding a metric to a scorecard*

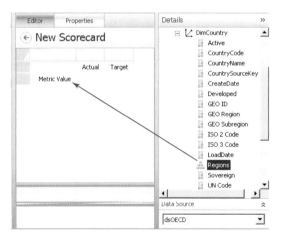

FIGURE 10-16 *Adding a dimension to a scorecard*

Right-click the PerformancePoint content list and choose New ➢ Filter ➢ Member Selection. Select the dsOECD data connection you created earlier by double-clicking it, and then click Select Dimension on screen that displays. Select the DimOECDStatistic.Statistics dimension hierarchy. Click Select

Members right-click All, and then choose Autoselect Members ➤ Select All Descendants, as shown in Figure 10-17.

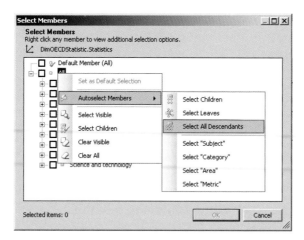

Leave the Default member selection blank and click Next. Choose Tree on the next screen. Name the filter Statistic and save it.

Repeat this process for DimDate.Year, using the member selection filter again, but only select the years 2000, 2005, 2008, 2009, 2010, and 2011 (which are the years we have data for). Name the filter Year and save it.

Finish by creating a new dashboard (right-click the PerformancePoint content list and select New ➤ Dashboard). Select 2 Rows and click OK.

FIGURE 10-18 *A basic scorecard with filters*

Drag the filters to the top row and then drag the scorecard to the bottom row. Connect them as described in Chapter 7 in the "Filters" section.

Rename your dashboard as **OECD Statistics**, right-click it, and deploy it to SharePoint. You should have a dashboard similar to the one shown in Figure 10-18. Not all data points have data for all years in this data set, so you may need to work through a few.

MDX FUNCTIONS FOR COMPARING AN ITEM WITH ITS PEERS

Note that this method of comparing the average of children to the maximum of children is a particular method of banding generally used to indicate inequality in a region. It is typically used in conjunction with a custom MDX formula to pull the average from the current level to compare an item with its peers. In MDX (Multidimensional Expressions), the formula to put in the target would look like the following:

```
MAX( [DimCountry].[Regions].CurrentMember.Parent.Children  ,
[Measures].[MetricValue] )
```

As this would show a Target even for those members without data, you may want to wrap it in a statement like so:

```
IIF( [Measures].[MetricValue] = NULL, NULL,
MAX( [DimCountry].[Regions].CurrentMember.Parent.Children  ,
[Measures].[MetricValue] )
)
```

The equivalent function to do a rank would be like the following:

```
IIF( [Measures].[MetricValue] = NULL, NULL,
RANK([DimCountry].[Regions].CurrentMember,
ORDER( [DimCountry].[Regions].CurrentMember.Parent.Children  ,
[Measures]. [MetricValue] ) )
)
```

CUSTOM INDICATORS IN PERFORMANCEPOINT

Custom indicators are relatively easy in PerformancePoint. For this example, you are going to use them to create conditional formatting, but you could as easily add your own images.

Working on the workspace created in the previous example, right-click the PerformancePoint content list and choose New ➤ Indicator. Choose Blank Indicator and then click OK. Leave the defaults of Standard and 3 levels, and click Finish.

You change the image by double-clicking the red-lined box, or change the background color by double clicking. For Level 1 (Worst) click background color, choose Red from the standard colors, and then click OK. Set Level 2 as Yellow, and set Level 3 (Best) as Green. Your indicator setup screen should look like Figure 10-19.

FIGURE 10-19 *Conditional formatting on an indicator*

The other banding methods are used less often. You use Band by Numeric Value of Actual when your actuals can only be certain values, and you use Band by Stated Score when using Analysis Services KPIs. The Worst Value setting is also used very seldomly; for most use cases with increasing indicators, 0 is the optimal value for this setting.

Name your indicator **ConditionalFormatting** and save it. Now, go back to your KPI, click the Target, and click Set Scoring Pattern and Indicator. Leave the defaults as they are and click Next.

Click the Workspace tab and choose the indicator you just created, as shown in Figure 10-20. Click Next and then click Finish.

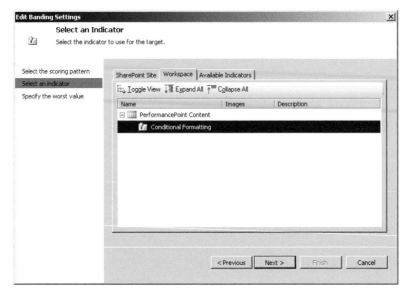

FIGURE 10-20 *Selecting an indicator*

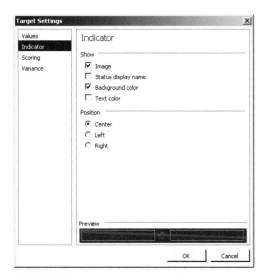

FIGURE 10-21 *Formatting a scorecard*

Save your KPI and go to your scorecard. By default the scorecard doesn't use KPIs' conditional formatting settings, so right-click any cell below the Target and choose Metric Settings. Click the Indicator tab and select the background color check box, as shown in Figure 10-21.

Click OK to see your scorecard. Notice that most values are red. The empty values are black because you didn't choose a color.

You are going to hide those values, so right-click again and choose View Settings. Select to the Filter tab select the Filter Empty Rows check box, and then click OK. The rows that are hidden still show on the scorecard in design mode, but they are highlighted in red to show that they will be hidden when the scorecard is deployed on a dashboard. Save your scorecard, go back to your deployed dashboard, and refresh it to see a similar dashboard to the one in Figure 10-22.

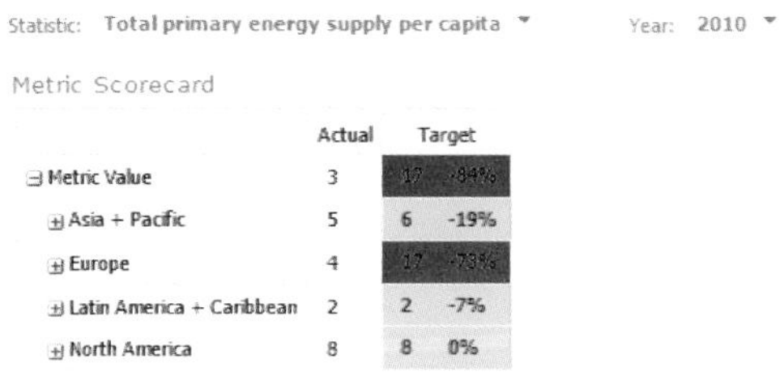

FIGURE 10-22 *A scorecard with conditional formatting*

Many times when using conditional formatting, you will remove the actual column and replace the variance with the actual value. This is a good way to save a lot of space—by showing only a single column, removing the variance, and using color instead of an indicator.

SUMMARY

In this chapter you learned the basic principles of using scorecards, and you worked through the practical implementations in both PerformancePoint and Excel. Scorecards are one of the most prevalent forms of business intelligence deployed today, and knowing how to build them is an essential part of your toolbox.

CHAPTER 11

Timelines

Providing an understanding how values change over time is one of the most fundamental functions of visualization, and the presentation of this type of information has evolved significantly since it was invented. Timeline visualizations serve as an aid to comprehension, allowing you to extrapolate and predict a trend. For example, if sales are consistently increasing by $100,000 per month over the last three months, it is easy for the human eye to imagine an increase over the upcoming months. Similarly, seasonality, such as the sales increases in the retail sector for the Christmas shopping season, becomes easy to see as a chart line rises and falls. Trends can be built into the charts as well as trendlines. Care must be taken when using trendlines to ensure that the user of the chart is kept aware of the fact that trends are derivations based on the data rather than actual measured values. Statistical predictions are another way of creating trendlines.

HISTORICAL USE OF TEMPORAL ANALYSIS

The earliest examples of timeline visualizations were in the mid-17th century, when Joseph Priestly created a timeline to compare the lifespan of various people, as illustrated in the "Timelines" section later in this chapter, and the convention of time being shown as running left to right, used to match the direction in which the names on the timeline have been read is one that we continue to use for visualizations. William Playfair, who you read about in Chapter 2, extended this usage by creating bar, column, and line charts to show changes over time. Although both bar and column charts are often used purely for comparison, their original use was to allow comparisons over time, or to show a progression over time.

Similarly, visualizing multiple trends over time creates a visual cue to related trends or contra-related trends. Seeing a correlation between an increase in profits related to a decrease in customer satisfaction might indicate a cost-saving measure that has affected product quality, and visualizations showing these changes over time aid in sparking that intuitive leap.

Traditionally, temporal analysis has been used by historians and in the medical field to track the progress of diseases both in individuals and in the population at large. In business, the biggest users of timelines have been in sales and finance departments where they track sales and profitability against costs.

TYPES OF TEMPORAL ANALYSIS VISUALIZATION

How you illustrate a change over time is primarily dependent on whether you have to do so in a static manner or whether you can create an animated visualization. Many early examples of showing a time change in the film industry used an animation of calendar pages being torn off a calendar, which is a great example of illustrating the passage of time, but it doesn't show any other data points. To show data points against the passage of time on a static medium (such as a printed chart, or indeed in a chart on a computer screen), one of the dimensions of the chart needs to be chosen to represent the passage of time. The convention is that this is done left to right. There are certain types of visualizations that use top to bottom (or even bottom to top); if you use one of these formats then include an indicator that helps the reader of the chart know that you have used an unconventional format.

Charts that use the horizontal axis to show position in time use the vertical axis to show the value of a data point. A data point can be represented as a point, a column, a line, or a bar.

The other ways of showing changes over time are animation and tiling—i.e., repeating a chart over a time axis. The following list introduces each of the chart types described later in this chapter:

- A *timeline* is the earliest form of temporal chart. It shows a change over time, generally from left to right, but sometimes also from top to bottom. The length of the line indicates the amount of time, as well as the start and end dates.

▨   A *line chart* traces a value continuously over time, but unlike a timeline, it varies its position vertically. Choosing between a line chart and the other charts is easy; if the values can be interpolated over time, such as a rise in temperature throughout a day, then a line chart is appropriate. If values cannot be interpolated—for example the chart is showing the seven days of the week, and the data has sales for only three of those days—connecting those points is inappropriate and misleading.

▨   A *bar chart*, with bars positioned vertically above each other, is a useful tool for showing discrete values that start and end at different dates. In the case of a bar chart, positioning on the vertical axis is a point in a series rather than an additive value. Graphically, a bar chart resembles a timeline in that it has a graphical element stretching between two points. If these points are on an axis of dates, the bar chart is a timeline.

▨   A *column chart*, in which columns are positioned horizontally next to each other, is useful for showing values where the addition of the individual values would be meaningful. An example is a chart for sales value, with each column representing the value of sales for a given time period, such as a financial month.

▨   A *combined chart* combines column and line charts, typically for showing percentages or trends.

▨   A *point or scatter plot* is useful for discrete values in which the addition, or "summing," of the individual values would make little sense. This type of chart is often used in scientific research or for the results of opinion polls. Additional data can be added to a chart of this type by changing the size of the point; this is called a bubble chart. (Bubble charts are the most commonly animated chart type, as showing a bubble growing and shrinking over time illustrates the changes over time very effectively—temporal analysis is one of the places where animation works well).

▨   *Tiling*—repeating the same chart, either horizontally or vertically, with each repetition showing a different point in time—is a way of increasing the available dimensions to show other values. Because both x- and y-axes are now available for non-time dimensions, the information available in a single chart increases at the expense of screen space and the size of each individual chart.

▨   *Animations* are the latest addition to temporal analysis. Showing changes in time by animating is an easy way to add an extra dimension to analysis without consuming additional space. Most typically combined with scatter plots, other ways of showing changes over time are also possible.

The following sections examine these visualizations in more depth and also describe how you can combine the different visualizations to better present your data.

TIMELINES

Joseph Priestly's timeline of lifespan shown in Figure 11-1, is the earliest example of this form of chart, and it shows many of the key features that we still use today. Note the labeled timeline—running from 600 BC to 0 AD. The length of the line between the birthdate and the date of death of each man shown on the chart offers an easy way to see the lifespan of each.

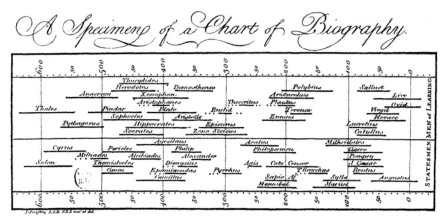

FIGURE 11-1 *An early timeline chart created by Joseph Priestly*

A timeline has a graphic—a bar or a line—to show the start and end dates of an event or series of events. Timelines are useful in instances where you do not need to show a metric but rather a sequence of events, using the length of the line to delineate the length of time that has passed and showing qualitative metrics. Sometimes the qualitative metrics can include great detail, especially in an interactive version of the timeline is available where detailed write-ups of the event can be expanded.

Timelines are visually very similar to both bar charts and Gantt charts. Which chart is used depends on the context. Timelines are used primarily where no other data points are being shown, and qualitative data, such as the names of people or battles, need to be highlighted. Bar charts are used where additional data need to be shown, for instance using the color of the bar to distinguish between different processes. Gantt charts are used to display dependencies in the process on the timeline.

FIGURE 11-2 *Another great example of the timeline is at the Imperial War Museum in London, in the bunker—this timeline runs from bottom to top, and interactively allows one to drill down into greater detail of events.*

Ease of Development

REPORTING TOOL	PREDEFINED CHART TYPE	EASE OF DEVELOPMENT
Excel	No	⬤
PerformancePoint	No	⬤
Power View	No	⬤
Reporting Services	No	◯
Silverlight/HTML5	N/A	◯

LINE CHARTS

Line charts are a very simple way of showing a value by positioning data points on the vertical axis and drawing a line through the various points. If you plot different data points this way, the various lines are called series. The relative positioning of these lines enables you to easily make additional comparisons, as shown in Figure 11-3. This early example of a line chart by William Playfair shows a classic use of a line chart—comparing imports and exports over time, with the area of the chart between the lines being an important additional data point. Because the imports are additive over time, the overall area enables you to compare whether for the period as a whole, England has imported or exported more goods.

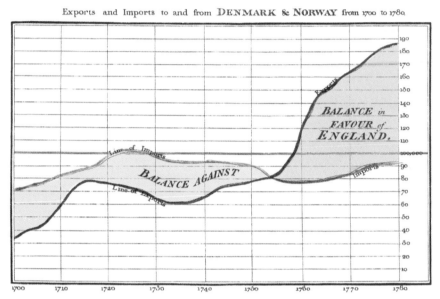

Exports and Imports to and from DENMARK & NORWAY from 1700 to 1780.

The Bottom line is divided into Years, the Right hand line into L10,000 each.

FIGURE 11-3 *An example of an early line chart by William Playfair*

Line charts are one of the most used and most useful chart types. They are present in almost every reporting tool, and they are used almost exclusively for showing changes over time. You must take care not to casually interpolate data between data points if the chart data is not contiguous. As an example, let's consider a store that trades Monday to Saturday, and is closed on Sundays. If a chart for the month included Sundays on the axis, it would be misleading to draw a line from the sales value on Saturday to the sales value on Monday via Sunday, because the chart would then show a sales value for a day that the store was closed.

The area chart version of the line chart simply shades in the gaps between various lines on the chart. However, note that many of the challenges inherent in attempting to judge area are present in this type of chart.

EASE OF DEVELOPMENT

REPORTING TOOL	PREDEFINED CHART TYPE	EASE OF DEVELOPMENT
Excel	Yes	●
PerformancePoint	Yes	●
Power View	Yes	●
Reporting Services	Yes	●
Silverlight/HTML5	N/A	●

BAR AND COLUMN CHARTS

Bar and column charts, as shown in Figure 11-4, are simply two versions of the same chart rotated 90 degrees. In a column chart the date is on the bottom axis. The additional series on the bar chart replaces the value used for the height on the column chart. However, the two charts are used very differently when it comes to temporal analysis. A bar chart uses the length of the bar to show a start and end date, with the position of the bar being the discrete item, whereas a column chart uses the length of the column to show a value. For temporal analysis, the date always runs from left to right. Some additional work is required in all the Microsoft tools to show the bar chart in the correct manner, as it has really been implemented as a column chart rotated 90 degrees. Figure 11-4 shows an example.

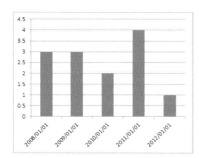 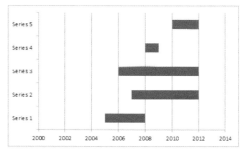

There are many additional ways of adding data to bar and column charts, such as using stacks and groups. These methods are discussed in Chapter 12.

FIGURE 11-4 *Bar and column charts are often confused, but the distinction is simple. Bars run from left to right, and columns from bottom to top.*

Both types of charts rely on the human eye being able to follow a straight line and make comparisons. It is always a good idea to add background lines to aid this process.

Ease of Development

REPORTING TOOL	PREDEFINED CHART TYPE	EASE OF DEVELOPMENT
Excel	Yes	●
PerformancePoint	Yes	●
Power View	Yes	●
Reporting Services	Yes	●
Silverlight/HTML5	N/A	●

COMBINED CHARTING

Using a line chart in combination with a column chart is one of the most powerful visualization techniques because it can be used either to show additional
or derived data points, such as profit margin as a percentage against sales
value or profit value, or it can be used to show a trend, such as a three-month
moving average. Choice of color in this combined form is very important; if
you have used multiple series that are differentiated by color, making sure
that the line and the chart for matched series have similar colors is essential.
Using different shades of the same color ensures that contrast is maintained
between the line and the chart while still keeping the relationship clear. An
example of using different shades of red and blue to match Sales Amount and
Gross Profit to their moving averages is shown in Figure 11-5.

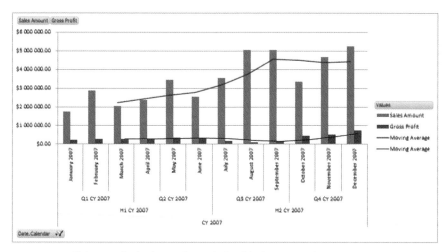

FIGURE 11-5 *Using matched colors to show relationships between series*

Ease of Development

REPORTING TOOL	PREDEFINED CHART TYPE	EASE OF DEVELOPMENT
Excel	Yes	●
PerformancePoint	Yes	●
Power View	No	●
Reporting Services	Yes	●
Silverlight/HTML5	N/A	●

SCATTER PLOTS AND BUBBLE CHARTS

A scatter plot is a chart of points, graphed on an x and y (horizontal and vertical) axis. For static temporal analysis, the horizontal axis will be always be the
time period of the chart.

A bubble chart is a refinement of the scatter plot. The horizontal position is
still time, but in addition to using position on the vertical axis to represent a
data point, the size of the bubble, its color, and, in some tools, its shape can
be used to represent data points.

Bubble charts have been used with great effect as animated tools. Rather than
showing time on the horizontal axis, another data point can be represented
on the horizontal axis, and the changes over time are shown by changing the
various values. The animation draws attention, as the bubbles grow or shrink,
and move around on the plot. However, it is vital that the animation can be
paused, and that the position on the timeline is shown, as shown in Figure 11-6.

Ease of Development

REPORTING TOOL	PREDEFINED CHART TYPE	EASE OF DEVELOPMENT
Excel	Yes	●
PerformancePoint	Yes	●
Power View	No	●
Reporting Services	Yes	●
Silverlight/HTML5	N/A	●

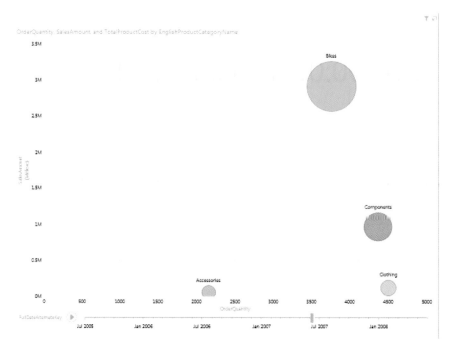

FIGURE 11-6   *A PowervView bubble chart*

TILING

Tiles are a series of similar charts, typically with one background filter applied to the charts in a series. In the context of temporal analysis, the background filter would be a discrete set of points in time, for example years or months. This is a technique that can be applied in Reporting Services with some amount of ease, by embedding a chart in a matrix, and PerformancePoint has the capability of doing this specifically for pie charts (the only possible advantage of having pie charts in PerformancePoint). However, the tool that truly shines with tiling is Power View, in which you simply drag a value to the Tile field to yield an exceptionally powerful visualization. The drawbacks of tiling are, of course, that much more screen real estate is needed when charts are repeated, and thus the charts themselves often end up smaller.

Ease of Development

REPORTING TOOL	PREDEFINED CHART TYPE	EASE OF DEVELOPMENT
Excel	No	●
PerformancePoint	No	◌
Power View	Yes	●
Reporting Services	No	●
Silverlight/HTML5	N/A	●

ANIMATION

Animation in cinematic effects, for instance time-lapse filming, has always been an exceptional way to show how things change over time. Animation has only recently been used to good effect in the visualization field.

Many business intelligence (BI) tools have used animation to show transitions; it's a nice visual effect, but it doesn't add any value or informational content. Instead, using animation to show changes over time is an effective use of the tool. There are several different ways of showing changes over time. The most popular and information-dense method is in a scatter or bubble plot, in which the x- and y-axes, the bubble size, and the bubble color can be used to show dimension values or metrics. A visualization with these criteria is five-dimensional (x-axis, y-axis, the size of the bubble, the color of the bubble, and the animated changes)—very informationally dense.

A further enhancement is to combine tiling and animation, which allows for a better use of screen real estate. When you combine tiling and animation, you only show a few tiles and move them along to illustrate the change over time. You will see how to do this in the section "A Data-Driven Timeline Using Reporting Services" later in this chapter.

Ease of Development

REPORTING TOOL	PREDEFINED CHART TYPE	EASE OF DEVELOPMENT
Excel	No	●
PerformancePoint	No	●
Power View	Yes	●

REPORTING TOOL	PREDEFINED CHART TYPE	EASE OF DEVELOPMENT
Reporting Services	No	●
Silverlight/HTML5	N/A	●

TOOL CHOICES, WITH EXAMPLES

Temporal analysis is one place where all the Microsoft tools have strengths. However, PerformancePoint is the most limited, and Power View's sole outstanding feature is animation.

PERFORMANCEPOINT SERVICES (PPS)

PerformancePoint supports column and line charts. When numeric values are combined with percentages, PerformancePoint automatically sets the chart type to a combined chart. Scatter plots, timelines, and animations are not supported at all.

The lack of a capability to combine line and column charts gratuitously is a serious hindrance, but PerformancePoint has another strength in temporal analysis in its internal awareness of the current date, and the ability to apply a formula to the date. The language used for this is called STP, short for Simple Time Protocol. After you have mapped a time dimension, STP allows for the addressing of dates. These will each be implemented either as connection formula or as formulas in a time intelligence filter.

Table 11-1 includes example formulae.

TABLE 11-1 STP Examples

TO DISPLAY	FORMULA	RESULT
Yesterday	`day-1`	The previous day relative to the current date.
Tomorrow	`day+1`	The next day relative to the current date.
The current quarter and today	`quarter, day`	A set of time periods consisting of the current day and current quarter.
Last 10 days	`day:day-9`	A 10-day range including today.
Last 10 days (excluding today)	`day-1:day-10`	A 10-day range NOT including today.

TO DISPLAY	FORMULA	RESULT
Same day last year	`(year-1).day`	Current date (month and day) for last year. For example, if the current date were December 10, 2010, then `(year-1).day` would show information for December 10, 2009.
Same month last year	`(year-1).month`	Current month for last year. For example, if the current month were December, 2010, then `(year-1).month` would show information for December, 2009.
Same range of a period of six months last year	`(year-1).(month-5): (year-1).(month)`	From 18 months ago to one year ago. For example, if the current month were December 2010, then `(year-1).(month-5): (year-1).month` would show information for the time period ranging from June 2009 to December 2009.
Same range of months to date for last year	`(year-1).firstmonth:(year-1).month`	From the first month of last year up to and including the month parallel to the current month this year.
Year to date	`yeartodate`	A single time period representing the aggregation of values from the beginning of the year up to and including the last completed period. The period corresponds to the most specific time period defined for the data source.
Year to date (by month)	`yeartodate.fullmonth`	A single time period representing the aggregation of values from the beginning of the year up to and including the last completed month.
Year to date (by day)	`yeartodate.fullday`	A single time period representing the aggregation of values from the beginning of the year up to and including the last completed day.
Parallel year to date	`yeartodate-1`	The aggregation of the same set of default time periods completed in the current year except for the prior year.

Although all the examples in Table 11-1 are lowercase, STP is not case sensitive, and you may find that casing the formula elements makes them easier to read. For instance, instead of year, put Year, and use FirstMonth instead of firstmonth.

Examples of PerformancePoint column, line, and combined charts are included in Figures 11-7, 11-8, and 11-9.

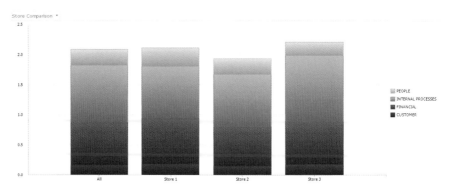

FIGURE 11-7 *A PerfomancePoint stacked chart showing a snapshot*

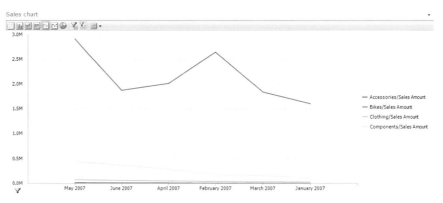

FIGURE 11-8 *A PerformancePoint line chart*

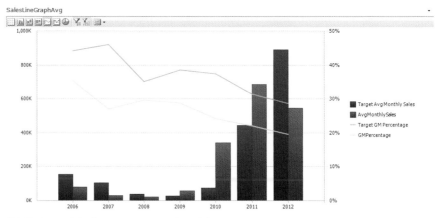

FIGURE 11-9 *A PerformancePoint combined chart*

The combination of a Time Intelligence filter using STP formulae and a combined line and column chart is very powerful. In Figures 11-10 and 11-11 you can see how selecting a time period in the drop-down enables you to change the connected graph

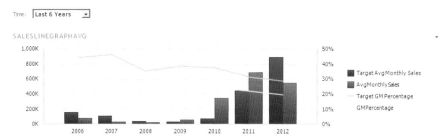

FIGURE 11-10   *A PerformancePoint chart filtered by an STP formula*

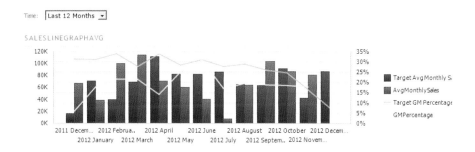

FIGURE 11-11   *The same PerformancePoint chart filtered by a different formula*

SQL SERVER REPORTING SERVICES (SSRS)

SQL Server Reporting Services (SSRS) enables you to have finely detailed control over the individual elements in the charts being displayed. SSRS supports line charts, column charts, combined line and column charts, bar charts, scatter plots, and—with a bit of ingenuity—timelines. The only visualization missing is the animation component.

Examples of SSRS column, line, and combined charts are shown in Figures 11-12, 11-13, and 11-14.

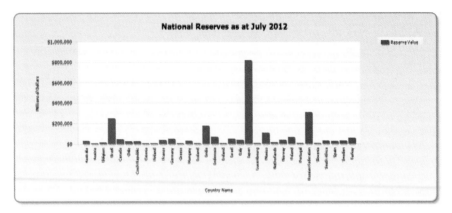

FIGURE 11-12 *A column chart in Reporting Services*

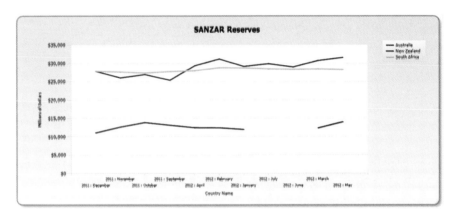

FIGURE 11-13 *A line chart in Reporting Services*

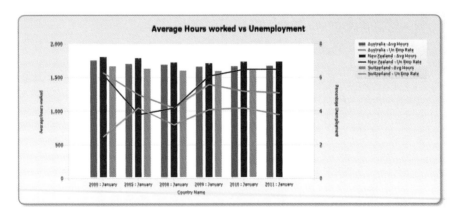

FIGURE 11-14 *A combined chart in Reporting Services*

There are some issues with the default representation shown in Figure 11-14: notably that the gaps in the dates have been skipped, and the data set looks continuous when it is in fact not. This is a feature of SSRS to watch for.

SSRS supports scatter plots natively, as illustrated in Figure 11-15. The default is to use different shapes for the markers, which is a nonstandard way of treating scatter plots. Some work with expressions is required to show the labels on the data points themselves.

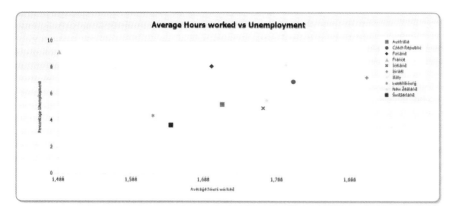

FIGURE 11-15 *A scatter chart in Reporting Services*

A traditional bar chart is shown in Figure 11-16, and the slight modification to the chart to show as a timeline is shown in Figure 11-17.

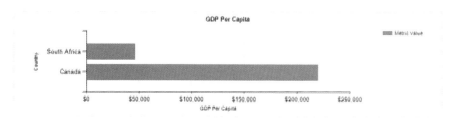

FIGURE 11-16 *A bar chart in Reporting Services*

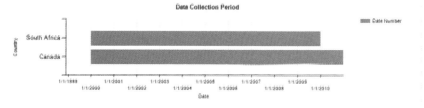

FIGURE 11-17 *A Timeline in Reporting Services*

EXCEL

Excel's repertoire of line, column and scatter charts is very similar to SSRS when it comes to temporal charts. Although the timeline capabilities are missing, Excel has a very important addition known as trendlines, which are statistical extrapolations of the trend of the chart series to date.

Examples of Excel column, line, and combined charts are shown in Figures 11-18, 11-19, and 11-20.

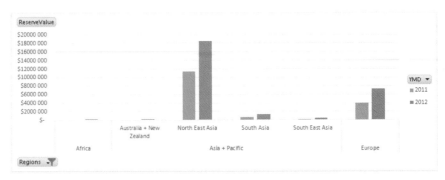

FIGURE 11-18 *An Excel column graph*

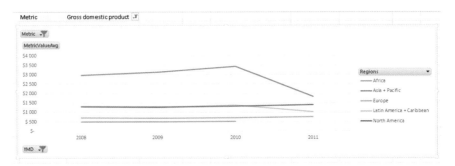

FIGURE 11-19 *An Excel line graph*

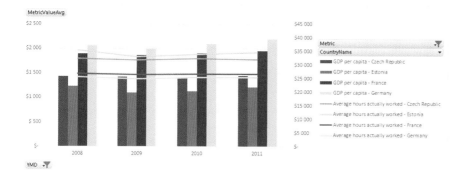

FIGURE 11-20 *An Excel combined graph*

The setup screen for the trendline is shown in Figure 11-21, and the resultant chart is shown in Figure 22.

Trendlines can be calculated by various methods:

- **Exponential:** Showing a curved line, this trendline is useful when data values rise or fall at constantly increasing rates.

- **Linear:** Use this type of trendline to create a best-fit straight line for simple linear data sets. A linear trendline usually shows that something is increasing or decreasing at a steady rate.

- **Logarithmic:** A best-fit curved line, this trendline is useful when the rate of change in the data increases or decreases quickly and then levels out.

- **Polynomial:** This trendline is useful when your data fluctuates as happens, for example, when you analyze gains and losses over a large data set.

- **Power:** Showing a curved line, this trendline is useful for data sets that compare measurements that increase at a specific rate.

- **Moving average:** This trendline evens out fluctuations in data to show a pattern or trend more clearly. A moving average uses a specific number of data points (set by the Period option), averages them, and uses the average value as a point in the line

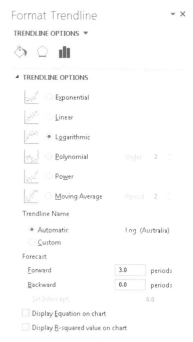

FIGURE 11-21 *Trendline options*

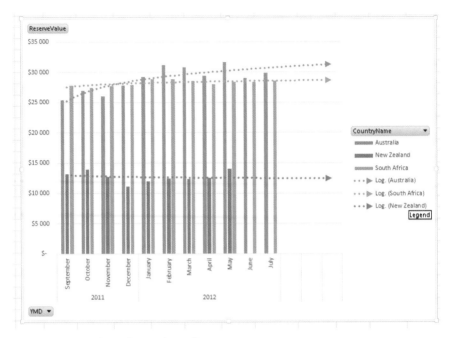

FIGURE 11-22 *A column chart with trendlines*

You have to add each trendline individually by right-clicking the series and choosing Add Trendline.

POWER VIEW

Power View has been designed for an interactive experience, and this truly makes it powerful for showing changes over time. The standard options for column, line, and bar graphs are all available in Power View. In addition, Power View enables both tiling and animation over time—truly a broad reach of visualization. The counterpoint to this, which is similar to PerformancePoint, is that there are limited customization options. Indeed, in terms of customizing how different components interact with each other, Power View has even fewer options than PerformancePoint.

In Figure 11-23, you can see a combination of bar, column, and line charts that are being filtered by a single slicer. The time required to build a visualization like this is much less than PerformancePoint, SSRS, or even Excel, as the connections are all built behind the scene.

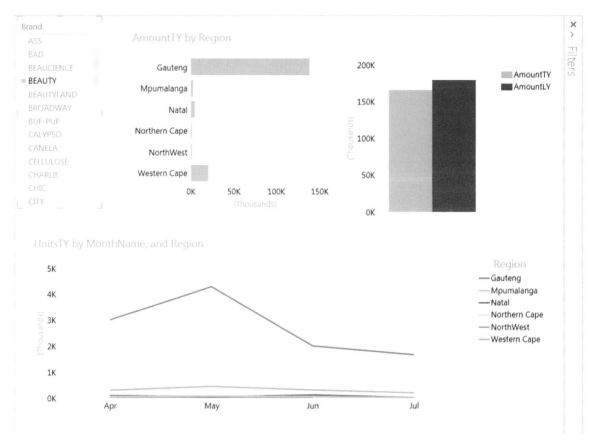

FIGURE 11-23 *A Power View analysis page*

You experience the power of Power View (forgive the pun!) when you apply the newer features. For one thing, tiling (automatically repeating the same graph and filtering by a value, which is possible in SSRS, and is exceptionally hard work in PerformancePoint and Excel) Is performed simply by dragging the tiled value into a box and having the tiles show up automatically. For a comparison over a discrete set of time values—for instance, months of the year—tiling is a great way to get a snapshot comparison, as shown in Figure 11-24.

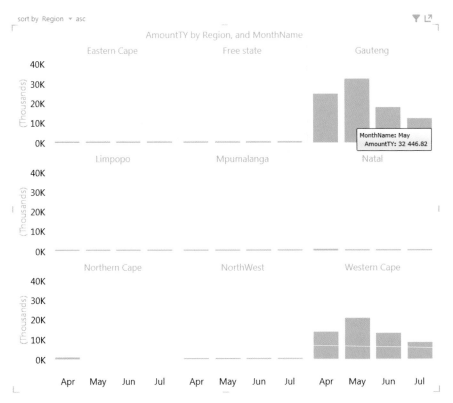

FIGURE 11-24 *Power View tiled charts*

Power View also has an animated scatter plot feature. This feature can't be used in combination with tiling, but is as easy to implement. Simply create a scatter plot chart and drag your date field to the Play Axis. The Play Axis is a slider along the bottom of the chart which can be used to set a point in time, or animate over the data points. Figure 11-25 shows a basic scatter plot, and Figure 11-26 shows—as much as is possible in a static image—the animation effects available. It is interesting to note how Power View shows the track of a particular data series over time when it is clicked upon—a very useful effect.

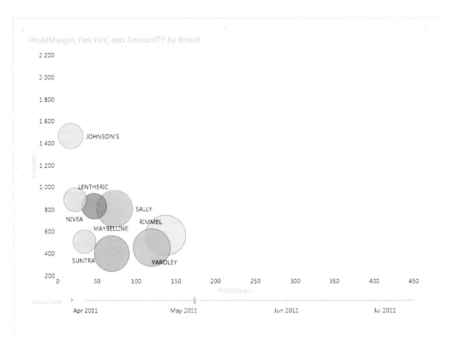

FIGURE 11-25 *A scatter plot with the animated Play Axis at the bottom*

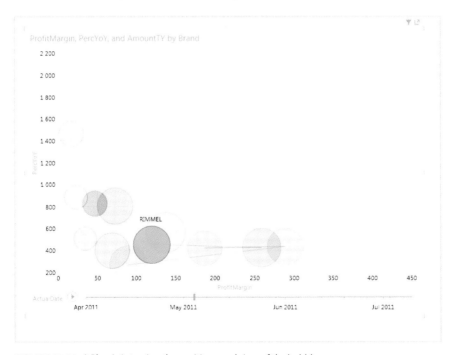

FIGURE 11-26 *A Play Axis tracing the positions and sizes of the bubbles*

IMPLEMENTATION EXAMPLES

The implementation examples in this section use the OECDPopulation PowerPivot model available from this book's web page (`www.wiley.com/go/ visualintelligence`), and called `OECDPopulationStats.xlsx`. Building the model is covered briefly in the next section, but refer to Chapters 5 and 6 for more details.

POWER VIEW ANIMATED SCATTER PLOT

Power View's best feature is the animated scatter plot. With a focus on interaction in general, the ability to drag a slider to animate changes in time (or just let it play), this visualization is Power View's raison d'etre. In this section you learn how to implement it.

Building a Model to Support Power View

Please see Chapters 5 and 6 for an introduction to building a PowerPivot workbook. This section requires at least Excel 2010 for the PowerPivot pieces, and Excel 2013 for Power View.

Power View requires a PowerPivot (or tabular) model to support the animation. You will need to set up a date table to allow the animations to work correctly. Create a connection to the VI_UNData database, and make sure you have imported the DimDate view, and the DimCountry, DimOECDStatistic, FactOECDNationalReserve, and FactOECDPopulation tables. Note that the DimDate view is near the bottom, and don't choose the DimDate table. Your sheet should look similar to Figure 11-27.

You need to set up the relationships to the DimDate view by first clicking the diagram button in the bottom right, and then creating relationships from the two fact tables to the DimDate, using DimDateID. You need to click on the DimDateID field on the fact table, and dragging it onto the DateID field on DimDate. Your diagram should look like Figure 11-28.

Right-click DimDate, and choose Go To which will take you to the table designer. In the Ribbon at the top, choose the Design tab and click the Mark as Date Table button, as in Figure 11-29.

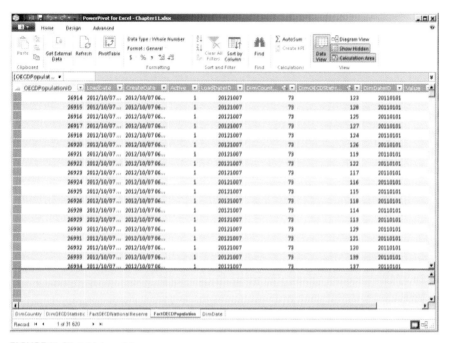

FIGURE 11-27 *Initial model setup*

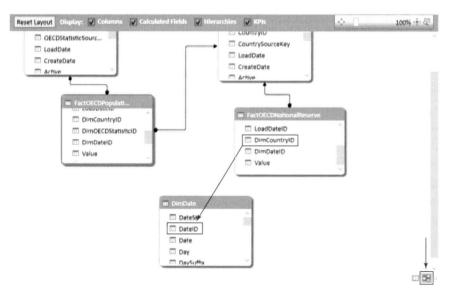

FIGURE 11-28 *The PowerPivot diagram designer*

FIGURE 11-29 *Marking a table as a date table*

Click OK in the next window. You need to fix up the sorting of the Month names by selecting the Month name column, and clicking Sort by Column on the Ribbon's Home tab. Choose MonthNumber, as in Figure 11-30.

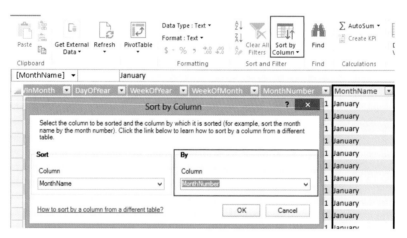

FIGURE 11-30 *Sort by columns*

Repeat the process for MonthNameFull.

Next, you need to set the row identifier. The row identifier is similar to the primary key in SQL Server, and is a number that uniquely identifies each row. Start by enabling the advanced tab. This option is found under the file menu, and is called Switch to Advanced Mode. Change to the Advanced tab, click Table behavior, then select OECDPopulationID in the drop-down box for the row identifier. Click the OK button.

Your final step is to create some measures that you are going to use in the scatter plot. You need to create a measure for each dimension value you are going to analyze. The three to analyze are Average Hours Actually Worked, GDP per Capita, and GDP per Hour Worked.

Create each of these on the FactOECDPopulation table, and use the following formulae:

```
AvgHours:=CALCULATE(
AVERAGE(FactOECDPopulation[Value])
, DimOECDStatistic[Metric]  = "Average hours actually worked"
)

GDPPerHour:=CALCULATE(
AVERAGE(FactOECDPopulation[Value])
, DimOECDStatistic[Metric]  = "GDP per hour worked"
)

GDPPerCapita:=CALCULATE(
AVERAGE(FactOECDPopulation[Value])
, DimOECDStatistic[Metric]  = "GDP per capita"
)
```

> **Each one of these formulae takes the average of the Value, filtered by a particular metric.**

You will do this by right-clicking Add Column. Rename the column to **AvgHours**. Paste the formula, starting with the equal sign, into the formula bar making sure to keep all the text of the formula on one line.

Save your workbook. Now that you have a Power View model, you are going to build out the animated scatter plot. Start by going back to Excel and clicking Power View on the Insert tab. On the new sheet that is created, drag GDPPerHour, AvgHours, and GDPPerCapita (in that order) from FactOECDPopulation in the field choice tab on the right to the value box, as shown in Figure 11-31.

FIGURE 11-31 *Dragging fields to the value box*

Change the chart type to a scatter plot (you do this in the Design tab, under Other Chart). Resize the chart to fill the screen. Drag GeoRegion from DimCountry to the Details box on the right side, and drag Date from DimDate to the Play Axis box (see Figure 11-32).

The result is an animated scatter chart, which you can play; alternatively, you can drag the slider to see data at a point in time. If you click a particular data item, you see the history for that item. Figure 11-33 shows an animated bubble chart.

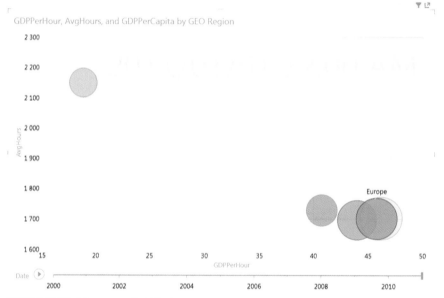

FIGURE 11-32 *Power View field choices*

FIGURE 11-33 *A Power View bubble chart*

COMBINING LINES AND COLUMNS IN EXCEL

In this section, you are going to track the relationship of Gross Domestic Product to population size over time. This example uses Excel 2013, which has a combined chart type that makes this process easier, but in earlier versions of Excel it is easy enough to simply change one of the chart series types to a line chart to create a combination chart.

Switch to Sheet 1, then start by clicking the Pivot Chart button on the Insert Ribbon, as shown in Figure 11-34.

FIGURE 11-34 *Excel Ribbon interface to add a pivot chart*

Choose Existing Worksheet and Use an External Data Source. Click Choose Connection, as shown in Figure 11-35.

The choice of a connection is a bit different between Excel 2013 and earlier versions. In the earlier versions, you select PowerPivot as the data source, but in Excel 2013 you must choose Tables and then select Tables in Workbook Data Model, as shown in Figure 11-36.

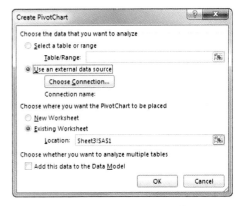

FIGURE 11-35 *Choosing a connection for a pivot chart*

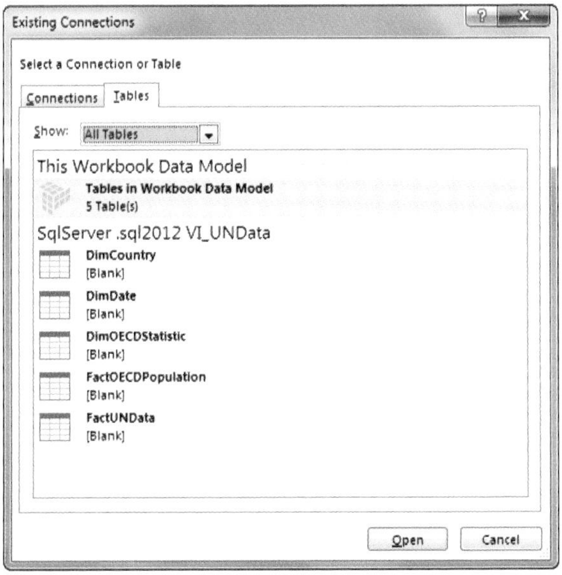

FIGURE 11-36 *Choosing a connection in Excel 2013*

At this point, you see an empty pivot chart on the left and the PivotChart Fields pane is on the right, but you need to add the appropriate fields to the chart. Start by adding the Value field from the FactOECDPopulation table to the Values block, and Metric from DimOECDStatistics to the legend, and YearName from DimDate to the Axis, as shown in Figure 11-37.

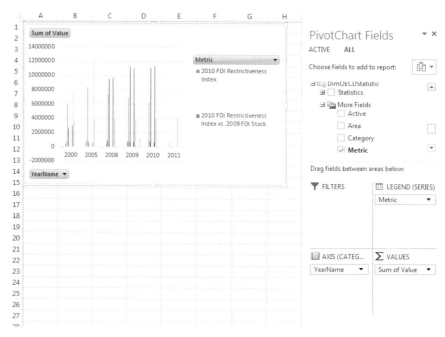

FIGURE 11-37 An Excel pivot chart

At this point, the chart isn't showing anything meaningful for analysis, just a selection of the metrics. Start narrowing down the selection by clicking Metrics in the pivot chart and selecting Gross Domestic Product and Population Levels. This restricts your data set to the values you want to compare. However, to compare them you need to format them to show a line and a column, and you need to set up secondary axes. In Excel 2010 and earlier, you do this by changing the chart series type individually, but in Excel 2013 if you right-click anywhere on the chart and select Change Chart Type, you are presented with the new chart selector window, as shown in Figure 11-38.

Set the chart type to Combo, and select Secondary Axis for Population levels. Click OK.

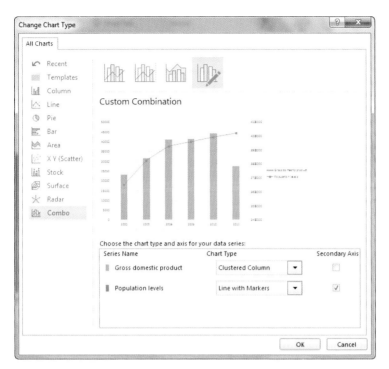

FIGURE 11-38 *Changing a pivot chart type*

This chart is a great showcase of one of the biggest fallacies in temporal analysis—points on the axis that have no data are hidden (for example Monday being followed by Wednesday because Tuesday had no data), thus altering the slope of the curve.

To fix this issue, you need to make several changes: Show the missing data points, limit the chart to the relevant dates, and add a trendline to interpolate the missing years.

To add the missing data points, right-click the chart area, and click PivotChart Options. Choose the Display tab, select the Show Items with No Data on Axis Fields option, and then click OK. All the years are now displayed, and you filter them by clicking YearName and choosing the years 2000 through 2012. The gross domestic product series is showing correctly as columns, but you need to add markers for the line chart to show noncontiguous values. Right-click the line and choose Format Data Series. If you're using Excel 2013, you should see

FIGURE 11-39 *The Format Data Series pane in Excel 2013*

a pane like the one in Figure 11-39; in earlier versions of Excel, you see pop-up window. Click the Paint icon, then choose Marker, and choose a series marker in Marker options—the default Square and size 5 will work nicely—and show the values of Population levels on the chart.

The final piece to this chart is showing interpolated values. This is where Excel truly shines over the other tools. Right-click on the line chart, and click Add Trendline—all the default values are fine (although you may want to play with the forecast feature!). Click OK. You see the final chart shown in Figure 11-40. You would, of course, finish off by formatting the axes appropriately.

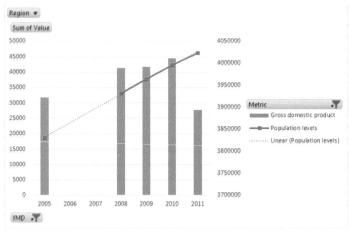

FIGURE 11-40 *An interpolated population chart*

A DRILLABLE LINE CHART IN PPS

In PerformancePoint, set up a data connection as described in Chapter 7, making sure to set up the time dimension correctly. You use the OECD_Data model that you setup in Chapter 7, and create an analytic chart. Right-click the library and click New ➢ Report. Choose Analytic Chart and then choose the data source you created. In the chart design screen, drag the YMD hierarchy from DimDate into the Bottom Axis column. Drag ReserveValue from Measures into the series. Finally, right-click the chart and select Report Type ➢ Line Chart with Markers.

To choose the appropriate data, click the All value on the bottom axis and then right-click next to it so you can select Filter ➢ Filter Empty Axis Items. At this point, you see a chart such as the one in Figure 11-41.

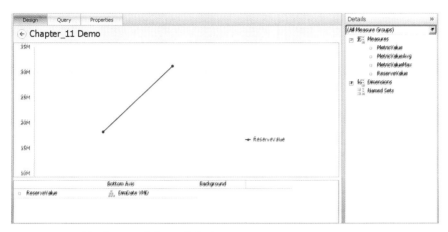

FIGURE 11-41   *A PerformancePoint analytic chart*

Once deployed, this chart is automatically drillable by clicking on the year to drill down to the months. You can create additional time series by using time intelligence filters. In order to make it interactive with the other components of PerformancePoint you need to add other dimensions to the background.

A DATA-DRIVEN TIMELINE USING SSRS AND DATA BARS

SSRS can do all the visualizations that you have worked with so far this chapter barring the animation, but it also has the capability of doing a timeline. This isn't a standard visualization in SSRS, but it is relatively easy to do. You use Report Builder to build the report, as described in Chapter 8. Start by creating a data source connection to the OECD_Data tabular cube in Report Builder and then creating a new data set.

To do so, open Report Builder and you will see the Getting Started Wizard. Click on Chart Wizard, then click Next on the following screen. Click New to create a new data source, then choose Microsoft SQL Server Analysis Services from the Select connection type drop-down, and enter **rsds_OECDDatain** the Name text box (this could be any name).

Click the Build… button. If you are using a local and unnamed Analysis Services instance, you can just enter "**.**" in the Server name box, otherwise enter the server you are connecting to. Finish off by choosing OECD_Data for the database name, and clicking OK. Click OK again and then click Next to create the data set.

In this data set, filter by the GDP per Capita metric, and add the YMD hierarchy, the Country Name hierarchy, and the MetricValue measure to the design surface, as shown in Figure 11-42. Add the DateSK column—this is an incrementing column that starts at 1 for the first date and has no gaps. It's ideal for calculating distances on a chart.

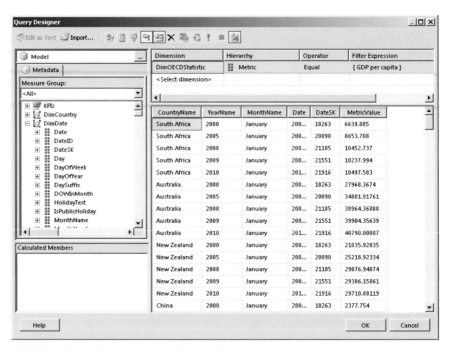

FIGURE 11-42 *The Reporting services data set designer*

This data set is going to be too large to work with easily, so filter it just for South Africa and Canada. You do this by dragging CountryName onto the filter pane at the top on the right, and then choosing South Africa and Canada from the drop-down. Click OK twice to close the designer when you're done.

You're just working on the chart, so remove the titleand footer from the report. You remove the title by clicking on it, and then hitting the Delete key, and you remove the footer by right clicking on it and choosing Remove footer.

Click the Chart option on the Insert tab, choose Chart Wizard, and in the window that displays select the data set you just created. Click next. Choose Bar, click Next, and then enter **CountryName** into the Categories and **DateSK** into the values column. Click the arrow next to the DateSK and choose Max as the aggregation value.

On the next screen choose the Generic style and then click Finish.

When the chart appears on the report design surface, drag the bottom-right corner to make the chart big enough to show all the values and then right-click the chart and click Change Chart Type. Scroll to the bottom to find the Range category. Choose the Range Bar chart type (it is fourth from the left).

Click the Low value that appears on the right side, and change it to use the DateSK field and to aggregate as Min, as shown in Figure 11-43.

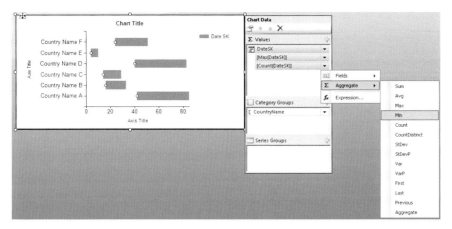

FIGURE 11-43 *Setting the DateSK field to aggregate as Min*

Format the chart by right-clicking near the vertical axis (around the CountryName labels). The words CountryName are repeated down the left hand side, next to the words Axis title, and you need to click between two of the lines containing CountryName. Then choose Vertical Axis Properties. Set the interval to 1 from Auto to show all the countries. Set the Axis title at the same time.

Next, right-click the bottom axis and select Horizontal Axis Properties. Deselect the Always Include Zero button. Set the minimum value to **18232** (This is the value of the first key in the data set, minus 30, to set the chart to display data points prior to the start of the data set), and the maximum to **22281** (this is the value of the last key in the data set), set the interval to 12, and then set the interval type to Months. Set the Axis title at the same time. On the same screen there is a text box for the Axis title, which will replace the words "Axis title" displayed previously. Make the axis title **Country**.

Run the report by clicking the Execute button and you see a display similar to Figure 11-44.

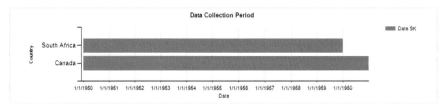

FIGURE 11-44 *Running the report*

It's immediately apparent that the dates are wrong. This is because the data set uses 1950/01/01 as the base date, and a date type in SSRS is based upon a date starting in 1900/01/01. If you create a new calculated field in which you add 18262 to the DateSK and then add 18262 to the minimum and maximum values, you get a chart such as that shown in Figure 11-45, which shows an accurate timeline for when data was collected for South Africa and Canada:

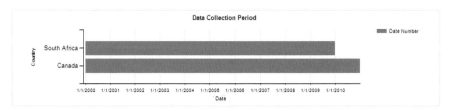

FIGURE 11-45 *Date ranges displayed in SSRS*

SUMMARY

In this chapter you learned about using visualizations to present data that changes over time, and the pitfalls to avoid. The different tools in the Microsoft stack are all good at displaying temporal data, but for different purposes: PerformancePoint is good with custom date ranges, Power View has an ani-mated bubble chart, Excel has trendline functionality, and Reporting Services can display timelines with ease.

CHAPTER 12

Comparison Visuals

Using a visualization to compare two or more objects either at a point in time or over a period is one of the oldest forms of visualization. In Chapter 11, a treatment of comparisons over time has been done, so this chapter focuses on point-in-time comparisons.

Comparing items of data and deciding which is better is one of the most common actions people take. This may take the form of ranking: for instance determining which of your stores are in the top 10% and which stores are in the bottom 10% by sales (or gross profit) allows you to determine the appropriate remedial action for the poorly performing stores, and apply what's been learned by the best 10% to your other stores.

Another comparison is comparing actuals against targets: For instance, while a store may be in the top 10% by sales, it could well have not achieved a target set for the period.

In this chapter you learn about several methods for comparing values visually: heatmaps (also called chloropleths), traditional bar charts, and pie charts, as well as bullet graphs, radar graphs, and matrices.

OVERVIEW OF POINT-IN-TIME COMPARISONS

The effect used to show *point-in-time comparisons* can take one or a combination of the following forms:

- Change in color (heatmaps, chloropleth, indicators)
- Change in width (bar charts)

- Change in height (column charts, prism charts)
- Change in position (scatter plots)
- Change in area (bubble charts, tree maps)
- Change in angular width (pie charts, donut charts)
- Change in length (radar charts)

Combinations of these formats to add data—for instance, color to show a change, and size of a bubble to show the absolute value—are very common.

PROBLEMS WITH POINT-IN-TIME COMPARISONS

The most common problem with comparison visualizations in popular media is that, despite being a snapshot of the comparison at a point in time, the time period is not listed. This can lead to confusion later on when the comparison has changed.

Figure 12-1 shows an example from VizWorld (`http://www.vizworld.com/2009/11/bad-infographic-mapping-emissions-country/`) that compares emissions. It has some of the problems mentioned in Chapter 2 with regard to the area of the bubbles (i.e., that the radius rather than the area has been used, and it hasn't been labelled).

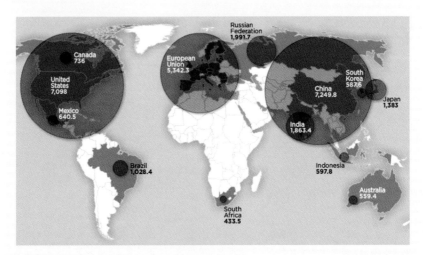

FIGURE 12-1 *A comparison visual with several problems*

PROBLEMS WITH CHLOROPLETHS

A *chloropleth* is a heatmap with the shapes of countries or states instead of blocks. Showing chloropleths using non-normalized numbers, for instance gross domestic product (GDP) instead of GDP per capita, often gives a misleading impression, showing a map of the population more than the figure being chosen. Figure 12-2 shows an example of this from the popular cartoon XKCD (`http://xkcd.com/1138/`).

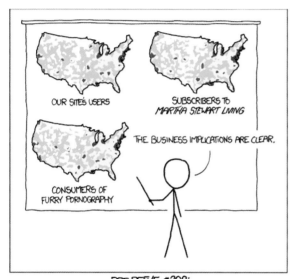

FIGURE 12-2 *XKCD showing the problem with heatmaps*

EXPLAINING PERSPECTIVE AND PERCEIVING COMPARISONS

How you perceive the difference between two objects is dependent on a variety of factors—the difficulty with using area as a comparison method is covered in Chapter 2, and the challenges of using 3D is covered in Chapter 1. Other factors include their relative positioning and ordering—putting two slices of a pie chart with similar but not identical values opposite each other can be hard to read. As you learned in Chapter 2, background images can also distort comparisons.

PIE CHARTS VERSUS BAR CHARTS

People commonly use pie charts as a comparison visual. However, you need to carefully think before using a pie chart. Figure 12-3 shows a pie chart. Look carefully. Is Slice B or Slice D bigger?

It's fairly difficult to determine which slice is larger. While, as shown later, ordering the pie chart by value will assist in this comparison, there are better methods. Compare Figure 12-3 to Figure 12-4, a column chart of the same values.

In Figure 12-4, it's much easier to determine which column is larger, and it's also easier to tell the absolute values.

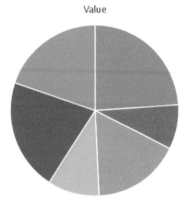

FIGURE 12-3 *An Excel pie chart with similar-sized slices*

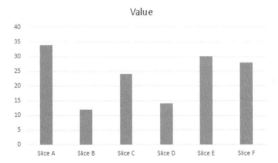

FIGURE 12-4 *An Excel column chart with the same values*

Another option is a stacked column. With a stacked column, as with a pie chart, it aids perception greatly to order the numbers by value. You can see by this by comparing the pie chart in Figure 12-5 with the stacked chart in Figure 12-6.

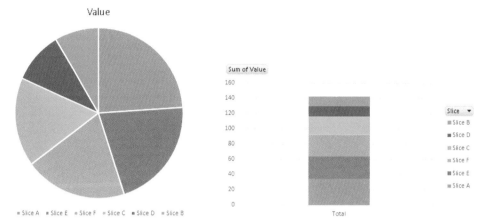

FIGURE 12-5 *A pie chart ordered by value*   FIGURE 12-6 *A stacked chart*

It's easier to see the total value in the stacked chart, but that comes at the expense of the ease of comparing the individual items (although that's still possible). Also, comparing individual items to the total value is now easier. Which of these charts you choose depends on the message you are trying to convey.

> Ordering values by magnitude is always a good idea for legibility.

EASE OF DEVELOPMENT

REPORTING TOOL	PREDEFINED CHART TYPE	EASE OF DEVELOPMENT
Excel	Yes	●
PerformancePoint	Yes	●
Power View	Yes	●
Reporting Services	Yes	●
Silverlight/HTML5	N/A	●

BULLET CHARTS

Bullet charts have been popularized by Stephen Few, and are an excellent way of having multiple comparison points. Chapter 16 deals with them more extensively, but this chapter includes an implementation in Reporting Services (SSRS).

Figure 12-7 shows a basic example of a bullet chart.

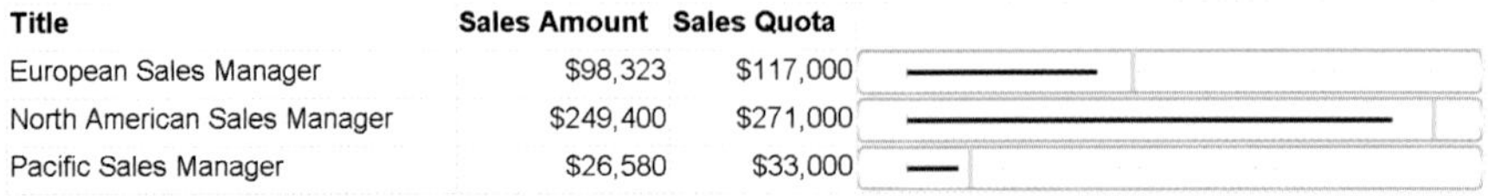

Title	Sales Amount	Sales Quota	
European Sales Manager	$98,323	$117,000	
North American Sales Manager	$249,400	$271,000	
Pacific Sales Manager	$26,580	$33,000	

FIGURE 12-7 *A bullet graph in SSRS*

Ease of Development

REPORTING TOOL	PREDEFINED CHART TYPE	EASE OF DEVELOPMENT
Excel	No	
PerformancePoint	No	
Power View	No	
Reporting Services	No	
Silverlight/HTML5	N/A	

RADAR CHARTS

A radar chart is a way of comparing data along multiple axes. In a radar chart, each point is represented as a distance from the center. The order and choice of data points is quite important in this type of graph, as adjacent nodes should be related in some manner, and the slope of the graph has meaning. In the chart of education ratings for the Scandinavian countries shown in Figure 12-8, the ratings for men and women have been chosen to be opposite each other, allowing for each comparison, and science was picked to be between math and reading, as science ability can be considered highly influenced by ability in math and reading.

The high slope for women up to science versus the flat one for men is an interesting contrast.

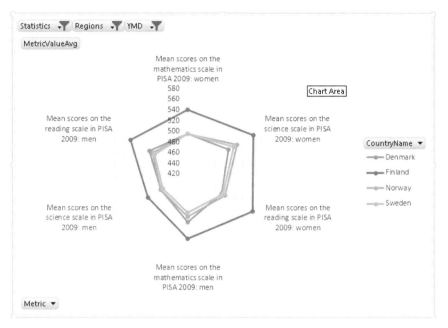

FIGURE 12-8 *A radar graph of Scandinavian education scores*

Ease of Development

REPORTING TOOL	PREDEFINED CHART TYPE	EASE OF DEVELOPMENT
Excel	Yes	●
PerformancePoint	No	●
Power View	No	●
Reporting Services	Yes	●
Silverlight/HTML5	N/A	●

MATRICES

A matrix of different comparisons is a very common visualization. A common use for them is on online shopping portals, such as the one from HTC in Figure 12-9.

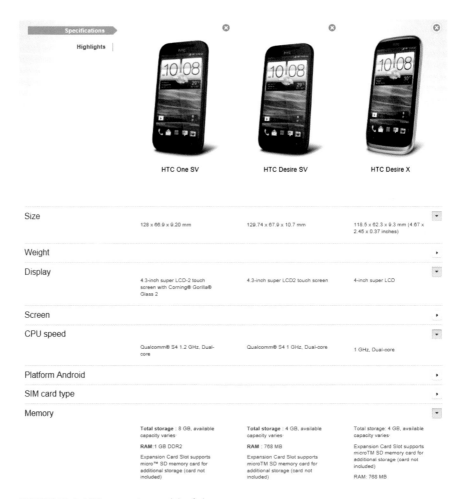

FIGURE 12-9 *HTC comparing models of phones*

Another form of matrix comparison is the bus matrix used in the Data Warehouse design, shown in Figure 12-10. By listing the dimensions along the top and the fact tables down the side, you can make an estimation of the difficulty of development of each area based upon the order in which they're done.

Facts/Dimensions

	Date	Time	Teller	Commission Earner	Business	Till	Product	Tender Type	Customer	BankAccount	Invoice Type	Cheque	Discount Auth User	Discount Reason	Invoice	Invoice Line Item	Return Reason	Return	Status	SwapType	Auth Till User	User action	Variance Reason
Invoice	X	X	X	X	X			X		X		X											
Invoice Line Item	X	X	X	X	X		X		X				X	X									
InvoiceTender	X	X	X	X	X			X	X	X		X		X									
Return	X	X	X	X	X			X	X					X		X		X					
Return Line Item	X	X	X	X	X		X	X	X						X	X							
Exchange					X										X		X		X				
Till Open	X	X			X	X														X			
Till Open User	X	X	X		X	X														X			
User Change	X	X	X		X																	X	X
Day End Recon	X	X	X		X			X												X			
Till Close	X	X	X		X	X		X												X			X

FIGURE 12-10 *A bus matrix*

PerformancePoint has an analytic grid, Excel has a pivot table, and SQL Server Reporting Services (SSRS) has a matrix for creating these comparison tables.

PerformancePoint's analytic grid is shown in Figure 12-11.

DimCountry Regions	Mean scores...	Mean scores...	Mean scores...	Mean scores...	Mean scores...	Mean scores...	Mean score i...	Expenditure...
⊟ Asia + Pacific	486.6788355	480.22512625	491.924246	498.81417825	4 ⌐Mean scores on the science scale in PISA 2009: men⌐ 375			13486.34791
⊞ Australia + New Zeal...	521.257136	512.413167	527.8930355	531.437763	497.334269	538.5145	517.890327	12784.503875
⊞ North East Asia	533.554451	524.13089	533.786862	545.447412	501.022974	539.934752	519.85773	14890.03598
⊞ South East Asia	370.646619	371.943281	378.124051	386.933775	383.272307	419.801983	401.705191	
⊟ Europe	500.24016836	489.31279244	498.47459548	499.33233656	470.32487992	511.73701368	493.273586473684	13368.6117674286
⊞ Central Europe	492.839797333333	485.913392	497.74769	503.9896165	464.320704833333	510.620712166667	490.947979333333	7550.1334078
⊞ Eastern Europe	468.91121	466.732419	476.746896	479.820981	436.875505	481.522416	459.395959	
⊟ Western Europe	504.447456388889	491.700391111111	499.923991722222	498.863874111111	474.184570222222	513.787702944445	495.9972164	15186.8862548125
⊟ Latin America + Cari...	416.930844666667	400.228196	426.071153333333	419.817264	415.921136333333	441.127491666667	428.796609333333	7166.3860415
⊞ Meso America	425.412094	411.76969	419.169678	412.724955	412.653217	437.578505	425.26531	7503.772083
⊞ South America	412.69022	394.457449	429.521891	423.3634185	417.555096	442.901985	430.562259	6829
⊟ North America	532.700246	520.832034	531.011766	526.367631	507.182212	541.527242	524.241845	20903.35796
⊟ North America	532.700246	520.832034	531.011766	526.367631	507.182212	541.527242	524.241845	20903.35796
Canada	532.700246	520.832034	531.011766	526.367631	507.182212	541.527242	524.241845	20903.35796

FIGURE 12-11 *A PerformancePoint analytic grid*

Ease of Development

REPORTING TOOL	PREDEFINED CHART TYPE	EASE OF DEVELOPMENT
Excel	Yes	●
PerformancePoint	Yes	●
PowerView	Yes	●
Reporting Services	Yes	●
Silverlight/HTML5	N/A	●

CUSTOM COMPARISONS

A custom comparison can take several forms. You can format the various charts in Excel and Reporting Services to a level that the chart is essentially a custom type.

For instance, Figure 12-12 is an example of a Christmas tree comparison.

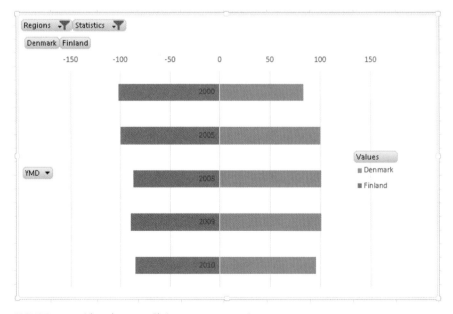

FIGURE 12-12 *A bar chart as a Christmas tree comparison*

Bullet graphs such as the one shown in Figure 12-13 are a custom comparison in Excel. This graph was developed by superimposing two bar graphs with a transparent background and a colored shape with a gradient.

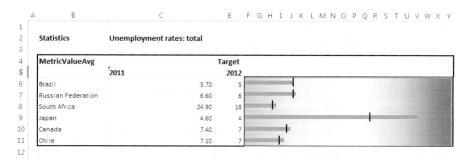

FIGURE 12-13   *A bullet graph in Excel*

Other custom visualizations include filled-up shelves shown in Figure 1-3 in Chapter 1, or the animated building in Figure 2-21 in Chapter 2. The animated buildings are essentially just prettified columns in a column graph.

Another custom visualization is the prism map also shown in Chapter 1.

TOOL CHOICES, WITH EXAMPLES

The Microsoft toolset is relatively good with comparison visualizations, and works well across the toolset. The only large gap is an automatically generated heatmap. While Excel can be used to generate a heatmap of sorts, it is far from use friendly. The InfoVis toolkit is discussed later in this chapter to show you what these heatmaps look like.

PERFORMANCEPOINT SERVICES

PerformancePoint is very good with the basic comparison visualizations. It has column charts, scorecards (the indicators covered in Chapter 13 are a form of comparison visual), and an analytic grid. It is, however, limited in that further customization is not possible. The interactivity of being able to slice your various comparisons by a scorecard —as shown in Figure 12-14—makes up for this in large part by making the experience of filtering the comparisons very easy.

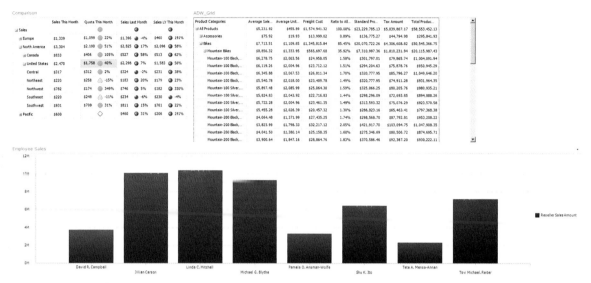

FIGURE 12-14   *A PerformancePoint dashboard*

SSRS

Reporting Services allows for great and finely detailed control over the individual elements in the charts being displayed. It enables you to easily create embedded charts (such as bullet charts) in table matrices. An example of embedding a bar chart in a matrix is shown in Figure 12-15.

This repeating (or tiling) of a chart is one of Reporting Services' greater strengths for comparing values.

EXCEL

Excel's greatest strength is in the level of control you have over a visualization's exact look. For instance, the pie charts shown in Figures 12-4 and 12-6 can have the individual slices pulled out to highlight items you are interested in, as shown in Figure 12-16, as well as a great deal of customization of how the labels are shown.

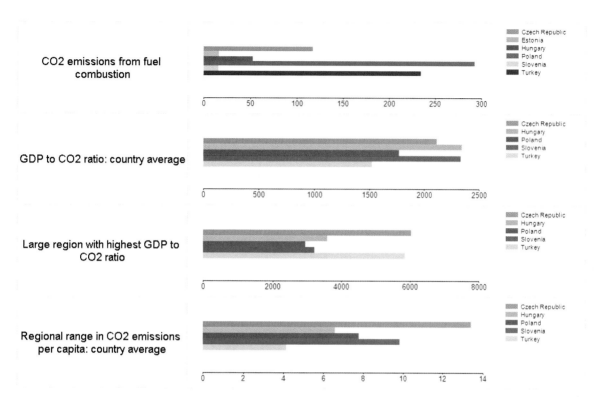

FIGURE 12-15 *Comparisons in Reporting Services*

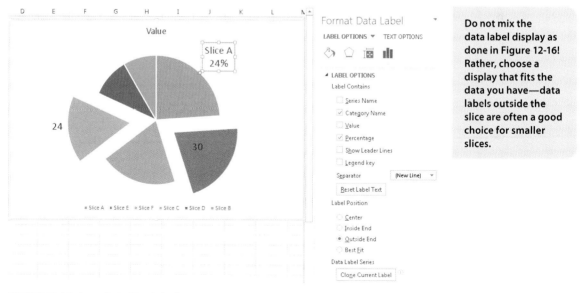

Do not mix the data label display as done in Figure 12-16! Rather, choose a display that fits the data you have—data labels outside the slice are often a good choice for smaller slices.

FIGURE 12-16 *An exploded Excel pie chart*

Another strength of using Excel is conditional formatting, which is used to create heatmaps, as well as the data bars. You can read more about heatmaps in Chapter 16, but an example of one is shown in Figure 12-17.

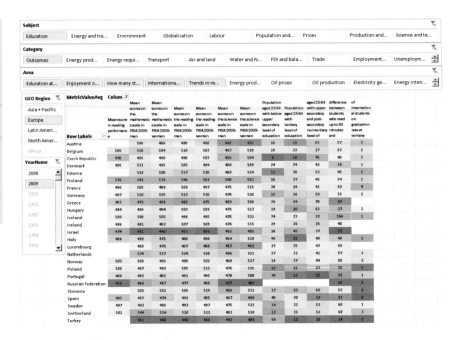

FIGURE 12-17 *A heatmap in Excel*

HEATMAPS AND COLUMNS

In Figure 12-17, the columns were set up individually with conditional formatting, as the numbers in the different columns are not comparable. Grand totals were also removed for this reason.

POWER VIEW

Power View is a good tool for interactive comparison visualizations. The automatic linking of column and bar charts on the same page is very useful. Just as with PerformancePoint, though, the level of control over the visualization is very limited. Figure 12-18 shows an example of a dashboard with a slicer, a table of data, and column and bar charts interacting with each other. Active regions are shown in blue, and inactive in a grey-blue.

FIGURE 12-18 *A Power View dashboard*

HTML5

Working in HTML5 gives you the ability to build your own visualizations. The prism map referenced earlier is one example, but all the other examples previously listed are possible—with an additional amount of work, of course. Figure 12-19 shows a heatmap chart built using the InfoVis toolkit. InfoVis is an open source HTML5 library available at `http://philogb.github.com/jit/`. The chart in the figure is based on countries for which we have both National Reserves and GDP per capita in 2009.

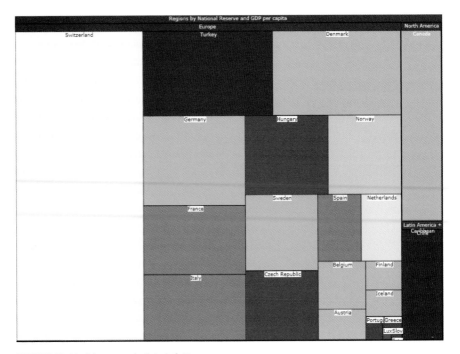

FIGURE 12-19 *A heatmap built in InfoVis*

IMPLEMENTATION EXAMPLES

The implementation examples in this section use the OECD_Data model, so be sure you have downloaded those from this book's web page on Wiley.com.

PERFORMANCEPOINT: COLUMN GRAPHS

PerformancePoint is the easiest tool to set up. To create the column chart for this example, create a data source, as explained in Chapter 7, right-click your PerformancePoint content list, and then create a new report. Choose Analytic Chart from the window that appears and finish off by choosing your data source. At this point you should see the Dashboard Designer window like the one in Figure 12-20.

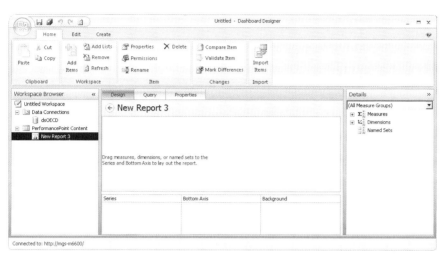

FIGURE 12-20 *Dashboard designer*

Drag MetricValueAvg to the Background, DimDate ➢ YMD to the background, DimCountryRegions ➢ Regions to the Bottom Axis, and DimOECDStatistics ➢ Statistics to the Series. You will find these by drilling down on Measures and Dimensions on the right-hand pane. Click the drop-down arrow next to DimDate and select 2009. Click the drop-down arrow next to Statistics and choose Foreign Population ➢ Foreign-born Nationals ➢ Foreign-born population. Finally, click the All member on the bottom axis to show the data at the region level. You should see a chart similar to Figure 12-21.

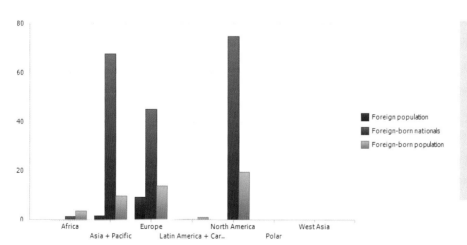

> When numbers can't be meaningfully added together, avoid stacked charts. For the same reason, there are times that a pie chart is not a meaningful representation, as the total figure and proportions are not meaningful.

FIGURE 12-21 *A PerformacePoint analytic chart*

EXCEL: MULTIPLE AXES AND SCALE BREAKS

The implementation examples in this section use the OECDPopulation PowerPivot model available from this book's web page, and called `OECDPopulationStats.xlsx`.

Sometimes it is difficult to show comparison for data—for instance, comparing the GDP per capita to the National Reserve value, as they are substantially different values, or comparing two countries that are very different. For instance, the chart shown in Figure 12-22 has these two measures for Switzerland and for Estonia, and Estonia's Reserve value is barely visible:

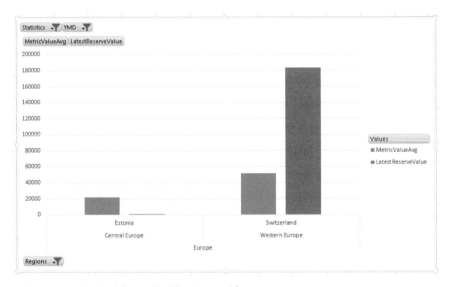

FIGURE 12-22 *An Excel chart with difficult-to-read figures*

MULTIPLE AXES VERSUS SCALE BREAKS

When two or more axes are shown together on a chart, the chart is said to have *multiple axes*. These will be shown on each side of the chart, and the series on the chart will be associated with one or the other of the scales.

A *scale break* is shown when, for example, only sections of a scale are shown on the chart. For instance, a chart might only display values from 0–100 and 90000–100000. This enables a comparison of figures that are different in scale.

Open `OECDPopulationStats.xlsx`. Switch to sheet 1, then start by clicking the Pivot Chart button on the Insert Ribbon, as shown in Figure 12-23.

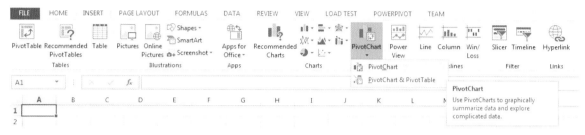

FIGURE 12-23 *Excel Ribbon interface to add a pivot chart*

Choose Existing Worksheet and Use an External Data Source. Click Choose Connection, as shown in Figure 12-24.

The choice of a connection is a bit different between Excel 2013 and earlier versions. In the earlier versions, you select PowerPivot as the data source, but in Excel 2013 you must choose Tables, and then select Tables in Workbook Data Model, as shown in Figure 12-25.

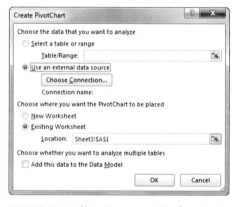

FIGURE 12-24 *Choosing a connection for a pivot chart*

FIGURE 12-25 *Choosing your workbook model*

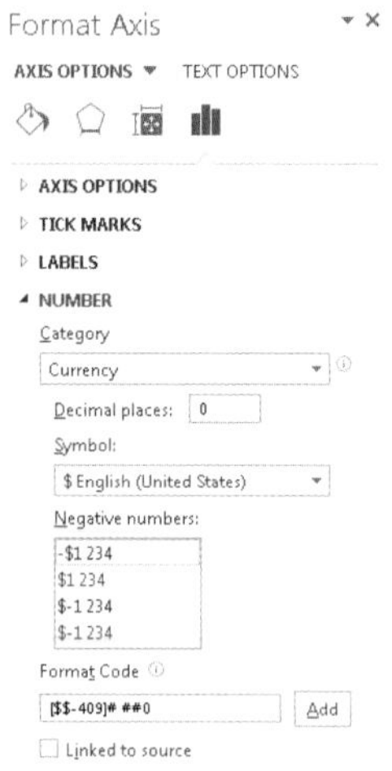

Format Axis

AXIS OPTIONS ▼   TEXT OPTIONS

▷ AXIS OPTIONS
▷ TICK MARKS
▷ LABELS
▲ NUMBER
Category
Currency
Decimal places: 0
Symbol:
$ English (United States)
Negative numbers:
-$1 234
$1 234
$-1 234
$-1 234
Format Code ⓘ
[$$-409]# ##0   Add
☐ Linked to source

FIGURE 12-26 *Formatting a number in Excel*

AXIS OPTIONS ▼   TEXT OPTIONS

▲ AXIS OPTIONS
Bounds
Minimum   1.0   Auto
Maximum   1.0E6   Auto
Units
Major   10.0   Auto
Minor   10.0   Auto
Horizontal axis crosses
● Automatic
○ Axis value   1.0
○ Maximum axis value
Display units   None ▾
   ☐ Show display units label on chart
☑ Logarithmic scale Base 10
☐ Values in reverse order
▷ TICK MARKS
▷ LABELS
▲ NUMBER
Category
Currency
Decimal places: 0
Symbol:
$ English (United States)
Negative numbers:
-$1 234
$1 234
$-1 234
$-1 234
Format Code ⓘ
[$$-409]# ##0   Add
☐ Linked to source

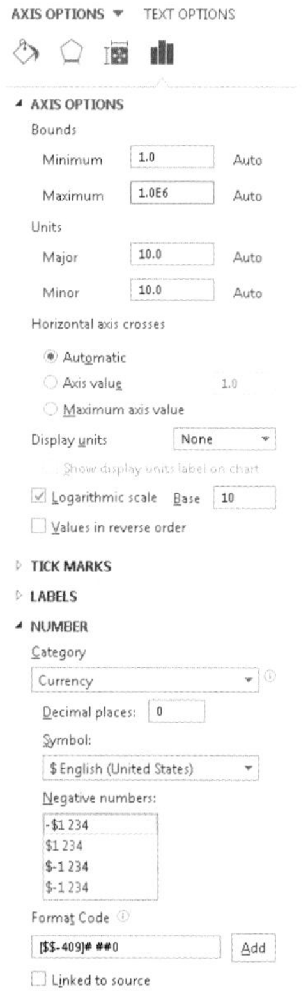

FIGURE 12-27 *Formatting the secondary axis in Excel*

At this point, you see an empty pivot chart on the left and the PivotChart Fields pane is on the right, but you need to add the appropriate fields to the chart. Drag MetricValueAvg and LatestReserveValue to the Values field in the right-hand pane.

Next, drag the DimOECDStatistics ➢ Statistics Hierarchy onto the Filter pane. Click the arrow next to the word Statistics on the chart, and drill down to Production and Income ➢ Production ➢ Size of GDP ➢ GDP per Capita, and then click OK.

Drag DimDate ➢ YMD onto Filters, click on the arrow next to the word YMD, select 2011, then press OK.

Drag DimCountry ➢ Regions to the Axis field on the right-hand pane. Click the arrow next to the word Regions on the chart, then click Select multiple items. Untick the All check box, and then tick Europe ➢ Central Europe ➢ Estonia and Europe ➢ Western Europe ➢ Switzerland.

Right-click on the word Europe that appears on the bottom of the chart, then click Expand/Collapse, and then Expand to CountryName. This will finish the chart shown at the beginning of this section.

For the first problem, you can put the one series onto a second axis by right-clicking the series and then selecting Format Data Series. On the screen that displays, set the axis to Secondary. Notice that some of your data has disappeared. To fix this, change the Gap Width to 400% and then go to the other series and change the Gap Width to 100%. The widths of the two series changes so that they can always be seen.

Next, right-click the right axis, choose Format Axis, and then change to the Axis Options tab in the Format Axis pane. Change the Number format to Currency, check that the correct currency (US$) is chosen, and set the Decimal places to 0. Your setup screen should look like Figure 12-26.

Now, do the same for the axis on the left. In this case, there is one additional setting you want to set—check the box next to Logarithmic Scale. (See Figure 12-27.)

The Logarithmic Scale option sets your axis to show in multiples of 10, which nicely compresses the data values. It requires some skill on the part of the reader to know that the values on the two axes scale differently, so be careful when using this technique.

The chart is as shown in Figure 12-28, but you still have to apply formatting to make it readable.

Having two axes enables you to show different scales, but it does mean that your reader needs to pay attention to the scales when reading the visualization. Figure 12-29 shows how the relationships change when using data for all of Europe. The left axis stays the same, but the values on the right axis do not.

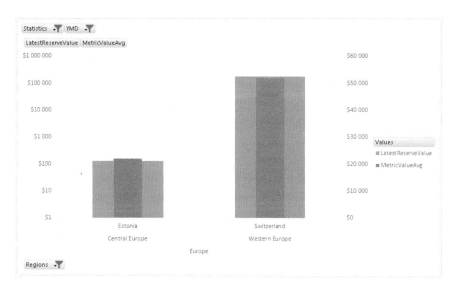

FIGURE 12-28 *Two axes superimposed*

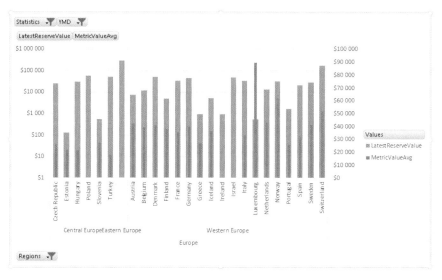

FIGURE 12-29 *A change in only one axis*

This is of course not a scale break, which you may be familiar with from Reporting Services (which has it as a built-in option).

There are some (relatively tricky) ways of getting scale breaks to work in Excel: The one you are going to work through now is reliant on being able to create custom measures. This is a feature specific to Excel 2013—in Excel 2007 and 2010 you need to download a tool called OLAPPivotTableExtensions from `http://olappivottableextend.codeplex.com/`. You will be continuing to use the same pivot table you used in the previous example.

OTHER SCALE BREAK TRICKS

Jon Peltier has some great alternative tricks to building a scale break, which are based on the data residing within Excel and not a cube. He calls them Panel Charts, and you can read more about them at `http://peltiertech.com/Excel/ChartsHowTo/PanelUnevenScales.html`.

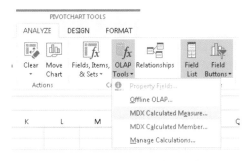

FIGURE 12-30 *Adding an MDX Calculated Measure*

Start by removing your current measures from the pivot table. Alternatively, if you are creating a new chart, make sure to add the YMD hierarchy to the filters section, filter for 2011, add the Regions hierarchy to the Axis category, and filter for Switzerland and Estonia.

Next, choose the appropriate scale break values. Given how low the value for Estonia is, you can set the upper scale break to 2000. You will do this by going to OLAP Tools on the Ribbon's Analyze tab and choosing MDX Calculated Measure, as shown Figure 12-30.

As shown in Figure 12-31, call your new measure LowerReserve and put it in the FactOECDNationalReserve measure group. Use the following code—all it does is set any value higher than 2000 to 2000.

```
CASE WHEN  [Measures].[LatestReserveValue] > 2000 THEN  2000 ELSE
[Measures].[LatestReserveValue] END
```

Add this measure to your pivot table by dragging the field name from the right-hand pane onto your pivot table. Now right-click the axis on the right side and choose format Axis. Set the number format to currency, and set the maximum to 4000. Because you are splitting the axis in two, this setting is always double the maximum value for the lower reserve.

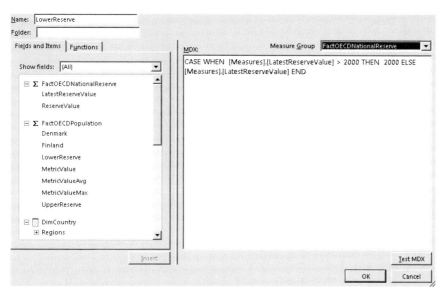

FIGURE 12-31 *Calculated measure text*

Next, create a new measure called UpperReserve in exactly the same manner as LowerReserve. This value instead has a lower limit. Setting this lower limit is crucial—any chart item with a value between the upper end of the Lower value (2000) and the lower end of the Upper value disappears off the chart. In this case, with just two values, you can be fairly arbitrary, and 150000 works. Use the following code:

```
CASE WHEN  [Measures].[LatestReserveValue] > 150000 THEN
[Measures].[LatestReserveValue] ELSE NULL END
```

The difference here is that the value at the bottom end is getting removed from the chart. Add Upper Reserve to the chart and switch it to the secondary axis.

The trick is to set the minimum and maximum bounds of the axis so that it appears above the other chart items. In this case, set the maximum to 200000 and the minimum to -228571 (-200000 plus an offset value of 1 seventh—you often need to tweak this offset).

Your chart should currently look like Figure 12-32.

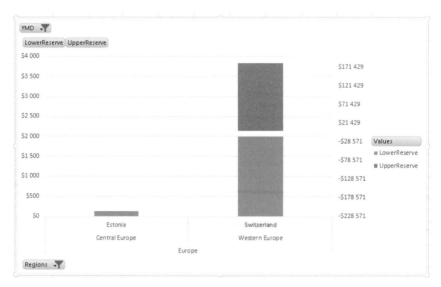

FIGURE 12-32 *The chart with double scales*

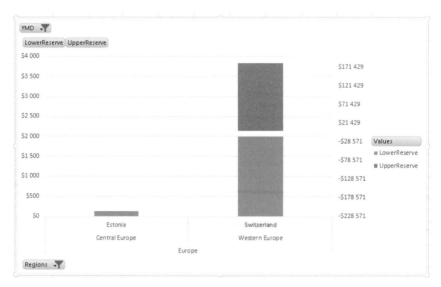

FIGURE 12-33 *Removing labels from a chart*

It isn't immediately apparent that what we are doing is a type of scale break technique. To make that more evident, first hide both axis titles and add data labels. You can do this by right-clicking each axis, choosing Format Axis, and then setting the Label Position to None, as shown in Figure 12-33.

Add data labels by right-clicking an axis and choosing Add Data Label. After you've added the labels, right-click and choose Format Data Label, set the number format, and also set the position to Inside End, as in Figure 12-34.

After that, change the font in the Home Ribbon where you'd normally do it. The final step is to set a gradient to show that the two series are related. Using one stop at 15% away and keeping to the very distinct colors illustrates that the two sections can't be compared. Figure 12-35 shows the gradient setup.

FIGURE 12-34 *Changing label position*

FIGURE 12-35 *Setting gradient stops*

Obviously, you need to do this twice—once for each series—and your final chart should like the one shown in Figure 12-36.

To get back to the Axis options (for instance, if you change the selection of countries and need to adjust the axis maximum and minimum), you have to go through the chart format area because you have hidden the axis. (See Figure 12-37.)

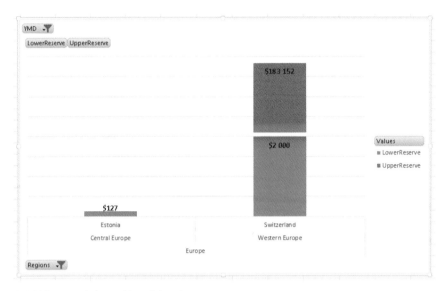

FIGURE 12-36 *A chart with scale breaks*

FIGURE 12-37 *Changing axis options*

Adding all the countries of Europe creates a rather messy chart. You can tidy it up by clicking the individual $2000 labels and deleting them. There is still data missing, and to bring that missing data onto the chart, you need to change the lower value for the upper reserve. This approach requires some manual effort to get these values set to 100% correctly.

SLICERS AND NUMBERS TABLES

You can dynamically set the scale break values if you have a numbers table in your cube, use that numbers table as the data source for your slicer, and then use that numbers table as your limit. This qualifies as an advanced topic—more information can be found at `http://markgstacey.net`.

EXCEL: RADAR CHARTS

Excel radar charts are very easy to set up. From a new sheet, click Insert ➤ Pivot chart. Select the external data connection option, and choose the connection to OECD_Data. If you need assistance, refer to Chapter 5.

On your new pivot chart, add MetricValueAvg to the values and drag DimDate ➢ YMD to the filters. Add DimCountry ➢ Regions to the Series, and DimOECDStatistic ➢ Statistics to the Axis.

On the pivot chart, click the drop-down arrow next to YMD and select 2011. Then click the drop-down arrow next to Statistics and uncheck the Select All box.

Navigate to Globalisation ➢ Trade ➢ and select International Trade in Services and International Trade in Goods and click OK.

Right-click Globalisation on the chart, choose Expand/Collapse, and then choose Expand to Metric.

Your chart should look like Figure 12-38.

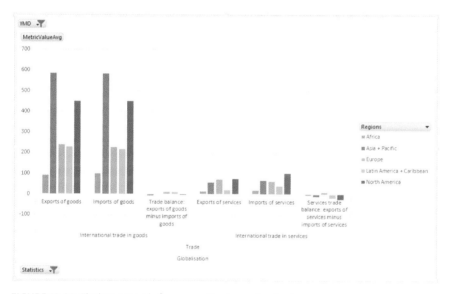

FIGURE 12-38 *The basic chart before converting to a radar chart*

To convert this to a radar chart, right-click the chart, choose Change Chart Type, and then pick Radar chart from the list of charts, and click OK. Your chart changes, as shown in Figure 12-39.

This chart is one that works better as a column chart. Give careful thought before using radar charts.

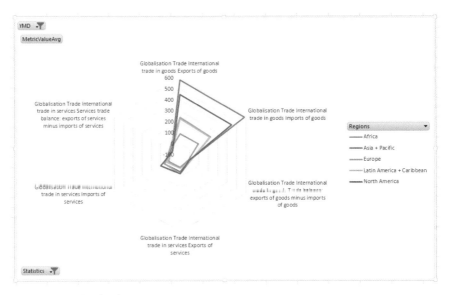

FIGURE 12-39 *A radar chart*

SSRS: A BULLET CHART

Reporting Services has a chart very closely related to the bullet chart—the gauge chart—which you use to create the bullet chart.

Start by creating a data source connecting to the OECD tabular model, and then create a new data set, and call it dsOECD. Pull the MetricValueAvg measure onto the design surface, drag DimOECDStatistics ➢ Statistics onto the parameters, and select the Production and Income ➢ Productivity ➢ Size of GDP ➢ GDP per hour worked metric. Check the parameter box.

Now drag DimDate ➢ YMD onto the design surface, and choose 2011. Drag DimCountry ➢ Regions ➢ CountryName onto the design surface.

Your design surface should look like the one shown in Figure 12-40.

The next step is to set a target, so you need to create a calculated measure. In this case, you are going to create two measures: one target being the best GDP per hour worked across the planet, and another one for the best GDP for the Sub Region. To create a calculated measure, right-click in the box in the lower-left corner, and choose New Calculated Member. Your code will be the following:

```
CASE WHEN [Measures].[MetricValueAVG] = NULL THEN NULL ELSE
MAX( [Measures].[MetricValueMax], [DimCountry].[Regions].[All])
END
```

And the screen should look like Figure 12-41.

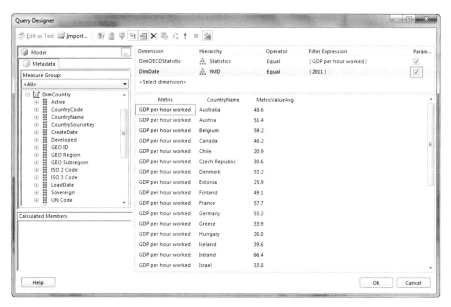

FIGURE 12-40 *A dataset query window for Analysis Services*

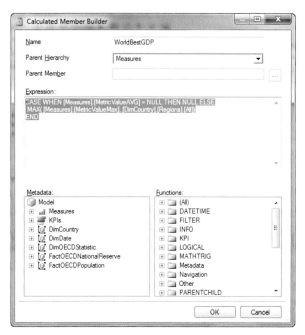

FIGURE 12-41 *Adding a calculated member*

Create another new calculated member, and use the following formula:

```
CASE WHEN [Measures].[MetricValueAvg] = NULL THEN NULL ELSE
MAX(
{(([DimCountry].[Regions].CurrentMember.Parent).Children}
 ,[Measures].[MetricValueMax]
 )
END
```

Your screen should look like the one in Figure 12-42.

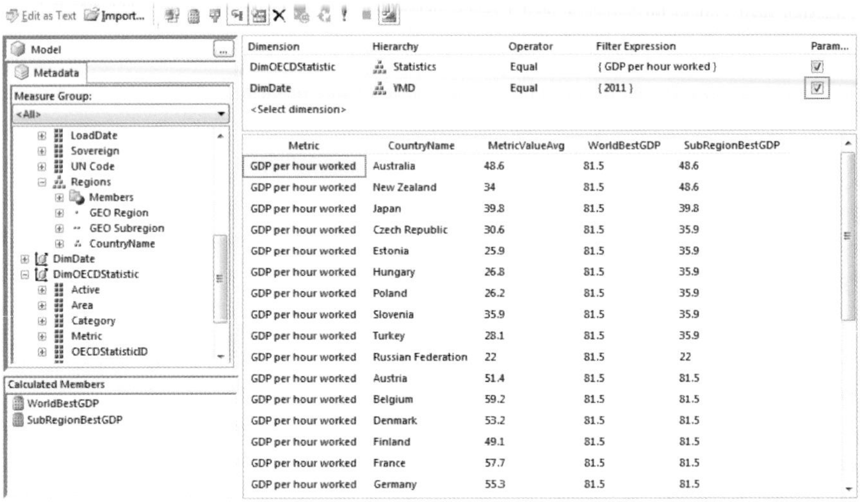

FIGURE 12-42 *Calculated column*

You now have two target values to use for the bullet graph. Click OK twice and then remove the footer and the title on the report.

In the Insert tab, click Matrix ➢ Matrix Wizard. Choose the dsOECD dataset you just created. Add Country Name to the Row group, and MetricValueAvg to the values, and click Next. Uncheck Show Subtotals and Grand Totals on the next screen and click Next. Finally, choose the generic style and click Finish.

On the table that appears, right-click the Metric value column, and choose Insert Columns ➢ Right. Click the new cell that appears, parallel to the Country Name, and from the Ribbon choose Insert ➢ Gauge. Click the cell again to make the gauge choice screen in Figure 12-43 appear, choose the linear bar, and then click OK.

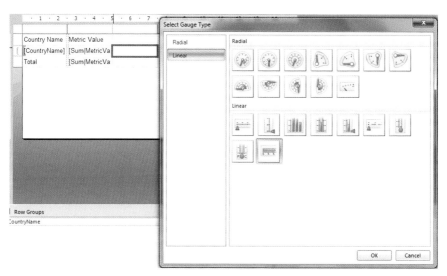

FIGURE 12-43 *Inserting a gauge chart*

Enlarge the row and column to make working easier, as shown in Figure 12-44.

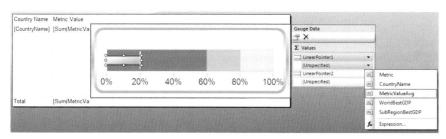

FIGURE 12-44 *Formatting the gauge chart*

Right-click the gauge and choose Gauge Properties. Select Back Fill and set it to solid and white. Click the gauge, click the arrow next to Unspecified below LinearPoint1, and set it to MetricValueAvg.

Repeat the process for LinearPoint2, and set it to WorldBestGDP. To add another point, select the first pointer on the graph, and then right-click just next to it on the white space, as shown in Figure 12-45.

Set the third pointer to SubRegionBestGDP. Your GDP values are not percentages, so right-click the

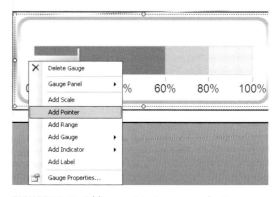

FIGURE 12-45 *Adding a pointer to a gauge chart*

scale, IOW the numbers along the bottom of the gauge, and choose Scale Properties. Select the Number tab, as shown in Figure 12-46, and choose Number in the Category list.

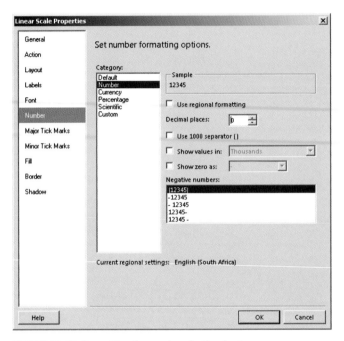

FIGURE 12-46 *Formatting the numbers for the chart*

A few final steps are all you have left to do. The background ranges are not relevant in this case—they are useful when percentages are being used. Delete each of the ranges (see Figure 12-47).

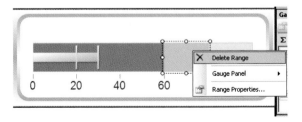

FIGURE 12-47 *Deleting the background for the range*

Now you have just some formatting to finish. For the LinearPointer1, click the arrow and choose Pointer Options. Change the width percentage to 25%, as shown in Figure 12-48.

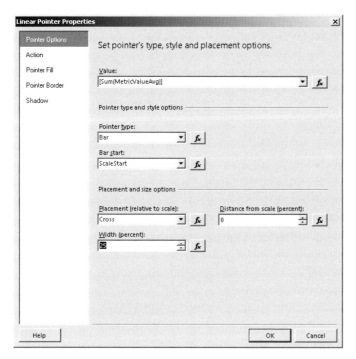

FIGURE 12-48 *Setting the size of the pointer*

Next, select the Pointer Fill tab and change the fill to solid black. Click OK, and get to the same settings for LinearPointer2. Change the width to 5% and the length to 80%, as shown in Figure 12-49.

Change to the Pointer Fill tab, and change the color to solid orange.

Repeat the process a third time for LinearPointer3; set the width to 5% and the length to 80%. Switch to the Pointer Fill tab, and set the color to solid blue.

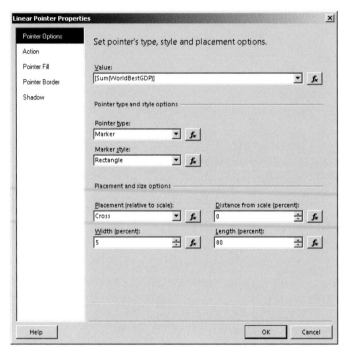

FIGURE 12-49 *Formatting the pointer*

To finish off, shrink the row that the bullet graph is embedded in, and run the report. Your report should look similar to the one in Figure 12-50.

REPORT FORMATTING

There are many things that you should do to this report to aid readability—modify color choice, change the numbers on the scale to be legible, use tick marks instead of numbers, or change the borders on the bullet graphs. These formatting modifications would all be additional to the basics of building a bullet chart. Also, instead of just purely ordering alphabetically, ordering by region would enable much better comparisons.

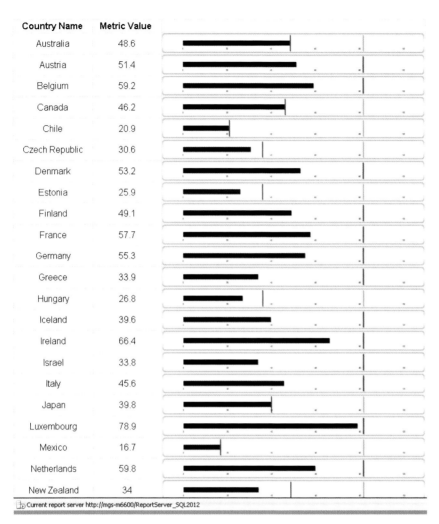

Country Name	Metric Value
Australia	48.6
Austria	51.4
Belgium	59.2
Canada	46.2
Chile	20.9
Czech Republic	30.6
Denmark	53.2
Estonia	25.9
Finland	49.1
France	57.7
Germany	55.3
Greece	33.9
Hungary	26.8
Iceland	39.6
Ireland	66.4
Israel	33.8
Italy	45.6
Japan	39.8
Luxembourg	78.9
Mexico	16.7
Netherlands	59.8
New Zealand	34

Current report server http://mgs-m6600/ReportServer_SQL2012

FIGURE 12-50 *A bullet chart*

HTML5

For your HTML5 visualization, you are going to implement the treemap visualization shown earlier in this chapter under the HTML5 examples. Although
you would typically use the C# web service from Chapter 9 to return the JSON
required, in this section you find out how to use SQL Server stored procedures

to create the JSON. You copy it manually, but it could just as easily be used to supply server-side code to create the JSON.

You will need the files available from this book's page on Wiley.com called `Chapter12_Treemap.js`. All the editing can happen in any text editor, such as Notepad++.

You will need the following:

- `Base.css`
- `Excanvas.js`
- `Jit.js`
- `Treemap.css`
- `Treemap.html`
- `Treemap.js`

`Treemap.html` simply references the appropriate JavaScript files.

`Treemap.js` contains the active code. The first section is the function `init()`, which is fired when the page is open. The code `var json={}` is the data piece—you will paste the code you get from SQL over the `{}`.

The next call is to initialize the `treemap` object:

```
var tm = new $jit.TM.Squarified({
    //where to inject the visualization
    injectInto: 'infovis',
    //parent box title heights
    titleHeight: 15,
    //enable animations
    animate: animate,
    //box offsets
    offset: 1,
    //Attach left and right click events
    Events: {
      enable: true,
      onClick: function(node) {
        if(node) tm.enter(node);
      },
      onRightClick: function() {
        tm.out();
      }
    },
    duration: 1000,
    //Enable tips
    Tips: {
```

```
      enable: true,
      //add positioning offsets
      offsetX: 20,
      offsetY: 20,
      //implement the onShow method to
      //add content to the tooltip when a node
      //is hovered
      onShow: function(tip, node, isLeaf, domElement) {
        var html = "<div class=\"tip-title\">" + node.name
          + "</div><div class=\"tip-text\">";
        var data = node.data;
        if(data.playcount) {
          html += "play count: " + data.playcount;
        }
        if(data.image) {
          html += "<img src=\""+ data.image +"\" class=\"album\" />";
        }
        tip.innerHTML =  html;
      }
    },
    //Add the name of the node in the correponding label
    //This method is called once, on label creation.
    onCreateLabel: function(domElement, node){
        domElement.innerHTML = node.name;
        var style = domElement.style;
        style.display = '';
        style.border = '1px solid transparent';
        domElement.onmouseover = function() {
          style.border = '1px solid #9FD4FF';
        };
        domElement.onmouseout = function() {
          style.border = '1px solid transparent';
        };
    }
  });
```

The parameters are the name of the div to insert the visualization into, the height, the title, whether or not to animate transitions, and how to enable left and right-clicks. All of these settings are available from the InfoVis examples at `http://philogb.github.com/jit/static/v20/Jit/Examples/Treemap/example1.html`.

It's a two-step process to generate the JSON you will paste in. The first step is a function that creates the individual child nodes, as follows:

```
ALTER FUNCTION dbo.fn_JSONCountryTree (@RegionName varchar(255))

RETURNS varchar(max)
AS
BEGIN
```

```
DECLARE @return varchar(max) = ''

DECLARE @tbl Table(CountryName varchar(255), JSON varchar(max),
FullJSON varchar(max))

INSERT INTO @tbl (CountryName, JSON)
select

countryname,


CASE WHEN ROW_NUMBER() over (order by countryname) = 1 THEN '' ELSE ',
' END +
'{
        "children": [],
        "data": {
            "GDP Per Capita": "' + CAST( CAST( round(fonr.value /
131.487000,0) as int) as varchar(10)) +   '",
            "$color": "' +  CASE CAST( ROUND( (FOP.Value -
17311.929220) / 7248.925672000,0) + 1 as int)
WHEN 1 THEN '#A50026'
WHEN 2 THEN '#D73027'
WHEN 3 THEN '#F46D43'
WHEN 4 THEN '#FDAE61'
WHEN 5 THEN '#FEE08B'
WHEN 6 THEN '#FFFFBF'
WHEN 7 THEN '#A6D96A'
WHEN 8 THEN '#66BD63'
WHEN 9 THEN '#66BD63'
WHEN 10 THEN '#1A9850'
WHEN 11 THEN '#006837'
END +'",
            "image": "",
            "$area": ' + CAST( CAST( round(fonr.value / 131.487000,0)
 as int) as varchar(10)) +   '
        },
        "id": "' + dc.CountryName  +  '",
        "name": "' + dc.CountryName  +  '"
    }'

            FROM DBO.FactOECDNationalReserve FONR
            INNER JOIN
            dbo.DimCountry DC
            on FONR.DimCountryID = dc.CountryID
            INNER JOIN dbo.FactOECDPopulation FOP
            on DC.CountryID = FOP.DimCountryID
            and fop.DimDateID = 20110101
            and FOP.DimOECDStatisticID = 197
            and FOP.value is not null
            where fonr.DimDateID = 20110901
```

```
              and [geo region] = @RegionName

              --and CountryName = 'Austria'
               order by CountryName asc


UPDATE @tbl
SET @return = @return+json,  FullJSON = @return



RETURN @return
END
go
```

In this code, the function takes a template JSON in the following format:

```
"{
        "children": [],
        "data": {
          "GDP Per Capita": "56",
          "$color": "#FDAE61",
          "image": "",
          "$area": 56
        }"
```

and uses values for the GDP per Capita and National Reserve to set the color and area. A `case` statement for 11 ranges of color is set up to set the color. There is also a chunk of code that appends each of the individual countries JSON to the `@return` variable. The `RowNumber()` call adds a comma to each entry except the first.

The following is the stored procedure that uses this function:

```
ALTER PROC TreeMapByRegion
as

DECLARE @return varchar(max) = ''


DECLARE @tbl Table(RegionName varchar(255), JSON varchar(max),
FUllJson  varchar(max))


INSERT INTO @tbl(RegionName, JSON)

select [GEO Region] ,
CASE WHEN ROW_NUMBER () over (order by  [GEO Region]) = 1 THEN ''
ELSE ',' END +
' {
        "children": [' +
```

```
dbo.fn_JSONCountryTree( [gEO rEGION]) + ' ],
        "data": {
          "GDP Per Capita": '  + cast( SUM(ROUND(FONR.Value /
131.487000,0)) as varchar(100)) +    ',
          "$area": '  + cast( SUM(ROUND(FONR.Value /  131.487000,0)) as
varchar(100)) +    '
        },
        "id": "'+[GEO Region]+'",
        "name": "'+[GEO Region]+'"
      }'


  FROM DBO.FactOECDNationalReserve FONR
              INNER JOIN
              dbo.DimCountry DC
              on FONR.DimCountryID = dc.CountryID
              INNER JOIN dbo.FactOECDPopulation FOP
              on DC.CountryID = FOP.DimCountryID
              and fop.DimDateID = 20110101
              and FOP.DimOECDStatisticID = 197
              and FOP.value is not null

                          where fonr.DimDateID = 20110901

GROUP BY [GEO Region]

UPDATE @tbl
SET @return = @return + JSON,
FUllJson = @return

SET @return = '{
    "children": [' + @return + ' ],
    "data": {},
    "id": "root",
    "name": "Regions by National Reserve and GDP per capita"
    }'

select @return


GO
```

This code calls the previous function for each region, and inserts the result into a table variable using a JSON template. It then uses the same variable appending logic to put all the regions together into a single string, and adds the outside wrappers of the JSON format for the treemaps.

To finish off the work, simply paste the results of this query into `Treemap.js` where the `var json = {}` is. Double check to be sure the semicolon is after the last brace!

SUMMARY

In this chapter you learned about comparisons using visualizations. For the most part, all the Microsoft tools are good at this, and you have seen how to use them effectively. You have also learned more on using the treemap visualization introduced in Chapter 9.

CHAPTER 13

Slice and Dice:
Ad Hoc Analytics

The term slice and dice has been a synonym for business intelligence (BI) and probably predates that term. With the advent of online analytical processing (OLAP) tools, business users became able to manipulate large data sets, and apply summaries such as SUM and COUNT across custom groupings in real-time—this capability is what is known as *slice and dice*. A better term is really *ad hoc analytics* because slice and dice was originally used purely for tabular data, and later advances mean that more graphical visualizations can also be interrogated in the same manner. In this chapter, you will learn about the different types of ad hoc analysis and explore the value of each of the tools.

OLAP

OLAP stands for online analytic processing to distinguish it from *online transaction processing* (OLTP) and batch based analysis. The term was first coined by Edgar F. Codd in 1993. Microsoft joined the market in 1998 with Analysis Services and today has the biggest market share in OLAP. Later technologies, such as the column-store database used in PowerPivot and Analysis Services Tabular are not OLAP, but are presented in a very similar way to front-end tools to maintain backward compatibility.

EXPLANATION OF TERMS

The field of ad hoc analytics is vast and murky, with different vendors perpetuating their own terminology. Microsoft, as always, does the same, and it is important to understand the different way the tools are defined.

First, ad hoc analytics needs to be differentiated from the way the term analytics is used in general. The term is often used as a synonym for predictive analytics, statistical analysis, or machine learning. These fields (to some extent one and the same) are all based around the concept that an analysis is being done mathematically and probabilistically—far outside the scope of this chapter.

Instead, *ad hoc analytics* is the analysis by a person of a data set, by dynamically applying filters, grouping, and aggregations until a result is discovered. This process, as mentioned, is also called slice and dice, and (outside the Microsoft space) is called data mining as well. *Data mining* in that context is analyzing data to derive value. However, Microsoft has a tool as part of its Analysis Services called Data Mining Extensions and a language DMX, which are in fact a statistical toolset. This distinction is important as it can lead to some confusion!

Some other important terms that are often confused are covered next.

SELF-SERVICE BI

Self-service BI is another one of those hot industry topics with confusion attached.

In the first definition, self-service BI simply refers to the ad hoc analytic capability described in the preceding section. Data has been prepared, possibly in a data warehouse, loaded into a BI tool, perhaps OLAP or not, and then the business users are allowed to interact with the data in this controlled manner.

At the other end of the spectrum is the self-service user who is gathering his own data and then building his own reports. Typically, as seen in Figure 13-1, this is easy enough when a single source of data (such as an ERP system) is available, but this becomes much more difficult after multiple sources of data are required to be combined, such as a CRM and an ERP system, with the possibility of duplication and data mismatches.

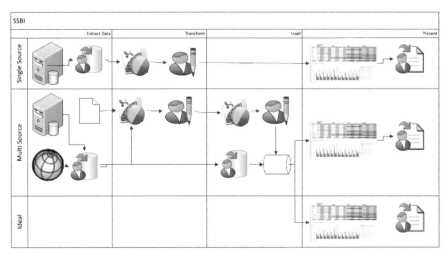

FIGURE 13-1 *Self-service BI lifecycles*

As with everything in life, the best approach is often a middle-ground: allowing a Business Intelligence Competency Center (BICC) to do the large part of combining data and then opening the door to business departments to use the centralized data sources, but also to expand and integrate their own sources.

THE PLACE OF POWERPIVOT

A common misconception is that PowerPivot is a visualization tool. Aside from the ever-present table visualization, PowerPivot is not a visualization tool in the slightest—no graphs or charts are part of the toolset. Instead, PowerPivot is a data modeling and data integration tool aimed at a business user. Incorporating Microsoft's xVelocity engine, an in-memory column-store analytic database at its heart, and a new functional language called DAX (for Data Analysis Expressions). Where PowerPivot sits is as a bridge between users and IT. Business users can create their own analyses, combining data from the corporate data warehouse as well as their own formulae and possibly external data sources. They can start sharing these analyses with their team by publishing to a collaboration portal built in SharePoint and using PowerPivot services to do the calculations. The final step in an enterprise BI scenario is when the business has decided that this analytic workbook is business-critical—which decision is often driven by usage metrics on the workbook in questions—and IT is asked to take it over. At this point, the workbook is imported into Analysis Services using Visual Studio, optimized using such techniques as partitioning, role-based security suiting the data within the workbook, and then deployed to a production server and monitored on an ongoing basis. Figure 13-2 shows a typical example of such an environment.

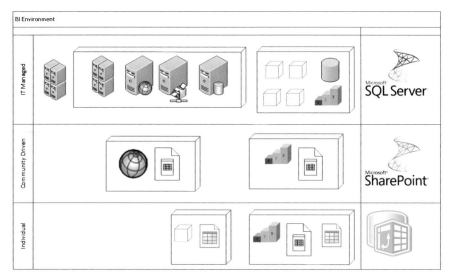

FIGURE 13-2 *BI environments using Microsoft tools*

PowerPivot thus sits as the glue holding many of the visualization tools together.

BISM

Microsoft talks about the Business Intelligence Semantic Layer (BISM) as the common term across the OLAP and column-store worlds. The semantic layers serve as a single common point to store calculations and business terms—this means that when a calculation changes due to changing accounting regulations or other reasons, it can be changed in a single central location rather than having to edit every report and dashboard containing the calculation.

DEFINITIONS

There are several terms in general use as verbs when doing ad hoc analytics—each of these will be covered in the section ahead—these terms are used throughout the book, and indeed the industry, so this will be a useful section. The terms are:

- Pivot
- Drill down (Drill up is the reverse)
- Drill through
- Drill across (not to be confused with cross drill)
- Slice

Pivoting

Excel popularized the pivot table, an indispensable tool for any analysis. Pivoting refers to the ability to drag any field into rows or the columns, and then view the data aggregated across those fields. Figure 13-3 shows a typical Excel pivot table and pivot chart beside each other.

FIGURE 13-3 *A pivot chart in Excel*

Ease of Development

REPORTING TOOL	PREDEFINED CHART TYPE	EASE OF DEVELOPMENT
Excel	Yes	●
PerformancePoint	Yes	●
Power View	Yes	●
Reporting Services	No	●
Silverlight/HTML5	N/A	●

Drill-down

A drill down requires a hierarchy, a predefined relationship between data values. The hierarchy that will always appear in any BI analysis (with many different versions) is the date hierarchy. In the most common date hierarchy, the calendar date will be defined as Year-Month-Day, with the drill down corresponding to that. Drill downs are most commonly shown with a "+" to allow drilling down. The inverse of a drill down is a drill up, which will collapse the expanded drill down, and this is most commonly shown with a "-". PerformancePoint analytic charts are an exception—drill down is achieved by clicking the dimension member name, and drill up requires a right-click. Figure 13-4 shows a drill down in Excel.

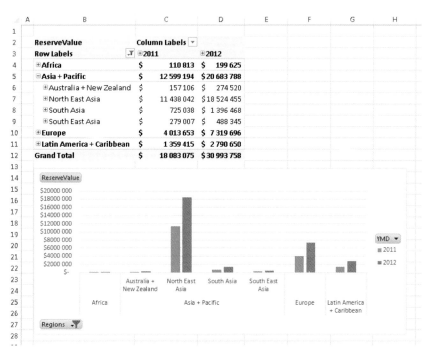

FIGURE 13-4 *Drilling down on a pivot table and linked pivot chart*

The display of the undrilled values next to the drilled values is by contrast to PerformancePoint, which replaces the values with the drilled-down ones (as you will see later in this chapter).

Ease of Development

REPORTING TOOL	PREDEFINED CHART TYPE	EASE OF DEVELOPMENT
Excel	Yes	●
PerformancePoint	Yes	●
Power View	Yes	●
Reporting Services	Yes	●
Silverlight/HTML5	N/A	●

Drill through

Drill through, although often confused with drill down, is distinct in that it often opens up a completely new visualization. This is a great technique for when you need to display information in a completely different format—for instance, you are looking at a management summary and you need to view the transaction detail. Excel provides a default drill-through action, which shows the detail from the underlying table—this is provided by double-clicking the data point you need to analyze further. A new sheet will be created with all the lines that contribute to the number you clicked, as you can see in Figure 13-5.

	A	B	C
1	Data returned for ReserveValue, Asia + Pacific - South Asia, 2011 (First 1000 rows).		
2			
3	[$FactOECDNationalReserve].[OECDNationalReserveID]	[$FactOECDNationalReserve].[Active]	[$FactOECDNationalReserve].[Value]
4	352	1	182375
5	353	1	183700
6	354	1	181633
7	355	1	177330
8			

FIGURE 13-5 *A table of data displayed by Excel after a drill through*

Reporting Services gives you much finer-grained control of drill through, allowing you to specify other reports or even URLs and JavaScript commands.

ANALYSIS SERVICES

Analysis Services in multidimensional mode allows for a large variety of drill-through actions to be defined on the cube, specifying which columns should be returned or sent to a report. Excel, Reporting Services, and PerformancePoint all support these actions, but they are not available in tabular mode SSAS and PowerPivot.

Ease of Development

REPORTING TOOL	PREDEFINED CHART TYPE	EASE OF DEVELOPMENT
Excel	Yes	
PerformancePoint	No	
Power View	No	
Reporting Services	Yes	
Silverlight/HTML5	N/A	

Drill across

A drill across is done by clicking one component on your screen and having another component update according to your selection. This is distinguished from the traditional filters and the slicers we will discuss next because the drill-across item contains data—for instance, clicking a line in a scorecard that has a red indicator and having the chart alongside update automatically is a drill-across. An example of a drill-across is shown in Figure 13-6.

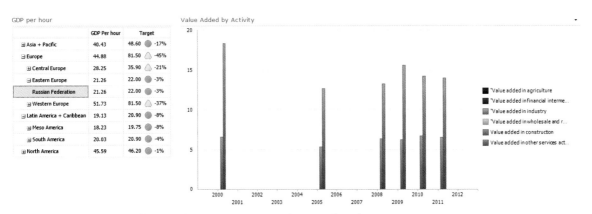

FIGURE 13-6 *Drilling across from a PerformancePoint scorecard to an analytic chart*

Ease of Development

REPORTING TOOL	PREDEFINED CHART TYPE	EASE OF DEVELOPMENT
Excel	No	●
PerformancePoint	Yes	●
Power View	Yes	●
Reporting Services	No	●
Silverlight/HTML5	N/A	○

Slicing and Slicers

A slicer is very similar in concept to a drill across, except that the slicer doesn't contain any information. It is a new way of showing a multiselect filter. One innovation is that slicers change color depending on whether data is contained within the data set. Figure 13-7 shows a slicer in Excel: It is easily apparent that although North America and Latin America are not selected, they do contain data that could be used if they were selected; Polar and West Asia do not contain data.

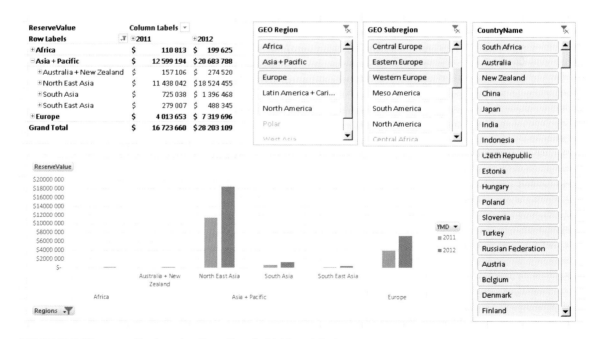

FIGURE 13-7 Slicers operating in conjunction with a pivot table and chart

Ease of Development

REPORTING TOOL	PREDEFINED CHART TYPE	EASE OF DEVELOPMENT
Excel	Yes	●
PerformancePoint	No	●
Power View	Yes	●
Reporting Services	No	●
Silverlight/HTML5	N/A	●

TOOL CHOICES WITH EXAMPLES

Ad hoc analysis is an area where the Microsoft tools diverge quite sharply. Reporting Services is not designed for this at all, and PerformancePoint shines on guided analysis. Excel, including PowerPivot and Power View, is truly the best tool for unguided analysis and data discovery.

PERFORMANCEPOINT: ANALYTIC CHARTS

PerformancePoint is great for guided analysis when known conditions are exceeded or not met, for instance when a particular store does not meet a sales target, or an item is overstocked and some further analysis is required. The ability to drill down to the particular store and then do an analysis on how many salespeople are allocated to that store or break down the stores sales by product is one of the key strengths of PerformancePoint. Figure 13-8 shows an analytic chart that drills across to the UK sales figures and drills down to the months for 2007.

Right-clicking October 2007 brings up a context menu that enables us to do a Decomposition Tree and determine what figures make up that low sales figure in October. As you can see in Figure 13-9, a large amount of additional information can be gleaned from the Decomposition Tree.

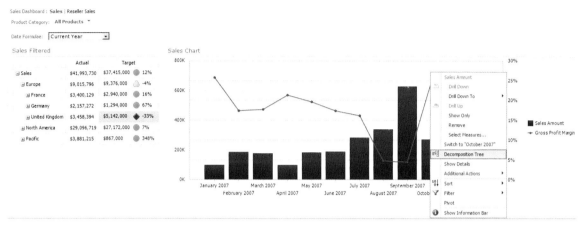

FIGURE 13-8   *Opening a Decomposition Tree from an analytic chart*

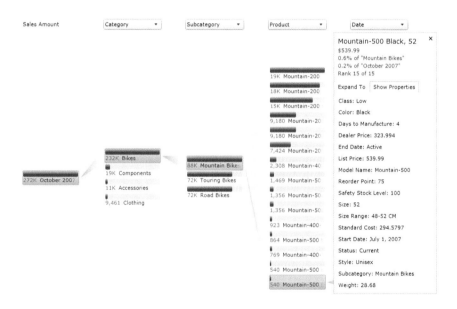

FIGURE 13-9   *A PerformancePoint Decomposition Tree*

The analytic chart can also be rearranged significantly to view alternate rollups. In Figure 13-10, I have drilled to November 2007 and filtered for the bottom 10 mountain bikes by Sales Amount. Immediately apparent is that although we have a spread of low-selling bikes, the Mountain-400 W Silver is a very profitable bike, so when talking to the store about doing a promotion, that is most likely the bike to focus on first.

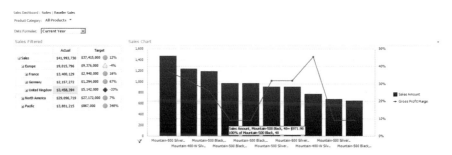

FIGURE 13-10 *Additional analysis within PerformancePoint*

One key factor to always remember with PerformancePoint analytic charts is that they are dependent on having well-designed hierarchies to create a rich visualization environment.

PERFORMANCEPOINT: DRILL ACROSS

PerformancePoint has an exceptional strength in that it allows for drill across to non-PerformancePoint components that are on the same dashboard.

A great example is combining GIS visualizations from SQL Server Reporting Services (SSRS) and filtering them by the PerformancePoint scorecard on the same page, as shown in Figure 13-11.

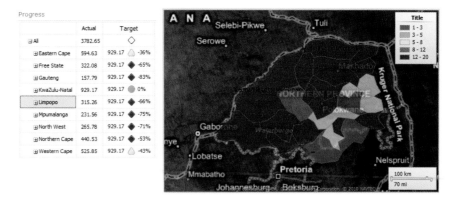

FIGURE 13-11 *Combining PerformancePoint and Reporting Services*

This cross-filtering works only from a PerformancePoint scorecard, not the analytic chart. It can, however, be used to filter an analytic chart by a scorecard.

EXCEL PIVOT TABLES

Excel pivot charts are by far the most widely known of the slice and dice tools, and they have a flexibility that none of the other Microsoft tools do. Excel pivots can be created against any data contained within Excel, but they do work much better when they have a solid data model to work from.

The pivot tables can be built up manually, but it is a lot more work because each level has to be added individually, and the subtotals removed. An example of such a pivot is shown in Figure 13-12.

There are other benefits to putting the data into a model first: centrally controlling the structure is the first benefit, the additional calculation power of DAX becomes available, and the data volumes that can be handled increase exponentially. The improved interface is shown in Figure 13-13.

Finally, when Excel pivots are deployed to Excel Services in SharePoint, they can be connected to PerformancePoint scorecards—the scorecard row values connect up to the slicers and change their values.

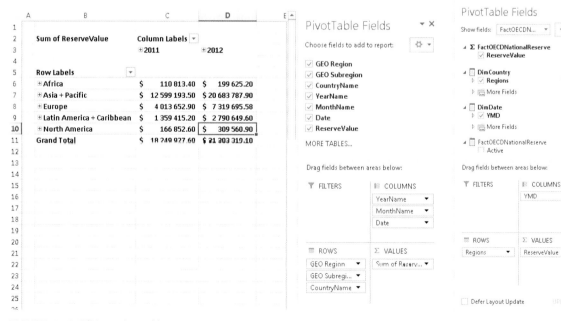

FIGURE 13-12 *Editing a pivot table*

FIGURE 13-13 *The Pivot-Table Fields task pane, where fields are added to the table*

SSRS DRILL DOWN AND DRILL THROUGH

Reporting Services has the capability of doing both drill down and drill through. Each one of these has to be built in manually—the drill down is not particularly complex, but the drill through does require some work. Figure 13-14 shows the drill down enabled.

Year Name	Month Name	Date	⊞ Africa	⊞ Asia + Pacific	⊞ Europe	⊞ Latin America + Caribbean	⊞ North America
			Total	Total	Total	Total	Total
⊟ 2011	⊞ December	Total	$27,885.10	$3,193,457.20	$999,249.87	$349,463.50	$42,766.40
	⊞ November	Total	$27,699.40	$3,194,497.00	$983,479.13	$341,846.40	$42,251.50
	⊞ October	Total	$27,419.40	$3,110,122.10	$1,004,709.08	$334,081.80	$41,141.40
	⊞ September	Total	$27,809.50	$3,101,117.20	$1,026,214.83	$334,023.50	$40,693.30
	Total		$110,813.40	$12,599,193.50	$4,013,652.90	$1,359,415.20	$166,852.60
⊞ 2012	Total		$199,625.20	$20,683,787.90	$7,319,695.58	$2,790,649.60	$309,560.90
Total			$310,438.60	$33,282,981.40	$11,333,348.48	$4,150,064.80	$476,413.50

FIGURE 13-14 *A Reporting Services matrix with drill down enabled*

Figure 13-15 shows the setup screen for creating an action. Individual fields within the report table get passed to the report that is linked to, which gives a great deal of control over how the action works to the report designer.

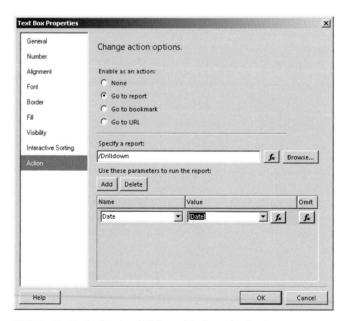

FIGURE 13-15 *Configuring drill through in Reporting Services*

POWER VIEW

Power View is a data exploration tool, embedded within both Excel 2013 and SharePoint (installed from SQL).

Obviously, as a data exploration tool, it is squarely aimed at slice and dice analytics. It does require a data model to create these interactive dashboards.

Power View has a few key benefits over the other tools:

- Automatically connected slicers
- Integrated graphics (for instance, pictures of products)
- Tiled views
- Animations
- Integrated maps

Although they are great features and very welcome, Power View's great disadvantage is that it is impossible to integrate with the other tools. It is purely a standalone tool.

Figure 13-16 shows slicing by region and drill across by selecting specific months, as well as a tiled view of products.

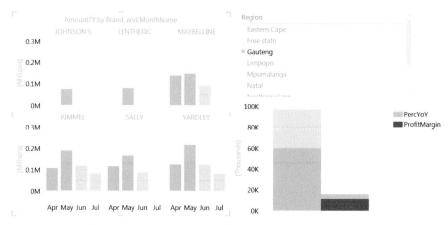

FIGURE 13-16 *A Power View report sliced by specific months*

In Figure 13-17, tiles with product images are used to slice the sales amounts in the column graph below:

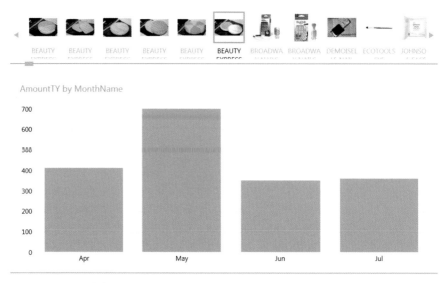

FIGURE 13-17 *A tiled view in Power View*

IMPLEMENTATION EXAMPLES

The implementation examples all use the OECD_Data model, so be sure you have downloaded them from this book's web page on Wrox.com.

SSRS: DYNAMIC MEASURES

Although Reporting Services isn't as dynamic as the other tools by default, it is an exceptionally powerful toolset, and some measure of ad hoc analytics can be enabled by using expressions.

For the purposes of this exercise, we will build the report by pulling in all the data we require and then use expressions to choose which items to use. You can also create dynamic queries, which will often perform much better.

Start by creating a new report in Report Builder and connecting to the OECD_Data tabular model. Create a new data set named **dsOECD** and pull the following fields onto the design surface:

- Measures ➢ Reserve Value

- Measure ➤ MetricValueAvg

- Measure ➤ MetricValueMax

- Measure ➤ MetricValue

- DimCountry ➤ Regions

- DimDate ➤ YMD

- DimOECDStatistic ➤ Statistics

Your query designer should look similar to Figure 13-18.

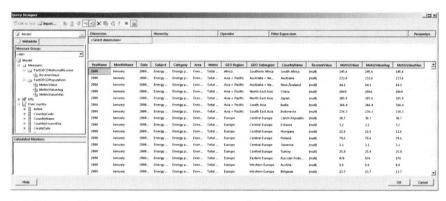

FIGURE 13-18 *The Report Builder query design screen for Analysis Services*

Next, create three new parameters: Measure, X-Axis, and Y-Axis. Use XAxis and YAxis for the actual name, and use X-Axis and Y-Axis for the prompt. For the Measure parameter, add the Available Values shown in Table 13-1. The Value fields are going to match the cube fields exactly so that this report can be used with PerformancePoint later. Set the default to ReserveValue.

TABLE 13-1 Measure Values

LABEL	VALUE
Reserve Value	ReserveValue
Metric Value Avg	MetricValueAvg
Metric Value Max	MetricValueMax
Metric Value	MetricValue

For the X-Axis and Y-Axis parameters, use the values Table 13-2. Set the X-Axis default to Year and the Y-Axis default to GeoRegion.

TABLE 13-2 Measure Values

LABEL	VALUE
Year	Year
Month	Month
Date	Date
Subject	Subject
Category	Category
Area	Area
Metric	Metric
Region	GeoRegion
Subregion	GeoSubregion
Country	CountryName

This sets up the basics for the report. Next, you create the dynamic fields that will use the parameters. Right-click dsOECD and click Add Calculated Field. Call the new field Measure and then put the following expression into the expression box (as you can see in Figure 13-19).

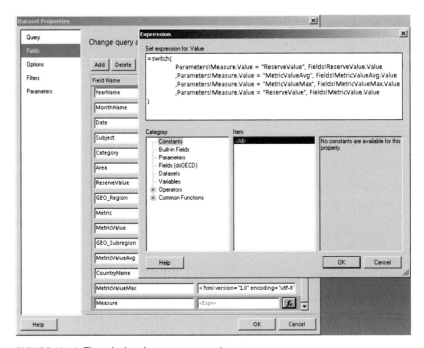

FIGURE 13-19 *The calculated measure expression*

```
=switch(
      Parameters!Measure.Value = "ReserveValue",
            Fields!ReserveValue.Value
      ,Parameters!Measure.Value = "MetricValueAvg",
            Fields!MetricValueAvg.Value
      ,Parameters!Measure.Value = "MetricValueMax",
            Fields!MetricValueMax.Value
      ,Parameters!Measure.Value = "ReserveValue",
            Fields!MetricValue.Value
)
```

This piece of code sets the value of the Measure field to the value of the field chosen by the user. Next, we will do the same for the X-Axis and Y-Axis fields. Create two new calculated fields called XAxis and YAxis. The code for the X-Axis is shown in the following snippet:

```
=switch(
      Parameters!XAxis.Value = "Year", Fields!YearName.Value
      ,Parameters!XAxis.Value = "Month", Fields!MonthName.Value
      ,Parameters!XAxis.Value = "Date", Fields!Date.Value
      ,Parameters!XAxis.Value = "Subject", Fields!Subject.Value
      ,Parameters!XAxis.Value = "Category", Fields!Category.Value
      ,Parameters!XAxis.Value = "Area", Fields!Area.Value
      ,Parameters!XAxis.Value = "Metric", Fields!Metric.Value
      ,Parameters!XAxis.Value = "GeoRegion", Fields!GEO_Region.Value
      ,Parameters!XAxis.Value = "GeoSubregion",
            Fields!GEO_Subregion.Value
      ,Parameters!XAxis.Value = "CountryName",
            Fields!CountryName.Value
)
```

The code for the YAxis is very similar, as you can see:

```
=switch(
      Parameters!YAxis.Value = "Year", Fields!YearName.Value
      ,Parameters!YAxis.Value = "Month", Fields!MonthName.Value
      ,Parameters!YAxis.Value = "Date", Fields!Date.Value
      ,Parameters!YAxis.Value = "Subject", Fields!Subject.Value
      ,Parameters!YAxis.Value = "Category", Fields!Category.Value
      ,Parameters!YAxis.Value = "Area", Fields!Area.Value
      ,Parameters!YAxis.Value = "Metric", Fields!Metric.Value Value
      ,Parameters!YAxis.Value = "GeoRegion",Fields!GEO_Region.Value
      ,Parameters!YAxis.Value = "GeoSubregion",
            Fields!GEO_Subregion.Value
      ,Parameters!YAxis.Value = "CountryName",
            Fields!CountryName.Value
)
```

Now finish by adding a new column chart, using the fields as shown in Figure 13-20.

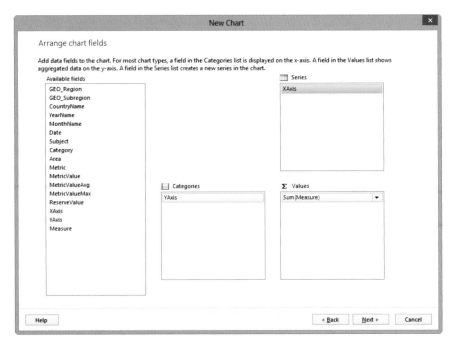

FIGURE 13-20 *Laying out the chart*

Choose the generic template, click Finish, and run the report to see a report such as the one shown in Figure 13-21.

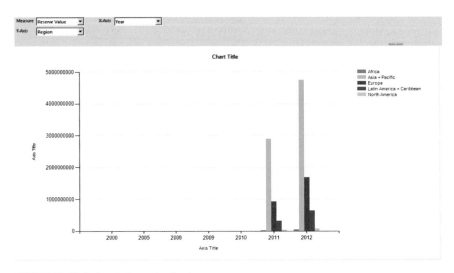

FIGURE 13-21 *A chart in Reporting Services*

There are some very obvious limitations with this report—years are rolled up months as opposed to the last value for the year, the formatting is not correct—but the obvious first issue is that the report is exceptionally slow and it will always return all the data. To rectify these problems, go back to the data set; add the Regions, YMD, and Statistics hierarchies to the filter; and click the Parameterize button, as shown in Figure 13-22.

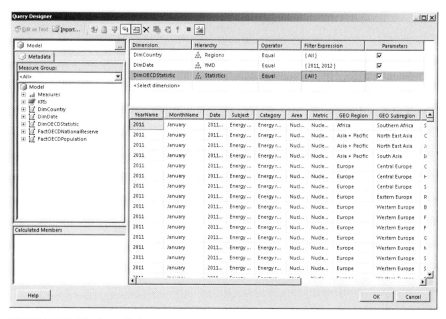

FIGURE 13-22 *The Query designer*

This process enables you to parameterize the query and will serve as a basis for connecting PerformancePoint to Reporting Services.

To finish this exercise, you will make the chart title dynamic and label the axes correctly.

Start by right-clicking the Axis Title running along the left of the chart, and clicking Axis Title Properties. Click the Fx button next to the chart title; then replace the wording with **Parameters!YAxis.Label**, as shown in Figure 13-23. The default, if you choose from the parameters at the bottom, will be Value, but generally speaking, Labels will be more user-friendly.

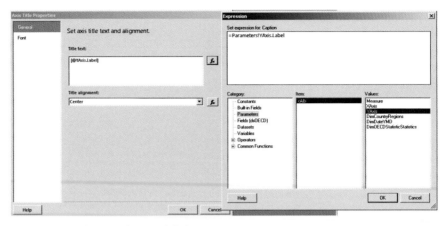

FIGURE 13-23 *Changing the Y axis label*

Repeat this for the XAxis and for the Chart title, using `="SUM of " + Parameters!Measure.Value`

Format the axis to have thousands separators as well, and the chart will appear as in Figure 13-24 when run.

> Assuming that the rollups will always be a SUM is dangerous, and in this example, there are indeed measures that are MAX and AVG. In a complete solution, the rollups will also be dynamic.

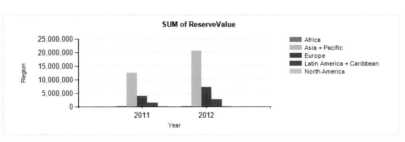

FIGURE 13-24 *A better formatted SSRS chart*

INTEGRATING PPS AND SSRS ON A SINGLE PAGE

> PerformancePoint can handle both Native mode and SharePoint Integrated mode reports from Reporting Services.

One of the strongest uses for PerformancePoint is combining PerformancePoint content with Reporting Services or Excel Services content and having them interact. In this exercise, you will create a Date Filter, a scorecard showing values for average hours actually worked by region, and then embed the report created in the previous section. You will also set up the scorecard such that the region changes the region in the report. The date filter will allow your user to select a date on a calendar, and will display all the months of that year on the report.

Start by opening up Dashboard Designer. If you have not used Dashboard Designer before, you will open it up from the front page of a Business Intelligence Center in SharePoint, choosing the Create Dashboard tab and clicking Start using PerformancePoint services to bring up the Run Dashboard Designer button. Set up the data connection and map the date dimension as described in Chapter 7. Name the data connection **dsOECD**.

Right-click the List name (PerformancePoint content). Choose New ➤ Filter and then Time Intelligence Connection formula. Click OK.

Click Add Data Source; then choose the dsOECD data source. Click Next and select the Time Intelligence Calendar. Click Finish and name the filter **Months of Year**.

Next, select PerformancePoint Content ➤ New ➤ KPI, and call the KPI **Average Hours Worked Per Year**. Change the number formats for both actual and target from Default to Number, and remove the decimal spaces.

For the actual, click 1 (Fixed Values) under Data mappings; then change the source to dsOECD and click OK. Choose MetricValueAvg under Select A Measure; then click New Dimension Filter and choose DimOECDStatistic.metric. Click OK, and choose Average Hours Actually Worked by clicking Default Member (All) and selecting it from the list. Make sure to deselect the default. Your setup should look like Figure 13-25.

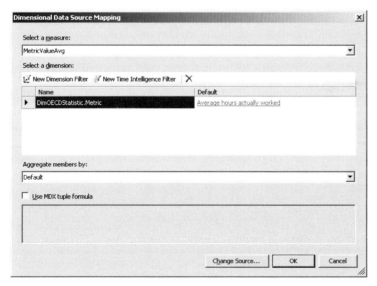

FIGURE 13-25 *Setting up a measure in PerformancePoint Dashboard Designer*

Repeat this process for the target, but also add a dimension filter for DimCountry.Regions and choose All instead of Default Member (All). Your setup should look like Figure 13-26.

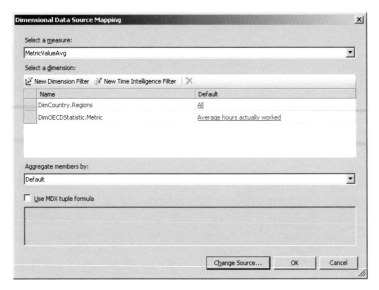

FIGURE 13-26 *Adding filters*

This process will create a target that is the average of all the countries.

Next, create a new scorecard by choosing "Blank scorecard" from the templates. Add the KPI to the new scorecard by dragging it onto the design surface, and add the DimCountries ➢ Regions hierarchy by dragging it onto the KPI name on the scorecard. Call your scorecard **Average Hours**, and it should appear as it does in Figure 13-27.

The final step before creating the dashboard is to link to the Reporting Services report. Right-click the PerformancePoint content list, choose New ➢ Report, and then choose Reporting Services.

A setup screen will appear—if you are using Native mode Reporting Services, put in the server name. If you are running a named instance, you will need to go to the Reporting Services Configuration Manager to obtain the name. Once you have set it up, click the Browse button to choose the report, as shown in Figure 13-28.

	Actual	Target	
⊟ AverageHoursWorkedPerYear		⬤	
⊞ Africa		1,750 ◇	
⊞ Asia + Pacific	1,748	1,750 △ 0%	
⊞ Europe	1,716	1,750 △ -2%	
⊞ Latin America + Caribbean	2,192	1,750 ⬤ 25%	
⊞ North America	1,724	1,750 △ -1%	
⊞ Polar		1,750 ◇	
⊞ West Asia		1,750 ◇	

Editor Properties

⟵ Average Hours

FIGURE 13-27 *A scorecard in PerformancePoint*

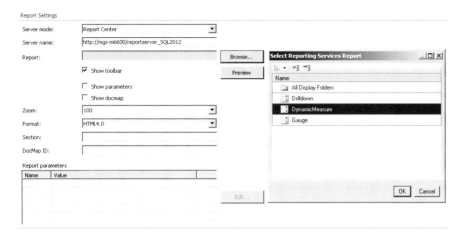

FIGURE 13-28 *Integrating Reporting Services into PerformancePoint*

Choose the report you created in the previous section; then click OK.

PerformancePoint allows you to override the defaults used for the report, as you can see in Figure 13-29.

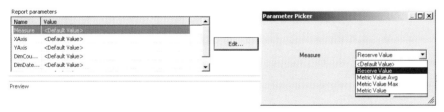

FIGURE 13-29 *Setting SSRS parameters in PerformancePoint*

Choose Reserve Value for the measure, Month for XAxis, and Country for YAxis; and leave the rest. Give your report a name and save it.

Now create the dashboard. Right-click the PerformancePoint content list and choose New ➢ Dashboard. Use the Header, 2 Columns template. Drag the Months of Year filter to the top section, the Average Hours scorecard to the left section, and the report you just created to the right section. Note that these will be in the Details window on the right!

> **Reporting Services in Integrated mode requires you to know the URL of the SharePoint server as well as the URL of the report in SharePoint. This URL format will be different depending on the version of SQL server you have installed.**

Click Average Hours and choose Create Connection from the Ribbon. If you don't see the Create connection button, change to the Edit tab in the Ribbon at top. Set Get Values From to Header - (1) Months of Year; then change to the Values tab and set the source to Member Unique Name. Click the Connection Formula button and type **Year**. This will set the filter to the year of the date selected in the calendar. Finish by clicking OK on both screens.

Repeat the process for the report. Click DynamicMeasures and choose Create Connection from the Ribbon. Set Get Values From to Header - (1) Months of Year; then change to the Values tab and set the source to Member Unique Name. Change the Connect To to DimDateYMD.

Click the Connection Formula button and type **Year**. Finish by clicking OK on both screens.

The final step is to link the scorecard to the report. Click DynamicMeasures and choose Create Connection from the Ribbon. If you can't see Create Connection in the Ribbon, change the tab in the Ribbon to Set Get Values from to Left Column - (1) Average Hours. Switch to the Values tab and set the source to Member Row: Member Unique Name. Change the Connect To to DimCountryRegions.

When a row is clicked on in the scorecard, this step will send the underlying unique name from the cube to the report, and hence filter the report. Give your dashboard a name. Right-click and deploy to SharePoint. Choose a date in 2011, as that is the last year for which there is average hourly data available.

TROUBLESHOOTING

This is a fairly complex section, and many people (including the author) have issues on the first deploy. The error messages can also be misleading, as an incorrect setup will sometimes lead to an error saying that you do not have permission to view the data. In order to troubleshoot, remove the connection to the parameters one by one until you have isolated the parameter that is the cause. A common cause of this is PPS sending a value that SSRS does not have in its list, for instance [Measure] being used instead of [Measures], or the underlying hierarchies not matching.

Clicking Asia/Pacific in the scorecard will show you a chart similar to the one in Figure 13-30.

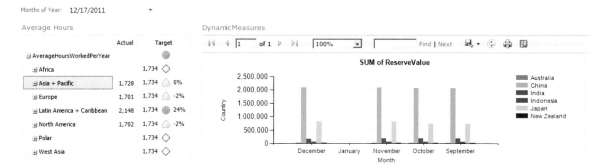

FIGURE 13-30 *An integrated dashboard*

DATES

Reporting Services doesn't handle dates as well as Excel or PPS, and in order to sort the months correctly, a month number field will be needed.

POWER VIEW: EXPLORING DATA

In order to use Power View, you will need to start by creating a data model.

Open a new Excel workbook and on the PowerPivot tab, click the Manage button. (See Chapter 5 for enabling PowerPivot if the tab is not visible.) Click the From Database button, choose SQL Server, and enter the location of your SQL Server. Choose the VI_UNData database from the drop-down and click Next. Choose Select From A List Of Tables; select the DimDate, DimCountry, DimOECDStatistic, FactOECDPopulation, and FactUNData tables; and click Finish. Rename the Value column to **ValueSource**. In FactOECDPopulation, choose the Value field, click the arrow next to Autosum, and choose Average. Right-click ValueSource and select Hide it from client tools, and then rename the Average of Value calculated measure to **Value**. You rename this by editing in the formula bar everything before the ":=".

This satisfies the bare minimum of building the model—in a full implementation, you would spend some time tidying it up.

Once you have your model set up, creating a Power View report is simple: Go the Insert tab in the Excel Ribbon and click Power View. Start by dragging the Value field from FaceOECDPopulation to the Fields box, Geo Regions from DimCountry to Tiles, and then CountryName to Fields. You will need to resize the chart and should see something similar to Figure 13-31.

FIGURE 13-31 *A tiled Power View report*

Drag Value from FactOECDPopulation to the whitespace next to the table, which creates a new table, and change it to a bar chart. By dragging CountryName to the Axis field, the bar chart will now become interactive, as seen in Figure 13-32.

FIGURE 13-32 *Filtering a Power View report*

This chart is still meaningless as it is simply a sum of all the different statistics. Start by clicking the CHART button on the Filters section, and filtering this chart to show just the GDP per capita. You will need to drag Metric to the Filter section and select the metric, as shown in Figure 13-33.

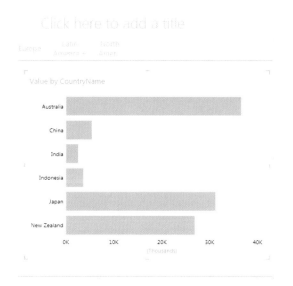

FIGURE 13-33 *Choosing a metric*

Click on the table on the left (The table and not the chart you edited above), and add a filter to show GDP per hour worked; then add another table below it by dragging value onto the white space. Add a country name and a filter to show average hours actually worked. These tables will all then be sliced by the chart. Each table and chart will be filtered by a different metric value.

Finish by dragging value to the whitespace beneath the chart. You may need to clear some space, which you can do by selecting the corner of the title text box, deleting it, and then resizing the main box. Drag Metric onto this new table; filter by the three metrics GDP per hour worked, GDP per capita, and Average hours actually worked; and then change it to a column chart. Move Metric to Legend, and drag YearNumber to the Axis of the chart. This will give you an interactive dashboard similar to the one in Figure 13-34. Clicking either of the charts will update the other chart with that selection, as well as the tables.

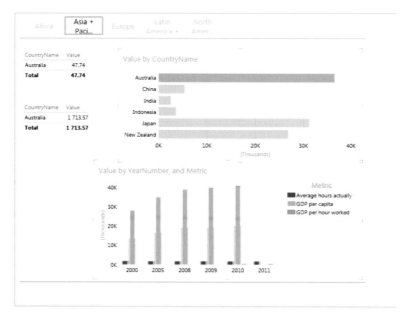

FIGURE 13-34 *An interactive Power View report*

SUMMARY

In this chapter you learned how to build interactive visualizations to support ad hoc analytics, using all the Microsoft tools. These visualizations are commonly more used by power users, but applying predetermined analysis paths helps guide less experienced users.

CHAPTER 14

Relationship Analysis

Relationship analysis is a visualization form you are probably more familiar with than you know. The earliest exposure you would have had to a visualization of this type would have been a family tree. Understanding how relationships work, and being able to tell at a glance which of a set of objects is dependent on another, is an old but growing area. Especially given the advent of social media, networks are taken to represent influence; for instance, a marketer may be more inclined to market to people with many followers on twitter than to those with only a few followers. Being able to analyze this is thus is a key differentiator. This chapter skips the pieces of heavy lifting that often sit underneath these analyses. The tools that would be used for this analysis include graph databases.

VISUALIZING RELATIONSHIPS: NODES, TREES, AND LEAVES

The two different types of relationship analysis we are going to cover in this chapter are network graphs, which show items at the same level and how they interrelate, and hierarchical or tree structures, which show the relationships from the top down. Trees and hierarchies have technical differences in detail, but for the purposes of visualization, you can treat them the same. You will be familiar with the Analysis Services hierarchies already from Chapter 13, so those types of visualization will be excluded.

COLOR PYRAMID

Figure 14-1 shows one of the very first relationship diagrams (created by Johann Heinrich Lambert in the 1760s), which illustrates the color relationships. His "Farbenpyramide" differed fairly substantially from the color relationships we use today, but it was an influential work.

FIGURE 14-1 *Farbenpyramide*

Both types of visualizations have various flavors. This chapter covers four of them, with very different uses.

The network map is used purely to show relationships without any value attached to the network. This is useful especially in the social media analysis context, where the connection between items in the network, known as nodes, is the sole arbiter of value. Other older uses for the network graphs include the representation of computer networks, telecommunication networks, and transport networks. In some of the versions of the network graph, direction is included.

A color wheel, which is a wheel divided into sections with the relationships shown as lines connecting the sections, has an added dimension in that it can show the size of a relationship. This is useful when showing, for example, trade balances.

Tree structures are used to represent top-down hierarchies. Organization charts and family trees are the most well-known examples of tree structures.

The strategy map visualization, made famous by Robert S. Kaplan and David P. Norton in their article, "The Balanced Scorecard—Measures That Drive Performance," is a very specific version of a tree chart. The implementation of this tool in Performance Point also lends itself to other uses.

NETWORK MAPS

A network map shows the connections between objects visually—these connections could be physical (as in the case of computer networks or railway tracks), or they could be more abstract (as in the case of social media networks).

NETWORK GRAPH THEORY

Network graph theory is another of the discoveries by the mathematician Leonhard Euler, first published in his book, *Seven Bridges of Königsberg*, in 1763. In the problem statement he worked through in this book, there are seven bridges, and he needed to determine if one could cross each bridge twice during a walk. A vertex (or node) is called odd if it has an odd number of arcs (or edges) leading to it, otherwise it is even, and if a network has more than two odd vertices, it does not have an Euler path—that is, one cannot walk the path and cross each bridge twice.

The easiest place to see a network map is at `http://inmaps.linkedin.com/`. This tool analyzes your LinkedIn network and gives you a network graph of your connections. An example of my network is shown in Figure 14-2.

If your network is fairly large, the limitations of network maps at scale are quickly apparent. As a node is added, performance degrades as a function of the number of connections of that node rather than as a function of the number of nodes. The readability of the graph quickly degrades as well. In the zoomed-out view, the categories blur into one another; when the view is zoomed in, only in the outskirts of the network graph are the relationships immediately apparent.

Creating data for a network map is relatively straightforward: It is simply a list of pairs, each pair being the two nodes, and with an edge that is the connection between the nodes. In order to render network graphs, it is worth considering rendering order. You might assume that drawing all the nodes first and then connecting them up will work—and indeed it will—but you are likely to end up with a severely non-optimal layout. Luckily, most tools available to you handle this fairly well.

Ease of Development

REPORTING TOOL	PREDEFINED CHART TYPE	EASE OF DEVELOPMENT
Excel	No	●
PerformancePoint	No	●
Power View	No	●
Reporting Services	No	●
Silverlight/HTML5	N/A	●

COLOR WHEEL

Primarily, a color wheel is a wheel divided up into sections as categories; secondarily, it shows links between the sections. It's a similar concept to the network map, but it's a condensed version. When you build a color wheel, you will almost certainly have to build it interactively to show only one relationship at a time, otherwise the lines overlap and look chaotic. A great example of an interactive version of a color wheel is shown in Figure 14-3.

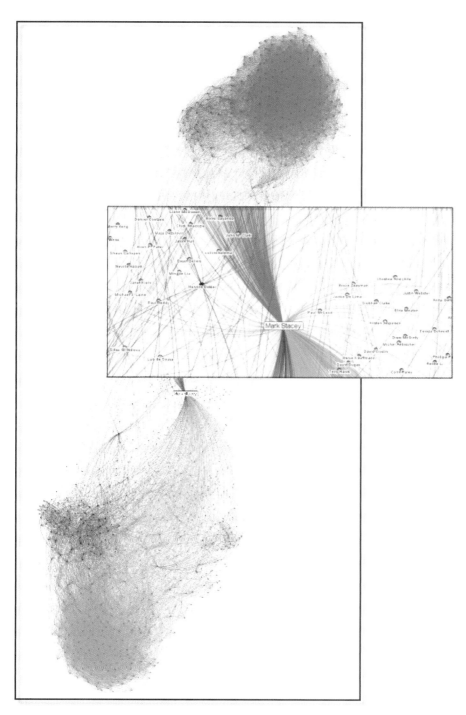

FIGURE 14-2 *The author's LinkedIn network*

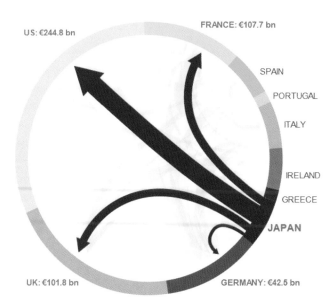

FRANCE: €107.7 bn

US: €244.8 bn

SPAIN

PORTUGAL

ITALY

IRELAND

GREECE

JAPAN

UK: €101.8 bn

GERMANY: €42.5 bn

FIGURE 14-3 *A color wheel showing trade balances from http://www.bbc*
.co.uk/news/business-15748696 (Source: bbc.co.uk © BBC)

Ease of Development

REPORTING TOOL	PREDEFINED CHART TYPE	EASE OF DEVELOPMENT
Excel	No	●
PerformancePoint	No	●
Power View	No	●
Reporting Services	No	●
Silverlight/HTML5	N/A	●

Another consideration related to color wheels is not having too many categories. Representing the entire world in this manner would likely be confusing
and chaotic for end users.

TREE STRUCTURES: ORGANIZATION CHARTS AND OTHER HIERARCHIES

Tree structures are used everywhere in our world. The most ubiquitous example in the corporate world is the organization chart. Figure 14-4 shows a proto-typical organization chart that was built in Visio.

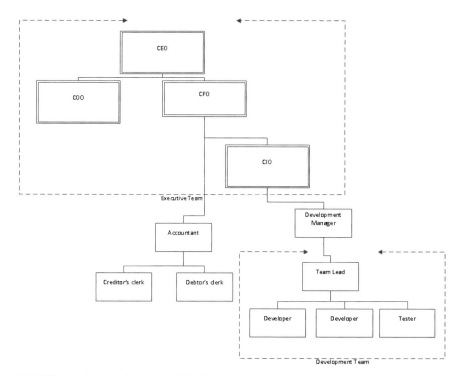

FIGURE 14-4 *Organization chart built in Visio*

A standard drill-down tree structure is another example. This type is exten-sively covered in the earlier chapters and is excluded from the following Ease of Development table.

Ease of Development

REPORTING TOOL	PREDEFINED CHART TYPE	EASE OF DEVELOPMENT
Excel	No	⬤
PerformancePoint	Yes	⬤
Power View	No	⬤
Reporting Services	No	⬤
Silverlight/HTML5	N/A	⬤

STRATEGY MAPS

Strategy maps are, in many ways, a refinement of the tree structure. The hierarchy of an organization's strategy is shown visually; the key addition is that each block of the strategy map is dynamically linked to data. Figure 14-5 shows a prototypical strategy map next to a scorecard that it is mapping.

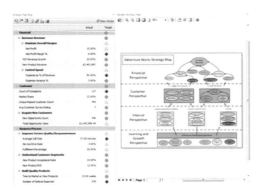

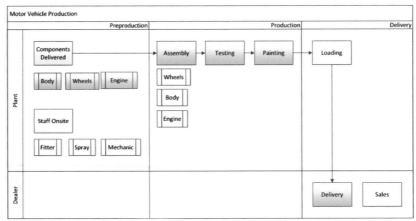

FIGURE 14-5 *A standard strategy map based on the balanced scorecard is shown on top, and at the bottom the same tools are used to show a process map*

Ease of Development

REPORTING TOOL	PREDEFINED CHART TYPE	EASE OF DEVELOPMENT
Excel	No	●
PerformancePoint	Yes	●
Power View	No	●
Reporting Services	No	●
Silverlight/HTML5	N/A	●

TOOL CHOICES

Relationship analysis is an area in which the Microsoft stack is especially poor. PerformancePoint has some native capabilities in the form of Decomposition Trees and strategy maps, and there is an add-in for Excel, but outside of that, any relationship analysis must be coded. The techniques necessary to do that are covered later in this chapter.

PPS DECOMPOSITION TREE

PerformancePoint is great for showing how a particular metric is broken down—not just by predefined hierarchies, as in the drill-down capabilities, but also with the Decomposition Tree, which allows for a continual drill down by alternative hierarchies in a tree format.

You want to know the best part? The Decomposition Tree is available at any time to you. All you have to do is right-click and choose Decomposition Tree, as shown in Figure 14-6.

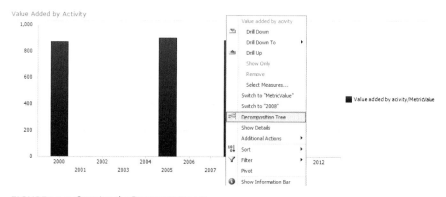

FIGURE 14-6 *Opening the Decomposition Tree*

The Decomposition Tree displays (like the one shown in Figure 14-7), allowing your end users to drill down on the various dimensions and see the makeup of the values they are examining.

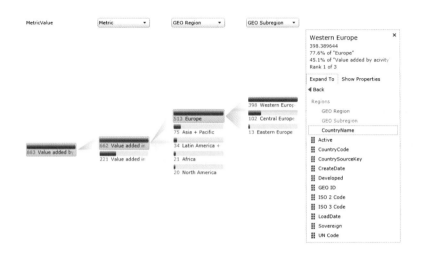

FIGURE 14-7 *A PerformancePoint Decomposition Tree*

DATA SOURCES

It's important to note that the majority of features in PerformancePoint—including the Decomposition Tree—only work when PerformancePoint is connected to an Analysis Services cube or Tabular data model.

EXCEL AND NODEXL

Excel itself does not have any support for network diagrams, but a downloadable add-in called NodeXL is available. You can download this tool from `http://nodexl.codeplex.com/`.

The NodeXL add-in is an Excel template into which you paste your data. In the simplest format, you can paste a list of edges and change the widths based on some value. In Figure 14-8, the edges are trade values between South Africa and other countries, and the width of the lines is the log of the distance from the trade value to the minimum trade value.

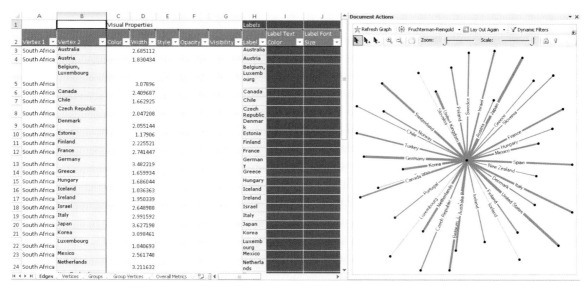

FIGURE 14-8   *The NodeXL template with data entered*

As you add more root nodes (that is, nodes that are connected to multiple nodes), the layout becomes more important. In Figure 14-9, Australia's trade exports have been added. NodeXL makes working with a large number of connections fairly easy, as you can click on a node to highlight what it is connected to. NodeXL also enables you to drag the node around to improve the layout.

PERFORMANCEPOINT SERVICES (PPS) STRATEGY MAPS

PerformancePoint has a great toolset for custom strategy maps because it can link any data in PerformancePoint to custom shapes in Visio. The most common example of this is to implement a Kaplan and Norton balanced scorecard, as shown in Figure 14-10.

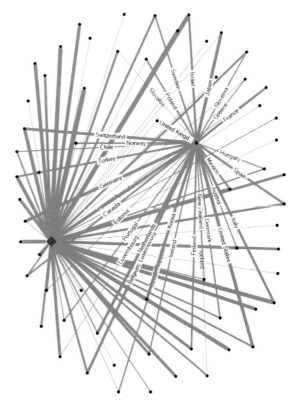

FIGURE 14-9   *Dragging a node around in NodeXL*

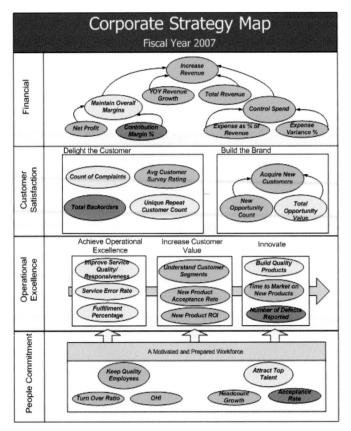

FIGURE 14-10 *A balanced scorecard in PerformancePoint*

More extensive use of this technology is great for visualizing flows such as manufacturing processes. Because PerformancePoint strategy maps are based on a user-customizable Visio diagram, almost any process can be visualized.

HTML5 STRUCTURE MAPS

The biggest challenge with the NodeXL tool is that it is embedded only within Excel. You can build a network map equivalent on the web using the same libraries that we've been using and you were introduced to in Chapter 9, but there are also some great online tools. You can see examples at `https://www.google.com/fusiontables/Home/`.

The output of the network graph built in Fusion Tables is shown in Figure 14-11.

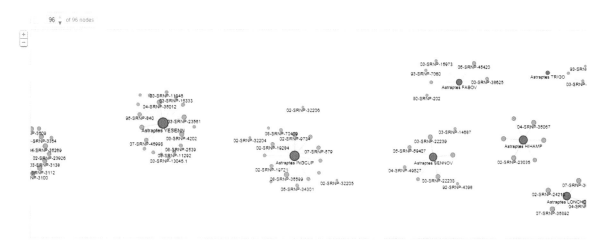

FIGURE 14-11 *Networks built in Fusion Tables*

IMPLEMENTATION EXAMPLES

The implementation examples use the OECD_Data model. You can obtain the datasets from the Wiley website; see Chapter 3 for information about installing them in the "Installing the Sample Databases" section.

BUILDING AN ORGANIZATION CHART IN PERFORMANCEPOINT

To create custom visualizations in PerformancePoint, you use the Strategy map feature, which requires you to first build a scorecard and then create a Visio document to which you link the key performance indicators (KPIs) in the scorecard. You can read about creating scorecards in Chapter 10.

In this example, you create custom rollups of OECD (Organization for Economic Development) statistic metrics and associate them with organizations. The organizations in this example are going to be our own creation, and this shows the power of this approach in PerformancePoint. The data points you will be using will be GDP per hour and Purchasing Price Parity in the Production category, and Mean score in reading performance in the Education category.

In the PerformancePoint Content section of the Business Intelligence Center in SharePoint, create a new PerformancePoint KPI in the Items section of the ListTools tab in the Ribbon. This action launches the Dashboard Designer.

Choose Blank KPI in the Select a KPI Template dialog and click OK. Name the KPI **GDP per hour**.

The next step is to create a new data source in Data Connections pointing to Analysis Services. Name the data source **dsOECD**. Fill in the SSAS server and instance name, and then select the OECD_Data database and Model cube.

On the Time tab of the new data connection, set up the time dimension. Select DimDate.Date under Time Dimension. Choose 2012-01-01 as the reference member. The Hierarchy level is Day and the Reference Date is 2012-01-01. In the bottom section, map the Date member level to the Day time aggregation.

On the KPI, click the 1 (Fixed Value) link in the Actual row/Data Mappings column. Click Change Source, change to the dsOECD data source, and then click OK.

For the Actual, you are going to use the MetricValueAvg measure. Add a new Dimension Filter, and choose DimOECDStatistics.Statistics, as shown in Figure 14-12.

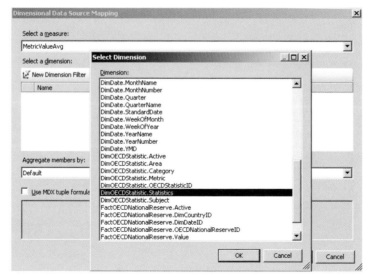

FIGURE 14-12 *Choosing a dimension to filter by*

Click the default measure and change the selection to GDP per hour, as shown in Figure 14-13. Be sure to uncheck Default Member (All).

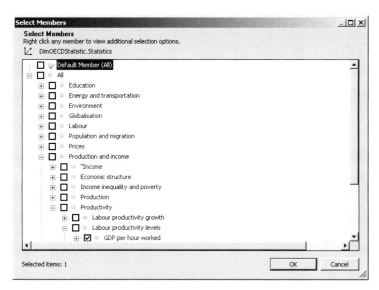

FIGURE 14-13 *Selecting the correct metric*

Repeat this process for the target, and replace MetricValueAvg with MetricValueMax as the target, as shown in Figure 14-14.

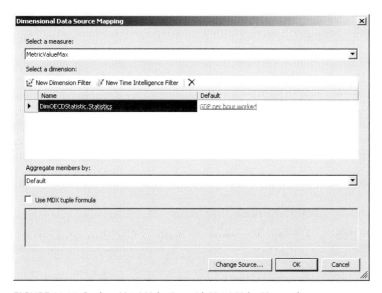

FIGURE 14-14 *Replace MetricValueAvg with MetricValueMax as the target*

Click OK and adjust the target values to 80% for Threshold 2.

Repeat this process for Purchasing Power Parity, which you find under prices, and Mean score in reading performance, located in education, giving you three total KPIs. Each one of these filters will filter the values of the measure to return only the recorded value for that metric.

Create a new blank scorecard by right-clicking PerformancePoint Content and then selecting New ➤ Scorecard. Add the three KPIs to the scorecard, as shown in Figure 14-15.

	Actual	Target	
GDP per hour	42.8086865967742	81.5	⬦ -47%
Purchasing Power Parity	138.374082047393	6236.547	◆ -98%
Reading Score	486.673088555556	535.877975	● -9%

FIGURE 14-15 *A PerformancePoint scorecard*

You now have a base scorecard, which you can map to shapes.

To do this mapping, you need a Visio diagram. Launch Visio and create a new drawing. Choose the flowchart category, and create a cross-functional flowchart. Drag in three Process items. Name all the items meaningfully, as in Figure 14-16.

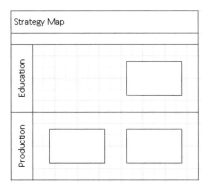

FIGURE 14-16 *A cross-functional flowchart in Visio*

Save the Visio document and go back to PerformancePoint's Dashboard Designer. Create a new report and choose Strategy Map. Choose the scorecard you just created, and then click Edit Strategy Map in the Ribbon's Edit tab. You see a screen you use to import the Visio document (see Figure 14-17).

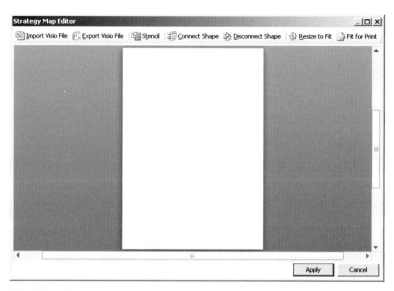

FIGURE 14-17 *Visio Import screen*

Import the Visio file you created earlier and click the top shape. Click the Connect Shape button and then double-click the Reading Score KPI. The shape updates with the name. Make sure to click the Target to ensure that it updates the color as well. You should see the updates shown in Figure 14-18.

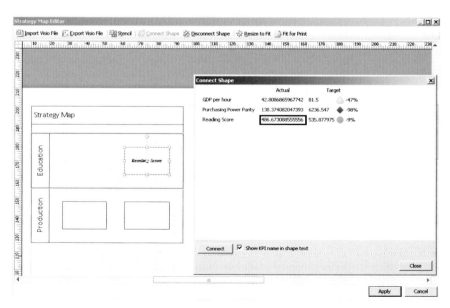

FIGURE 14-18 *Connecting shapes in Visio*

Close the Connect Shape dialog and click the Apply button. Your strategy map is ready to be embedded in PerformancePoint dashboards.

BUILDING A NETWORK MAP IN HTML5

For this network map, you use an online tool called Fusion Tables. Visit `https://www.google.com/fusiontables/Home/` and click See My Tables. You have to have a Google account to use this tool, so create one now if you don't have one.

Click Create ➢ More ➢ Fusion Tables (experimental), and then upload the `TradePartners.xlsx` workbook you were provided with. Click Next. The column names are in Row 1; click Next again and then click Finish. You have imported your data. Click Labs ➢ Network graph.

As the final step, click the drop-down next to Weight and choose the Weight option. A network graph similar to the one in Figure 14-19 is generated.

If you are using a Google apps account, you will need to enable this feature. Do so by going to `http://support.google.com/a/AppName` (where *AppName* is the name of your Google Apps domain) and log in. Click on the Organization & Users tab at the top, then Services in the new tab that appears below that one. Scroll down to Fusion Tables and switch it on. Finish by clicking the Save button at the bottom.

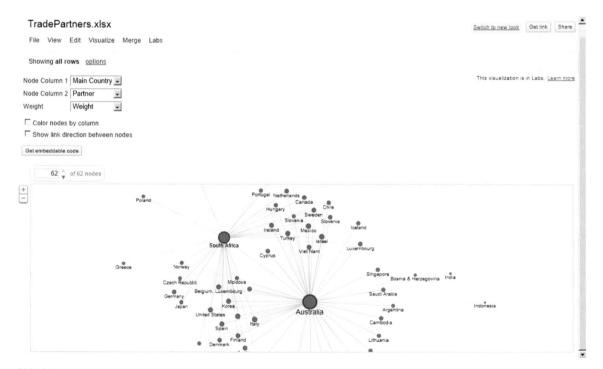

FIGURE 14-19 *A network graph*

This network graph is built on an HTML5 canvas, and you can easily embed it in your web pages. Although it doesn't have the interactivity of NodeXL, it does give you a very easy way of generating a web-friendly network graph.

COLOR WHEEL IN HTML5

For the color wheel, you are going to use a visualization called Sunburst from the JavaScript InfoVis Toolkit. You can download the toolkit from `http://philogb.github.com/jit/`. This basic example uses the Sunburst trivially. The code samples include an example of dynamically changing the color and width of the lines joining the nodes.

The following code samples assume that a JSON structure already has been setup, in a format like so:

```
"id": "node1",
      "name": "node 1",
      "data": {
        "$angularWidth": 13.00,
        "$color": "#33a",
        "$height": 70
      },
      "adjacencies": [
          {
            "nodeTo": "node3",
            "data": {
              "$color": "#ddaacc",
              "$lineWidth": 4
          }
        }
        ]

      }
```

The first piece of the JSON structure specifies the node properties: the Name and the definition of the node itself—its color, height, and angular width (the portion of the circle it occupies). Then, in the adjacencies node, the properties of each joining line are defined. In the preceding example, Node 1 is connected to Node 3 with a line width of 4 and an HTML code for color.

Each of these properties is then used to represent an item of data. For example, each node is a country, the angular width is the gross domestic product (GDP) of that country, and the width of the line is the size of the exports to that country. Figure 14-20 shows how it looks.

> **CODE SAMPLES**
>
> For this example, you will need to open the code sample files in the zip file called Chapter14.zip, as only excerpts of the code are included in this section, for brevity.

> A C# web service to output this JSON based on the OECD data source is discussed in Chapter 9.

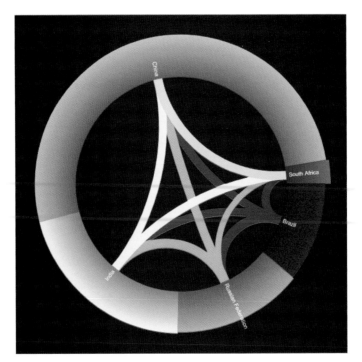

FIGURE 14-20 *The color wheel*

The implementation using the InfoVis library is relatively easy. The class is called Sunburst, and a complete sample is provided separately, and is available from the Wiley website. The code that is specific to the color wheel (called Sunburst by InfoVis) is shown.

```
var json = dpGetData();

//end
//init Sunburst
var sb = new $jit.Sunburst({
  //id container for the visualization
  injectInto: 'infovis',
  //Change node and edge styles such as
  //color, width, lineWidth and edge types
  Node: {},
  Edge: {},
  //Draw canvas text. Can also be
  //'HTML' or 'SVG' to draw DOM labels
  Label: {},
  //Add animations when hovering and clicking nodes
  NodeStyles: {},
  Events: {},
  levelDistance: 190,
  // Only used when Label type is 'HTML' or 'SVG'
```

```
    // Add text to the labels.
    // This method is only triggered on label creation
    onCreateLabel: function(domElement, node){},
    // Only used when Label type is 'HTML' or 'SVG'
    // Change node styles when labels are placed
    // or moved.
    onPlaceLabel: function(domElement, node){}
});
// load JSON data.
sb.loadJSON(json);
// compute positions and plot.
sb.refresh();
```

First, a JSON object is obtained and then the new object is instantiated. The outlines given here are the styling for the nodes, the edges, the labels, and any events. (The events are how the lines are hidden when a node is clicked.) `onCreateLabel` and `onPlaceLabel` are internal workings and can mostly be left alone. The library does the rest of the work.

The end result is a graphic that, when it's been clicked, looks like the one in Figure 14-21.

Note that the log of the trade amounts was used to size the lines.

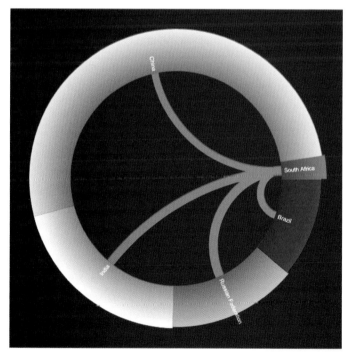

FIGURE 14-21 *An InfoVis color wheel*

SUMMARY

Relationship analysis is an area in which the Microsoft toolset falls far short. Luckily, this is fairly easy to remedy with free add-ins and web software. Each of the tools covered in this chapter has a different use case, so it is useful to be familiar with all of them.

CHAPTER 15

Embedded Visualizations

An embedded visualization, as the name suggests, is a visualization that is contained within some other content—typically, this *table of data* will be that most widely used of visualizations. Indeed, this book has made extensive use of this approach in the tables contained within every chapter, with indicators showing the ease of implementation. It is also possible to do these visualizations within a flow of text or perhaps within an application—but they are much less common. An example of an indicator embedded within an application is shown in Figure 15-1.

In this case, the indicators are being used as buttons that can be clicked on to set a status.

Common uses for embedded visualizations include highlighting problems such as highly divergent numbers that are likely to be a data-capture error, and ranking of various numbers such as all the stores within a region. Covered much more extensively in Chapter 10, indicators showing achievement against a target are another form of embedded visualization. Another great use is the ability to show multiple small charts, thereby allowing for a great deal of data to be displayed on a single page.

In this chapter, we will focus on the traditional tabular embedded visualizations—formatting of the table itself, embedding charts within cells in a table, and conditional formatting of cells according to value. You will also read about indicators and a specific type of embedded chart called a bullet graph.

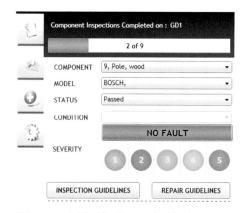

FIGURE 15-1 *Visualizations embedded in an application*

TABULAR DATA: ADDING VISUAL ACUITY

The primary reason to add any sort of visualization to a table to is draw attention to particular rows, columns, or cells in the table; or alternatively to show their relationship to other rows, columns, or cells. There are various ways of doing this—in the old paper chart world, using a highlighter was the only way, and this translates to the conditional formatting discussed in this chapter. Several other ways of highlighting the relevant data points are those not always traditionally thought of as visualization techniques—changing the font of a cell, making it bigger, and using italics or bold is one method; and adding borders is another. These small changes can make a huge difference in the reading of a chart.

For this example, I will use a very common scenario—you need to present a table of costs: to a potential client, your boss for budget approval, or possibly even at home while you decide on a holiday. In the following example, I use a fictitious consulting cost for a project, and the unformatted table is in Figure 15-2.

	A	B	C	D
1	Task	Rate	Cost	Hours
2	Phase 1 - Envisioning	Architect	88000	40
3	Phase 2 - Planning	Architect	176000	80
4	Phase 3 - Development	Architect	88000	40
5	Phase 4 - Deployment	Architect	44000	20
6	Phase 2 - Planning	Senior Consultant	42000	40
7	Phase 3 - Development	Senior Consultant	126000	120
8	Phase 4 - Deployment	Senior Consultant	84000	80
9	Phase 3 - Development	Tester	72000	40
10	Phase 4 - Deployment	Tester	144000	80
11	Total	Total	864000	540

FIGURE 15-2 *An unformatted table*

A few very basic formatting techniques applied make a huge difference in legibility: starting by sorting the data in the order that it will be read—in this case, most likely the task rather than the rate. Adding some white space on top and to the left, and adding a border around the entire cell with data will create the visual impression of a discrete table rather than a set of data. Changing the fonts to accentuate the important cells is important—in this case, the headers along the top and the total value are the most important, followed by costs and hours, and then the descriptions last. Little formatting items such as setting the currency are vital—without it, would you have known that these figures were South African rands and not U.S. dollars?

	A	B	C	D	E
1					
2	Task	Rate	Cost		Hours
3	Phase 1 - Envisioning	Architect	R	88 000.00	40
4	Phase 2 - Planning	Architect	R	176 000.00	80
5	Phase 2 - Planning	Senior Consultant	R	42 000.00	40
6	Phase 3 - Development	Architect	R	88 000.00	40
7	Phase 3 - Development	Senior Consultant	R	126 000.00	120
8	Phase 3 - Development	Tester	R	72 000.00	40
9	Phase 4 - Deployment	Architect	R	44 000.00	20
10	Phase 4 - Deployment	Senior Consultant	R	84 000.00	80
11	Phase 4 - Deployment	Tester	R	144 000.00	80
12	Total	Total	R 864 000.00		540
13					

FIGURE 15-3 *A formatted table of costs*

Adding borders to separate the costs as well as the phases will finish off the visual touches, as seen in Figure 15-3.

This is a much more legible chart, with only a couple of touches, but what will make it more readable yet is to include subtotals—in order to do that, we are going to pivot the table, and then finish touching it up. (You work with pivot tables in the "Embedding Visualizations in a Pivot Table" section later in this chapter.) The final result is shown in Figure 15-4.

		Architect		Senior Consultant		Tester		Total Cost (ex.)	Total Hrs
Items ▾		Cost (ex.)	Hrs	Cost (ex.)	Hrs	Cost (ex.)	Hrs		
Phase 1 - Envisioning	R	88 000.00	40					R 88 000.00	40
Phase 2 - Planning	R	176 000.00	80	R 42 000.00	40			R 218 000.00	120
Phase 3 - Development	R	88 000.00	40	R 126 000.00	120	R 72 000.00	40	R 286 000.00	200
Phase 4 - Deployment	R	44 000.00	20	R 84 000.00	80	R 144 000.00	80	R 272 000.00	180
Grand Total	R	396 000.00	180	R 252 000.00	240	R 216 000.00	120	R 864 000.00	540

FIGURE 15-4 *A pivot table*

Finishing off any table in this manner is essential before even diving into the rest of the visualization techniques—it is a subtle and yet powerful way of highlighting the data points you wish your audience to notice.

EMBEDDED CHARTS: SPARKLINES AND BARS

Embedding charts in a table is an excellent way to have a repeating set of data that can be easily compared—for instance, the growth of product sales over time or the trades of stocks over time.

In Figure 15-5, a sparkline has been used to show the national reserves of the BRICSA countries (Brazil, Russia, India, China, and South Africa) for the first 6 months of 2012.

ReserveValue	Column Labels ▾						
	⊟ 2012						
Row Labels ▾	⊞ January	⊞ February	⊞ March	⊞ April	⊞ May	⊞ June	⊞ July
Brazil	$ 227 743.00	$ 227 809.00	$ 234 639.00	$ 240 266.00	$ 245 509.00	$ 245 290.00	$ 248 259.00
China	$ 2 113 120.00	$ 2 142 100.00	$ 2 148 640.00	$ 2 142 760.00	$ 2 137 670.00	$ 2 149 840.00	
India	$ 172 938.00	$ 173 523.00	$ 174 098.00	$ 174 481.00	$ 173 936.00	$ 175 467.00	$ 176 415.00
Russian Federation	$ 295 334.00	$ 299 063.00	$ 301 611.00	$ 308 289.00	$ 309 003.00	$ 309 418.00	$ 307 261.00
South Africa	$ 28 809.70	$ 28 877.00	$ 28 533.10	$ 28 050.40	$ 28 364.70	$ 28 421.10	$ 28 569.20

FIGURE 15-5 *Sparklines embedded in a pivot table*

A couple of things are worth mentioning: The sparklines in this format are good for comparing patterns, and not absolute values—South Africa is just over 1% of China, and would not even show up on a chart at the same scale. An additional point is that (as is common with sparklines) the data has been shown superimposed on the text. Although this is an excellent space saver, care needs to be taken that the sparkline is still visible. In this case, using a lighter shade of gray for the text was sufficient.

THE INVENTION OF SPARKLINES

Sparklines were first introduced to the world in Edward Tufte's book, *Beautiful Evidence*, with several implementations making their way to the world. Luckily for us all, he never patented them, and they are now a native feature in Excel. If the Excel functionality isn't enough for you, more features are available in the free add-in, "Sparklines for Excel," at `http://sparklines-excel.blogspot.com/`.

Just as with line charts and column charts, columns can be used in sparklines.

Data bars are another visualization to be embedded inside a table, but in this case they are used to show a single value in the cell rather than summarizing the values of a series. Their usage on the same data set is shown in Figure 15-6.

Row Labels	January	February	March	April	May	June	July
ReserveValue							
Brazil	$ 227 743.00	$ 227 809.00	$ 234 639.00	$ 240 266.00	$ 245 509.00	$ 245 290.00	$ 248 259.00
China	$ 2 113 120.00	$ 2 142 100.00	$ 2 148 640.00	$ 2 142 760.00	$ 2 137 670.00	$ 2 149 840.00	
India	$ 172 938.00	$ 173 523.00	$ 174 098.00	$ 174 481.00	$ 173 936.00	$ 175 467.00	$ 176 415.00
Russian Federation	$ 295 334.00	$ 299 063.00	$ 301 611.00	$ 308 289.00	$ 309 003.00	$ 309 418.00	$ 307 261.00
South Africa	$ 28 809.70	$ 28 877.00	$ 28 533.10	$ 28 050.40	$ 28 364.70	$ 28 421.10	$ 28 569.20

FIGURE 15-6 *Databars embedded in a pivot table*

Sparklines and their variations are good for summarizing values over a series, and are often better for showing patterns rather than absolute values due to their extremely compressed nature, whereas data bars are good for showing absolute values.

Ease of Development

REPORTING TOOL	PREDEFINED CHART TYPE	EASE OF DEVELOPMENT
Excel	Yes	
PerformancePoint	No	
Power View	No	
Reporting Services	Yes	
Silverlight/HTML5	N/A	

CONDITIONAL FORMATTING

Conditional formatting is very similar to the data bars in an application—it is used to show the relationship of the value in a particular cell to the value in other cells by including a visualization in that cell. The value is denoted by the color in the cell. An oft-applied example in the accountancy world is red for losses and black for gains, leading to the phrases "in the black" and "in the red." Another use is to quickly show relative values by shading them along a color line—often green to red or blue to red—differing shades denote different values, in a similar way to a heat map.

In Figure 15-7, you can see the unemployment rates, with higher numbers shown in red:

	A	B	C	D	E	F	G	H	I
1									
2	Statistics		Unemployment rates: total ⊽						
3									
4	**MetricValueAvg**		**Column Labels**	▾					
5	**Row Labels**	⊽	⊞ 2000	⊞ 2005	⊞ 2008	⊞ 2009	⊞ 2010	⊞ 2011	
6	Brazil			12.70	9.30	7.30	7.70	6.30	5.70
7	Russian Federation			10.50	7.60	6.40	8.40	7.50	6.60
8	South Africa			23.30	23.50	22.90	23.90	24.90	24.90
9									

FIGURE 15-7 *Conditonal formatting on a pivot table*

Care in the choice of colors needs to be exercised, however. In the example in Figure 15-7, red for high unemployment and green for low unemployment are apt; in other examples, the assumption of red for bad, as people are wont to do, can be misleading. In Figure 15-8, red has been used for low population, yet China and India are definitely countries with worse population problems. Reversing the scale doesn't help because South Africa has a higher density population than Russia.

	A	B	C	D	E	F	G	H
1								
2	Statistics		Population levels					
3								
4	MetricValueAvg	Column Labels						
5	Row Labels	2000		2005	2008	2009	2010	2011
6	Brazil		171 279.90	183 383.20	189 612.80	191 480.60	193 252.60	194 932.70
7	China		1 269 117.00	1 307 594.00	1 328 276.00	1 334 909.00	1 341 335.00	1 348 010.00
8	India		1 053 898.00	1 140 043.00	1 190 864.00	1 207 740.00	1 224 614.00	1 241 948.00
9	Russian Federation		146 757.50	143 843.20	143 163.10	143 064.10	142 958.20	142 822.50
10	South Africa		44 760.38	47 792.79	49 319.36	49 751.50	50 132.82	50 384.55
11								

FIGURE 15-8 *Color can be misleading*

Ease of Development

REPORTING TOOL	PREDEFINED CHART TYPE	EASE OF DEVELOPMENT
Excel	Yes	●
PerformancePoint	Yes	●
Power View	No	●
Reporting Services	Yes	●
Silverlight/HTML5	N/A	●

INDICATORS

Indicators have been treated fairly extensively in Chapter 10, but they are in many ways simply a subset of the conditional formatting. Although the color is contained within a shape (which may have meaning), the color banding is essentially the same concept as coding the entire cell in a color. The advantage of an indicator is that it is a discrete item, and as such won't distract or overlay the numeric value.

Commonly, indicators are limited to fewer numbers than conditional formatting, so a problem with them both is rather more apparent: The numbers that are being shown have been banded into ranges, and as such you lose precision when displaying in this manner. As an example, let us consider the data set showing average hours worked per year—in the conditional formatting cells for 2011, it is very easy to rank the countries by color alone, but in the indicator set it is much harder. This problem doesn't disappear with the conditional formatting—look at cells H11 and C6 in Figure 15-9.

This banding of data into these buckets is in fact the greatest strength of indicators. Red icons mean they need immediate action, green icons can be ignored with safety, and yellow icons need to be investigated. Choosing the boundaries for these values is thus of utmost importance!

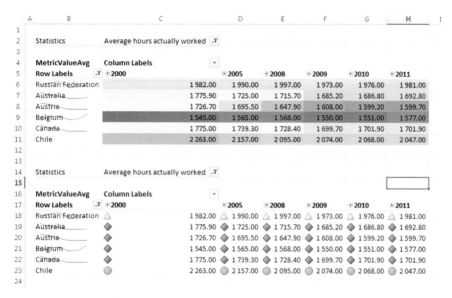

FIGURE 15-9 *Using indicators*

Ease of Development

REPORTING TOOL	PREDEFINED CHART TYPE	EASE OF DEVELOPMENT
Excel	Yes	●
PerformancePoint	Yes	●
Power View	Yes	●
Reporting Services	Yes	●
Silverlight/HTML5	N/A	●

BULLET GRAPHS

A bullet graph is really two or three embedded bar charts in a single cell, superimposed upon one another. They are very useful when you need to show a series of data points against targets or averages. For example, you may need to compare the total sales of each store within a region to each other, as well as to a target that is set for each store, and quite possibly the store average as well.

BULLET GRAPHS

Bullet graphs are the invention of Stephen Few, and his specification for what they should look like can be found online at `www.perceptualedge.com/articles/misc/Bullet_Graph_Design_Spec.pdf`. As always, Stephen Few is very fond of monochrome, so you may want to spruce up the design by using colors rather than gray scale.

The bullet graph in Figure 15-10 shows 2011 unemployment rates (the blue bar for each country) against a country-specific target (the black line—note that I made up the target), as well as against the overall target bands (the colored band at the back). Using a graph spread across the 20 columns in Excel is not necessary, but does give a nice visual cue to exactly how far the bullet graph is along the bands.

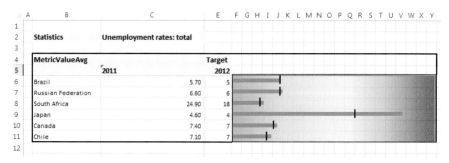

FIGURE 15-10 *Using a bullet graph*

Ease of Development

REPORTING TOOL	PREDEFINED CHART TYPE	EASE OF DEVELOPMENT
Excel	No	○
PerformancePoint	No	●
Power View	No	●
Reporting Services	No	◐
Silverlight/HTML5	N/A	○

TOOL CHOICES WITH EXAMPLES

Excel, PerformancePoint, and Reporting Services all allow for embedded for-matting of some description, while Power View does not. Excel is the leader in this section, with Reporting Services second, and PerformancePoint a long way behind.

EXCEL

Excel is the most widespread tabular display tool, and as such it has a very powerful set of visualizations; it is definitely the easiest tool to add embedded visualizations into. Covering data bars, sparklines, and conditional formatting, Excel may seem like the first choice in all cases—however there are some shortcomings.

Excel is great with conditional formatting—as shown in Figure 15-11, it is easy to add conditional formatting year by year to get a different scale when there are major data differences.

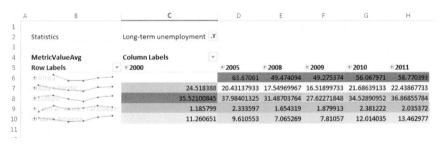

FIGURE 15-11   *Sparklines combined with conditional formatting in a pivot table*

However, when using a sparkline on the same graph, it won't dynamically get new data as they come in. Compare Figure 15-11 to Figure 15-12: the sparklines have shown up only for the data points we'd selected.

This same issue occurs with the bullet graph you saw earlier: It was made by superimposing two bar charts on top of one another, and it does not have the capability of dynamically resizing. Conditional formatting and indicators both have the capability of being dynamic, so they are great choices. As shown in Figure 15-13, Excel provides additional settings for applying conditional formatting.

	A	B	C	D	E	F	G	H
1								
2		Statistics	Long-term unemployment ⊤					
3								
4		MetricValueAvg	Column Labels ▼					
5		Row Labels ▼	⊞2000	⊞2005	⊞2008	⊞2009	⊞2010	⊞2011
6		⊞Africa		63.67061	49.474094	49.275374	56.067971	58.770393
7		⊞Asia + Pacific		24.518388	20.43137933	17.54969967	16.51899733	21.68639133	22.43867733
8		⊟Europe		35.52100845	37.98401325	31.48703764	27.62271848	34.52890952	36.86855784
9		⊞Central Europe		40.5900986	48.66661367		37.804775	30.28948367	39.4519905	41.61861717
10		⊟Eastern Europe		46.19108	38.451531	35.183184	28.71473	29.926106	32.760236
11		⊞Western Europe		33.27003831	34.18618265	29.17578372	26.67312944	33.14359383	35.51344483
12		⊞Latin America + Caribbean		1.185799	2.333597	1.654319	1.879913	2.381222	2.035372
13		⊞North America		11.260651	9.610553	7.065269	7.81057	12.014035	13.462977
14								

FIGURE 15-12 *Expanding a pivot table does not expand the sparklines automatically*

	⊞2005	⊞2008	⊞2009	⊞2010	⊞2011
	63.67061	49.474094	49.275374	56.067971	58.770393
8388	20.43137933	17.54969967	16.51899733	21.68639133	22.43867733
0845	37.98401325	31.48703764	27.62271848	34.52890952	36.86855784
0986	48.66661367	37.804775	30.28948367	39.4519905	41.61861717
9108	38.451531	35.183184	28.71473	29.926106	32.760236
3831	34.18618265	29.17578372	26.67312944	33.14359383	35.51344483
5799	2.333597	1.654319	1.879913	2.381222	2.035372
0651	9.610553	.065269	7.81057	12.014035	13.462977

Apply formatting rule to ...

◉ Selected cells

○ All cells showing "MetricValueAvg" values

○ All cells showing "MetricValueAvg" values for "GEO Region" and "YearName"

FIGURE 15-13 *Conditional formatting settings*

SQL SERVER REPORTING SERVICES (SSRS)

Reporting Services is a good choice for embedded visualizations—it is more work than Excel to generate, however; by embedding the visualization in a matrix, it will automatically repeat.

It also has a chart type that can easily be used to create bullet charts—the gauge chart.

Figure 15-14 shows a gauge chart that has been customized to be a bullet graph.

Title	Sales Amount	Sales Quota	
European Sales Manager	$98,323	$117,000	
North American Sales Manager	$249,400	$271,000	
Pacific Sales Manager	$26,580	$33,000	

FIGURE 15-14 *A bullet graph in SSRS*

Conditional formatting is also very easy with SSRS, as Figure 15-15 shows.

Title		Sales Amount	Sales Quota		
European Sales Manager	◆	$98,323	$117,000	▬▬▬▬▬	
North American Sales Manager	●	$249,400	$271,000	▬▬▬▬▬▬▬▬▬	
Pacific Sales Manager	◆	$26,580	$33,000	▬▬	

FIGURE 15-15 *Adding conditional formatting to an SSRS table*

Of course, being cautious with colors is imperative if you don't want your chart to end up being a cartoon canvas—use `www.colorbrewer.org` for a good selection of colors. As shown in the chart in Figure 15-15, using indicators is a more subtle and less garish way to show the data points.

PERFORMANCEPOINT

Although PerformancePoint is not a great embedded visualization tool, it is the most capable of the indicator tools with its scorecard component. And with a bit of work, conditional formatting can also be applied.

An example scorecard with both indicators and conditional formatting is shown in Figure 15-16.

Statistic: Total primary energy supply per capita ▼				Year: 2010 ▼	

Metric Scorecard

	Actual		Target		
⊟ Metric Value	3	◆ 17	17	-84%	
⊞ Asia + Pacific	5	● 6	6	-19%	
⊞ Europe	4	◆ 17	17	-73%	
⊞ Latin America + Caribbean	2	● 2	2	-7%	
⊞ North America	8	● 8	8	0%	

FIGURE 15-16 *Conditional formatting in PerformancePoint*

IMPLEMENTATION EXAMPLES

The implementation examples all use the OECD_Data model. See Chapters 4 and 5 for creating this data model.

EMBEDDING VISUALIZATIONS ON A PIVOT TABLE

Pivot tables are the most likely place for you to need visualizations; in this section you will create a new pivot table, add sparklines, and use conditional formatting. Data bars can be added in the same manner as conditional formatting.

> Combining too many of these visualizations in a single chart is overkill and should be avoided.

Start by creating a connection to the OECD_Data tabular model. Do this in Excel by going to the Data tab, clicking Connections, and then clicking Add. (You need to click Browse for more and then New Source if a connection does not exist already.) Your connection type will be Microsoft SQL Server Analysis

Services, and you will need to enter the name of the server to connect to. If it is on your local machine, using a dot (".") to mean "local" will suffice. Finish by choosing the correct model and clicking OK.

Then on the Insert tab, choose PivotTable. Your screen should look similar to the one shown in Figure 15-17.

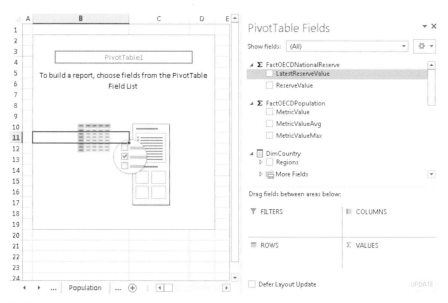

FIGURE 15-17 *Designing a pivot table*

Drag FactOECDNationalReserve ➢ LatestReserveValue to the Values box, DimCountry ➢ Regions to the Rows box, and DimDates ➢ YMD to the Columns box. Right-click in column A and choose Insert; then right-click in row 1 and choose Insert to give the table a border. Do some basic formatting, and set the value fields to use the currency format, as shown in Figure 15-18.

Finish the basic formatting by right-clicking Grand Total. If your pivot table is in A1, this will be D2—if you have left an empty row and an empty column surrounding your pivot table, this will be E3. All later cell references assumed that this cell is in E3 and choose Remove Grand Total. The LatestReserveValue is using a LastNonEmpty pattern, so it always shows the latest value, and Grand Total for the rows is simply repeating the 2012 value.

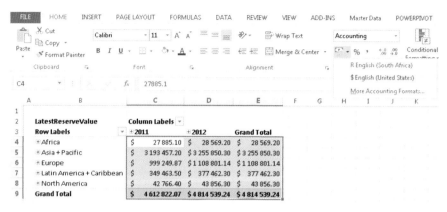

FIGURE 15-18 *Formatting currencies in Excel*

For sparklines, specifically, the data range is not dynamic, so expand both 2011 and 2012 before inserting them. Right-click 2011 Total and remove it by unticking Subtotal YearName. Insert another column by right-clicking in column A and choosing Insert—you will put the sparkline here. In B5, select Insert and then Line, as shown in Figure 15-19.

FIGURE 15-19 *Adding sparklines to a pivot table*

Choose the data range: D5 to O5, as shown in Figure 15-20.

To finish, you need to expand the sparkline to all the rows. In order to know how many rows to expand to, right-click Africa, choose Expand/Collapse, and then Expand Entire Field; then do the same with Southern Africa, as shown in Figure 15-21.

FIGURE 15-20 *Sparkline data range window*

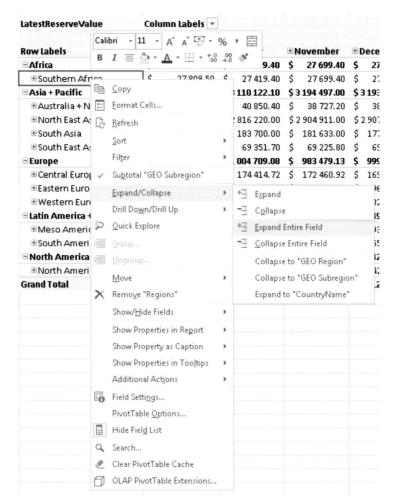

FIGURE 15-21 *Drilling down on a pivot table*

Finish by clicking the bottom-right corner of the cell with your sparkline in it and dragging it to the bottom of all your data, as shown in Figure 15-22.

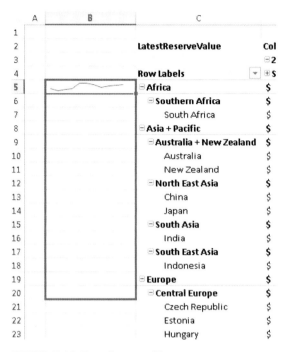

FIGURE 15-22 *Extending a sparkline*

Once you have done this, collapse the fields again to get a view similar to that shown in Figure 15-23.

FIGURE 15-23 *Sparklines in a collapsed pivot table*

Immediately apparent is the influence of the missing data in August 2012: Not all countries have submitted and it distorts the sparklines. Fix this by removing August completely in the Excel filters. Do so by clicking on the arrow next to the words "Column labels" and then ticking the multiselect tickbox. Find

August 2012 in the tree, and deselect it. This distorts the sparkline, so when you click the sparkline, a new context menu appears in the Ribbon, and you can edit the data, as shown in Figure 15-24.

FIGURE 15-24 *Changing sparkline data fields*

MISSING DATA

Missing data, such as that in this data set (there are data points missing in June and July as well), is one of the larger problems with aggregating large data sets. Using normalized aggregations such as arithmetic means or metrics such as GDP per capita are often required when doing this sort of analysis, rather than a pure SUM.

Another way of showing data is conditional formatting—the temptation is to simply highlight the whole data set and add conditional formatting, but doing this has a problem: the grand total will always be on one end of the spectrum, and the smallest point of the data set the other. Comparing the smallest country's reserve to that of all the OECD nations is not particularly helpful unless it's expressed as a percentage.

Instead, you will apply conditional formatting to each level independently. Start by clicking cell D5, choose conditional formatting in the Home Ribbon, and choose the Green-White scale, as shown in Figure 15-25.

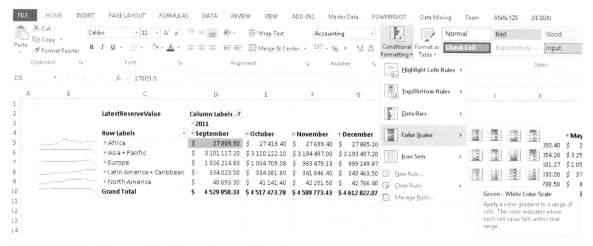

FIGURE 15-25 *Applying conditional formatting to a single cell*

A small icon will appear next to the cell you just formatted. Click it and set it to appear for all cells with the year and region, as shown in Figure 15-26.

Column Labels .T

	2011				2012	
	September	October	November	December	January	February
$	27 809.50	27 419.40	$	27 699.40	$	27 885.10	$	28 809.70	$	28 877.00
$	3 101 117.20					
$	1 026 214.83					
$	334 023.50					
$	40 693.30					
$	4 529 858.33					

Apply formatting rule to ...

◉ Selected cells

○ All cells showing "LatestReserveValue" values

○ All cells showing "LatestReserveValue" values for "GEO Region" and "MonthName"

FIGURE 15-26 *Expanding a conditional formatting selection*

Next, you will do the same for the level below that: the subregion. In this case, to differentiate between the levels, you will use a color scale from light to dark blue. So instead of choosing the same color scale, choose more rules. Set the rule up, as shown in Figure 15-27, making sure to set it to apply to all cells with the values Sub Region and Month, and choose two appropriately spaced blue values.

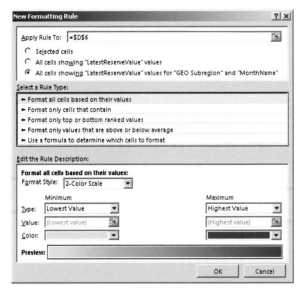

FIGURE 15-27 *Conditional formatting rules window*

Repeat this process at the country level, using yellow and red (you could choose any color you want, as long as it doesn't overlap with the existing color sets). The result is a table looking similar to the one shown in Figure 15-28.

Row Labels	September	October	November	December	January	February	March	April	May	June	July
Africa	$ 27 809.50	$ 27 419.40	$ 27 699.40	$ 27 885.10	$ 28 809.70	$ 28 877.00	$ 28 533.10	$ 28 050.40	$ 28 364.70	$ 28 421.10	$ 28 569.20
Southern Africa	$ 27 809.50	$ 27 419.40	$ 27 699.40	$ 27 885.10	$ 28 809.70	$ 28 877.00	$ 28 533.10	$ 28 050.40	$ 28 364.70	$ 28 421.10	$ 28 569.20
South Africa	$ 27 809.50	$ 27 419.40	$ 27 699.40	$ 27 885.10	$ 28 809.70	$ 28 877.00	$ 28 533.10	$ 28 050.40	$ 28 364.70	$ 28 421.10	$ 28 569.20
Asia + Pacific	$ 3 101 117.20	$ 3 110 122.10	$ 3 194 497.00	$ 3 193 457.70	$ 3 212 548.50	$ 3 238 983.70	$ 3 241 176.70	$ 3 238 054.20	$ 3 250 299.60	$ 3 234 358.40	$ 1 092 756.80
Europe	$ 1 026 214.83	$ 1 004 709.08	$ 983 479.13	$ 999 249.87	$ 984 189.12	$ 995 440.69	$ 1 004 446.55	$ 1 016 501.27	$ 1 055 927.69	$ 1 111 601.67	$ 794 711.61
Latin America + Caribbean	$ 334 023.50	$ 334 081.80	$ 341 846.40	$ 349 463.50	$ 348 631.30	$ 348 916.60	$ 356 731.20	$ 363 830.00	$ 371 057.10	$ 374 962.10	$ 379 010.30
North America	$ 40 693.30	$ 41 141.40	$ 42 251.50	$ 42 766.40	$ 42 674.50	$ 44 734.80	$ 44 653.90	$ 44 738.50	$ 45 379.30	$ 43 523.60	$ 43 856.30
Grand Total	$ 4 529 858.33	$ 4 517 473.78	$ 4 589 773.43	$ 4 612 822.07	$ 4 616 853.12	$ 4 656 952.79	$ 4 675 541.45	$ 4 691 174.37	$ 4 751 828.39	$ 4 792 866.87	$ 2 338 904.21

FIGURE 15-28 *Multiple conditional formatting rules applied to a pivot table*

It is important to note that the conditional formatting is relative to the data currently visible: drilling down on Europe. (Take note of the change in the coloring for South Africa, as seen in Figure 15-29.)

LatestReserveValue	Column Labels ⬜										
	⊟2011				⊟2012						
Row Labels ⬜	⊞ September	⊞ October	⊞ November	⊞ December	⊞ January	⊞ February	⊞ March	⊞ April	⊞ May	⊞ June	⊞ July
⊟ Africa	$ 27 809.50	$ 27 419.40	$ 27 699.40	$ 27 885.10	$ 28 809.70	$ 28 877.00	$ 28 533.10	$ 28 050.40	$ 28 364.70	$ 28 421.10	$ 28 569.20
⊟ Southern Africa	$ 27 809.50	$ 27 419.40	$ 27 699.40	$ 27 885.10	$ 28 809.70	$ 28 877.00	$ 28 533.10	$ 28 050.40	$ 28 364.70	$ 28 421.10	$ 28 569.20
South Africa	$ 27 809.50	$ 27 419.40	$ 27 699.40	$ 27 885.10	$ 28 809.70	$ 28 877.00	$ 28 533.10	$ 28 050.40	$ 28 364.70	$ 28 421.10	$ 28 569.20
⊞ Asia + Pacific	$ 3 101 117.20	$ 3 110 122.10	$ 3 194 497.00	$ 3 193 457.20	$ 3 212 548.50	$ 3 238 983.70	$ 3 241 176.70	$ 3 238 054.20	$ 3 250 299.60	$ 3 234 358.40	$ 1 092 756.80
⊟ Europe	$ 1 026 214.83	$ 1 004 709.08	$ 983 479.13	$ 999 249.87	$ 984 189.12	$ 995 440.69	$ 1 004 446.55	$ 1 016 501.27	$ 1 055 927.69	$ 1 111 601.67	$ 794 711.61
⊟ Central Europe	$ 176 959.40	$ 174 414.72	$ 172 460.92	$ 169 933.08	$ 168 672.90	$ 170 388.92	$ 170 846.45	$ 173 087.32	$ 169 399.44	$ 174 494.75	$ 176 312.06
Czech Republic	$ 25 663.40	$ 25 968.60	$ 26 188.50	$ 25 853.20	$ 25 794.00	$ 27 287.80	$ 27 373.60	$ 27 581.30	$ 25 547.80	$ 25 612.30	$ 25 452.90
Estonia	$ 131.49	$ 136.47	$ 139.28	$ 127.21	$ 134.90	$ 189.58	$ 174.68	$ 189.65	$ 187.75	$ 169.04	$ 180.25
Hungary	$ 33 522.30	$ 32 858.00	$ 30 508.00	$ 31 711.60	$ 31 581.00	$ 29 972.30	$ 29 775.20	$ 29 859.30	$ 29 114.10	$ 29 391.90	$ 29 076.40
Poland	$ 60 913.80	$ 61 277.60	$ 60 069.10	$ 60 461.20	$ 61 069.90	$ 61 791.00	$ 60 933.70	$ 62 865.20	$ 61 709.10	$ 63 481.10	$ 64 356.40
Slovenia	$ 554.01	$ 569.65	$ 535.04	$ 544.67	$ 598.30	$ 547.14	$ 505.58	$ 506.17	$ 511.89	$ 514.90	$ 546.21
Turkey	$ 56 174.40	$ 53 604.40	$ 55 021.00	$ 51 235.20	$ 49 494.80	$ 50 601.10	$ 52 083.70	$ 52 085.70	$ 52 328.80	$ 55 325.50	$ 56 699.90
⊟ Eastern Europe	$ 303 521.00	$ 301 728.00	$ 299 188.00	$ 296 673.00	$ 295 334.00	$ 299 063.00	$ 301 611.00	$ 308 289.00	$ 309 003.00	$ 309 418.00	$ 307 261.00
Russian Federation											

FIGURE 15-29 *Changing conditional formatting by drilling down*

ADDING CONDITIONAL FORMATTING TO A PPS SCORECARD

PerformancePoint also has conditional formatting, but it is by no means as intuitive as that in Excel. To do conditional formatting, a custom indicator needs to be created and then conditional formatting enabled on the scorecard.

Chapter 10 covered the creation of custom indicators in some depth, so they won't be covered here again.

SUMMARY

Embedding visualizations in applications and in tables is one of the most powerful ways to use them. The tools available from Microsoft to do this are quite powerful, and in this chapter you learned the techniques to apply them.

CHAPTER 16

Other Visualizations

Throughout this book you have learned about visualizations that you can implement using the Microsoft stack, and how to implement them. In this chapter you learn about other visualizations—many of these are not data-driven; instead, they are often drawn by artists or handcrafted by other professionals.

TRADITIONAL INFOGRAPHICS

As discussed at length in Chapter 1, data driven visualizations and infographics are very different in function, and they are often different in form as well. An infographic is typically static—in other words, if the data changes, the infographic doesn't update. Many infographics are simply images rather than being interactive.

An infographic is often used to tell a single story, with imagery chosen to fit that story. It might have numeric values attached to the images. An example infographic is shown in Figure 16-1.

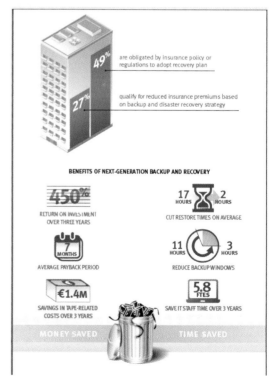

FIGURE 16-1 *An infographic promoting next generation backup and recovery*

PERIODIC TABLES

Mendelev's periodic table of the elements was a revolution in understanding of the elements—not just as a visualization, but also because he used the atomic weight—that is, how many protons were in the atom—as the underpinning, and isotypes are simply versions of the same element. The effect of the way Mendelev laid out the table cannot be overstated. As shown in Figure 16-2, being able to read the group (for example, beryllium and magnesium both in Group 2) across, and the periods (such as hydrogen and helium being the only two members of Period 1) down was of enormous value.

Group → / ↓ Period	1	2	3	4	5	6	7	8	9	10	11	12	13	14	15	16	17	18
1	1 H																	2 He
2	3 Li	4 Be											5 B	6 C	7 N	8 O	9 F	10 Ne
3	11 Na	12 Mg											13 Al	14 Si	15 P	16 S	17 Cl	18 Ar
4	19 K	20 Ca	21 Sc	22 Ti	23 V	24 Cr	25 Mn	26 Fe	27 Co	28 Ni	29 Cu	30 Zn	31 Ga	32 Ge	33 As	34 Se	35 Br	36 Kr
5	37 Rb	38 Sr	39 Y	40 Zr	41 Nb	42 Mo	43 Tc	44 Ru	45 Rh	46 Pd	47 Ag	48 Cd	49 In	50 Sn	51 Sb	52 Te	53 I	54 Xe
6	55 Cs	56 Ba		72 Hf	73 Ta	74 W	75 Re	76 Os	77 Ir	78 Pt	79 Au	80 Hg	81 Tl	82 Pb	83 Bi	84 Po	85 At	86 Rn
7	87 Fr	88 Ra		104 Rf	105 Db	106 Sg	107 Bh	108 Hs	109 Mt	110 Ds	111 Rg	112 Cn	113 Uut	114 Fl	115 Uup	116 Lv	117 Uus	118 Uuo
Lanthanides				57 La	58 Ce	59 Pr	60 Nd	61 Pm	62 Sm	63 Eu	64 Gd	65 Tb	66 Dy	67 Ho	68 Er	69 Tm	70 Yb	71 Lu
Actinides				89 Ac	90 Th	91 Pa	92 U	93 Np	94 Pu	95 Am	96 Cm	97 Bk	98 Cf	99 Es	100 Fm	101 Md	102 No	103 Lr

FIGURE 16-2 *The periodic table of elements*

Other forms of this periodic table have been used to illustrate other subject areas. The periodic table of fonts in Figure 16-3 is a stellar example. This visualization (including the option to purchase a print) is available here: `www.squidspot.com/Periodic_Table_of_Typefaces.html`.

Perhaps the most intriguing of the periodic table of elements visualizations is the one at `www.visual-literacy.org/periodic_table/periodic_table.html`, which is a periodic table of visualizations. This is shown in Figure 16-4.

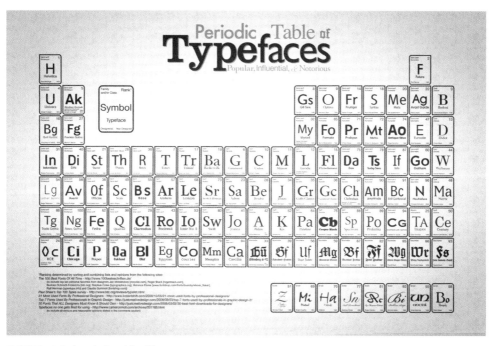

FIGURE 16-3 *A periodic table of fonts*

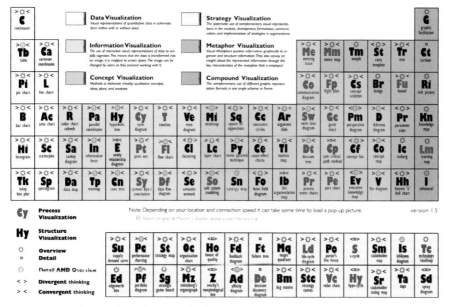

FIGURE 16-4 *The periodic table of visualizations*

SWIM LANES

Swim lanes, also called cross-functional flow charts in Microsoft Visio, are most often used to show process flows across different areas (see Figure 16-5). This flow shows a typical ETL (Extract, Transform, Load) process loading data from one system into a warehouse, and the data subsequently being used by the business information (BI) system.

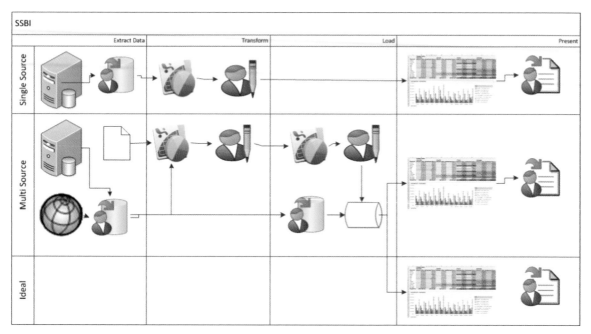

FIGURE 16-5 *A swim lane illustrating different ETL processes*

TRANSPORTATION MAPS

When trains and subways were first put into service, maps of their routes followed the same conventions as traditional maps. Shown to scale, there was often an enormous amount of wasted space on the map, as well as overlapping text when stations were close together. With the launch of the New York subway, which had more stations than ever before, something new was needed, and this was the novel concept of showing each station evenly spaced. That concept, along with color-coding the lines and removing the background graphics, made this map revolutionary in visualizations of travel routes. Figure 16-6 shows the original New York subway map. (You can obtain other New York subways maps through history at `http://nycsubway.org/wiki/Historical_Maps`.) Figure 16-7 shows a newer version of the subway map.

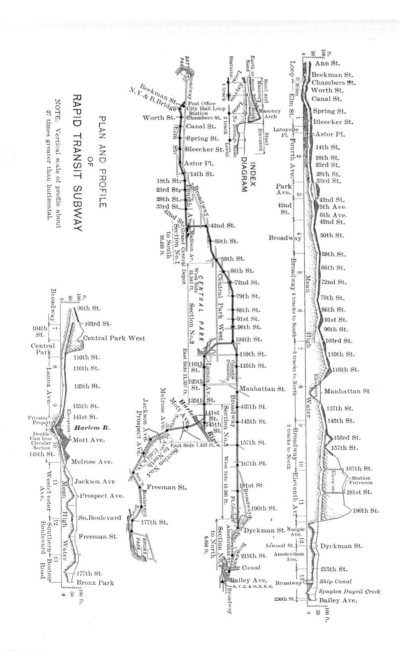

FIGURE 16-6 *The original NYC subway map*

FIGURE 16-7 *A newer NYC subway map*

MIND MAPS

Mind maps are a little outside the traditional visualization arena, but are very useful for brainstorming and framing your thoughts around a plan. A book's contents are easily planned in a mind map, and this book's original Table of Contents is shown as a mind map in Figure 16-8. You'll note that the book has evolved over time!

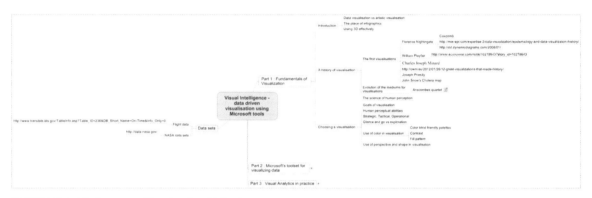

FIGURE 16-8 *Mind maps used for planning this book*

VENN DIAGRAM

A Venn diagram is a very simple visualization used in set theory, which has been widely adopted on the Internet. Two or three circles, each representing a group, are shown overlapping each other, with the overlap being the group (or set) of people or things that belong to all those groupings overlapping those areas. These circles are not shown to scale in the most common form of these diagrams. A widely shared example of a Venn diagram is shown in Figure 16-9. (It's become quite popular to use Venn diagrams for humor.)

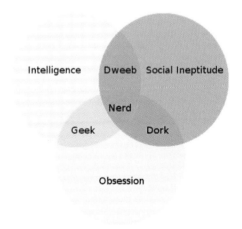

FIGURE 16-9 *A humorous Venn diagram*

CAD DRAWINGS

Computer aided design (CAD) is a massively growing field, especially with the growth of 3D printing. Originally CAD was commonly used only by engineers and architects on high-end workstations, but it has penetrated the world of design very deeply. A CAD drawing is shown in Figure 16-10.

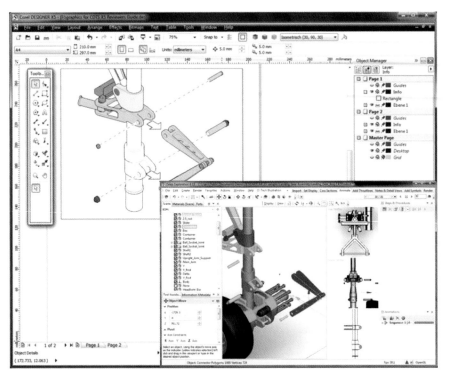

FIGURE 16-10 *Computer aided design—more complex than the average visualization*

3D MODELING

CAD is a form of 3D modeling, but the world of 3D has expanded vastly beyond just CAD with engineering precision. Games, such as the original Quake and all of its successors, are an obvious example, but 3D design has penetrated far further. Figure 16-11 shows an example of a 3D inspection program designed to run on a tablet computer and used to aid engineers in inspecting power pylons.

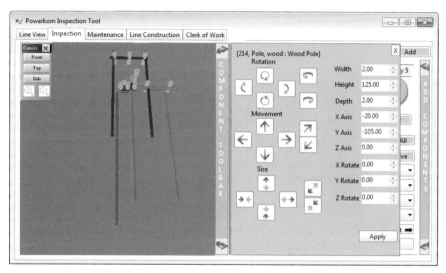

FIGURE 16-11   *The Orion inspection system developed by Aphelion Software*

FUNNELS

Funnels represent any process where the number of items decreases as the process progresses. They have widely been applied to the sales process—some leads turn into opportunities, some opportunities turn into negotiations, some negotiations turn into sales. The value in visualizing this as a funnel is showing the effectiveness of this process as well as showing which step has the lowest conversion ratio. If a salesperson has a wide pipeline in every step except turning negotiations into sales, perhaps he could use some assistance in closing or needs to attend a course on sales techniques. Figure 16-12 shows an example of a typical sales funnel. This funnel is built in Microsoft Reporting Services.

FIGURE 16-12 *A sales funnel developed in SSRS*

FLOW DIAGRAMS

The swim lanes discussed earlier in this chapter are a type of flow diagram. The instance shown in Figure 16-5 was specific to one process, but flow diagrams can be very conceptual. The following figures are two different flow charts: Figure 16-13 is a normal UML (Universal Modelling Language) flowchart, showing a start, end, and a couple of decision points and processes, whereas Figure 16-14 is a SharePoint workflow diagram that shows a workflow process.

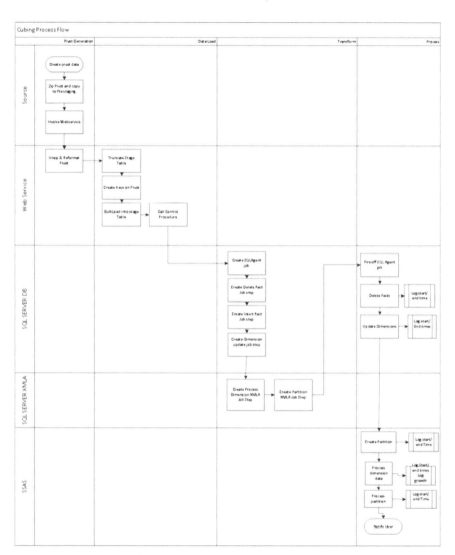

FIGURE 16-13   *A UML data flow*

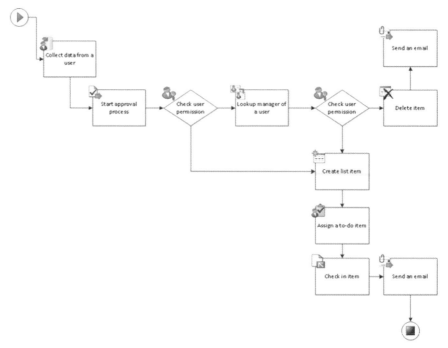

FIGURE 16-14 *A SharePoint workflow in Visio*

GEOGRAPHIC INFORMATION SYSTEM MAPS

Any data containing a latitude and longitude could technically be considered a Geographic Information System (GIS). The term GIS is typically used for those systems containing spatial data types and/or mapping capabilities.

On the Microsoft platform, SQL Server has had support for spatial data types since SQL 2008, and mapping support came along in Reporting Services for SQL 2008 R2, which included support for Bing Maps. You can see an example in Figure 16-15.

Further evolution in Office 2013 Power View has enabled people to create slicker maps directly in Excel (and SharePoint), as shown in Figure 16-16, which is an election-tracking template provided with Excel 2013.

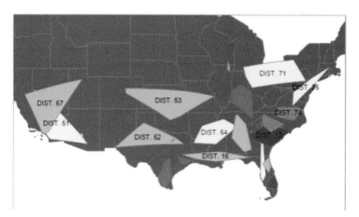

FIGURE 16-15 *A geospatial heatmap, or chloropleth, in SSRS*

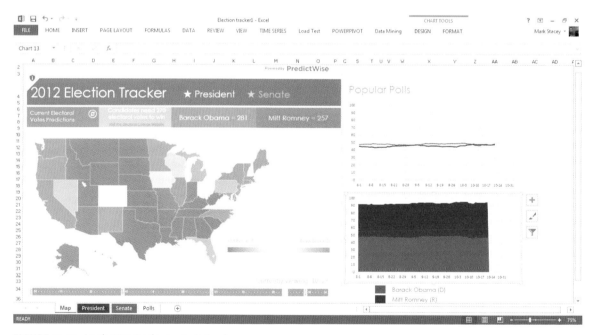

FIGURE 16-16 *An election-tracking map in Excel*

The various types of visualizations that can be done on maps (in other words, adding visualizations to maps as opposed to the different types of maps) include the following:

- **Chloropleth:** The different bounded areas are highlighted by changing the shading or color to represent a value.

- **Prism map:** Similar to a chloropleth, but in 3D.

- **Pin map:** Pins are shown on a map to highlight areas of interest.

- **Combined chart maps:** Instead of pins, some other chart type, such as a bar chart or pie chart, is shown to represent a value at that point.

Chloropleth and prism maps are often used for representing values such as population density or voters, but they are also good for representing sales or profitability in a state. The reporting services map shown in Figure 16-16 is a chloropleth, and Figure 16-17 shows a prism map. You can also see one at `www.pwinfographics.net`.

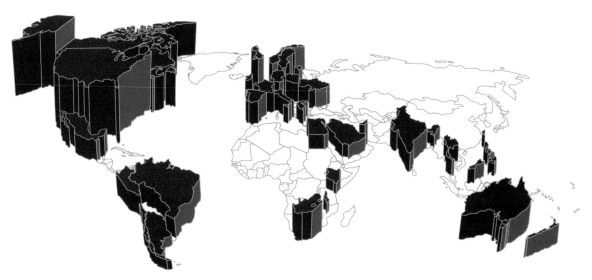

FIGURE 16-17 *A prism map*

Pin maps are good for navigation and orientation. Although they are used to represent data by having a variable number of pins, this is an inefficient use of space, and pin maps are often unreadable when the volumes become too high.

Showing charts on a map is another usage that is inefficient—especially as the prevalence is toward pie charts. The charts obscure the map itself, they are often too small to read easily, and they are often poorly distributed and obscure one another.

HEATMAPS

The chloropleth map shown in the previous section is in fact a specialized type of heatmap in which the size and shape of the individual items are based upon GIS shapes such as countries or states. A heatmap uses the color of the item to convey one dimension, and the size to convey another. This has often been used in stock-market analyses, where size is used to show either market capitalization, or the size of the investor's holding, and color has been used to show the performance of the share. Figure 16-18 is an example of a chloropleth.

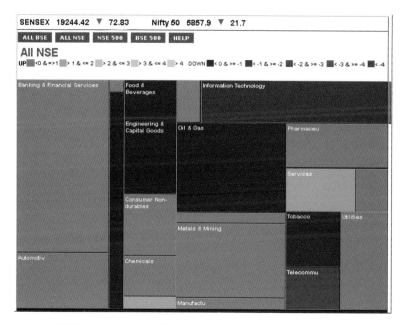

FIGURE 16-18 *A heatmap of stock prices*

SUMMARY

In this chapter you learned about some other common types of visualizations. Many of these, such as infographics and periodic tables especially, are likely to be handcrafted, and so won't be data driven—but they can still be useful in the decision-making process.

Choosing a Microsoft Tool

When working in the Microsoft business intelligence toolset, it's important to realize that you will not standardize on one tool for your visualizations. Each tool in the tool box has its own purpose, and you will frustrate yourself trying to make the wrong tool do the job of another—just as it would be frustrating to try to drive in a nail with a screwdriver. In this appendix, you discover the strengths and weaknesses of each tool.

STRENGTHS AND WEAKNESSES OF EACH TOOL

As mentioned in Chapter 2, the Microsoft toolset loosely follows the strategic/ tactical/operational levels, with a tool for each level. However, the correlation is loose, and with the launch of Power View as an application within SharePoint and a visualization within Excel, the tactical level has been split into two categories: PowerPivot in Excel for the data modeling, and Power View for the visualization. Consequently, the correlation between the toolset and the levels has become even weaker. This chapter explores the uses of each tool and shows you how to choose which to use.

PERFORMANCEPOINT

As described in Chapter 3, PerformancePoint Services (PPS) has its antecedents in the original Business Scorecard Manager. The strongest feature of PPS is the scorecard building component.

Many people struggle with trying to customize Analytic Grids to display data in a format that can be customized. Instead, use scorecards to gain control over the display of your data. Analytic grids are simply an interactive component rather than a high-fidelity display component.

PerformancePoint is directly aimed at the process of looking at a scorecard and quickly identifying where a problem exists, and then exploring prebuilt analysis paths to identify root causes of the problem.

A key point about PerformancePoint is that it is ideal for driving analysis from a monitoring point of view, clicking on a value in a scorecard to change values in associated charts and grids. It has the ability to have either a PerformancePoint Analytic Chart or an Excel Services or Reporting Services report embedded on the same page, and driven by the scorecard. Figure A-1 shows a mixture of PerformancePoint components, a map created within Reporting Services, and an Analytic Chart below. Clicking the scorecard updates the map as well as the chart, and the chart allows for additional drilling down.

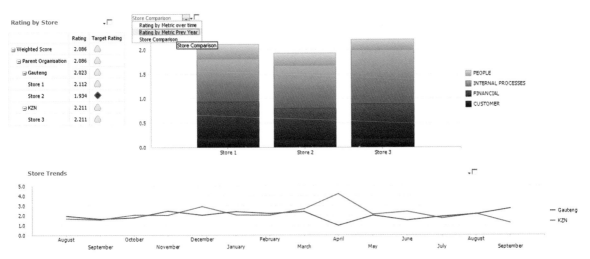

FIGURE A-1 *PerformancePoint interactive dashboard*

PerformancePoint is particularly poorly suited for printing, as the SharePoint elements, such as navigation and the Ribbon, are typically also printed.

REPORTING SERVICES

Reporting Services is squarely aimed at the high-fidelity reporting audience. It is more complex to develop than either PerformancePoint or Excel, and is typically a developer function, even when using Report Builder, but offers a level of control over the display not allowed in the other tools. A rather complex but exceptionally powerful expression language enables a developer to do exceptionally powerful conditional formatting.

In addition, Reporting Services and Power View are the only two tools that include mapping capabilities, and Reporting Services allows for much greater customization of the maps.

Reporting Services is often used where inclusion of specific formatting elements, such as logos, time of running reports, and so on, are required—for instance, in a monthly board pack that needs to be printed.

Figure A-2 shows an example Reporting Services front page.

FIGURE A-2 *A report showing the progress of initiatives in a government department*

EXCEL/EXCEL SERVICES

Excel is and has always been the domain of the analyst—someone who wants to interact with his data and have a dynamic visualization rather than a static one. Pivot tables and pivot charts, with slicers, enable a user to build an interactive dashboard, and the ability to publish on the web using Excel Services allows for the sharing of the analysis while preserving the interactivity. The inclusion of PowerPivot (in Excel 2010) and Power View (in Excel 2013) advances this interactivity greatly.

Figure A-3 shows an example of an Excel dashboard.

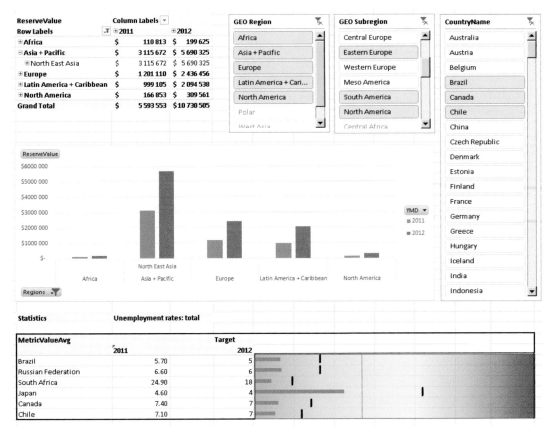

FIGURE A-3 *An interactive Excel dashboard including a bullet chart at the bottom*

POWER VIEW

Power View is designed for data exploration. You use this tool when you do not know what question you should be asking, but want to explore and discover patterns in your data. For developers, it is important to put away your assumptions about Report Builder when working with Power View, The approach is not really to give your users a prebuilt Power View report, but to give them a model that they can explore on their own—or with PowerPivot—to build a model and explore it using Power View.

An example of Power View's killer feature—the animated bubble chart—is shown in Figure A-4. (The animation doesn't show in the figure here, of course, but it really is animated!)

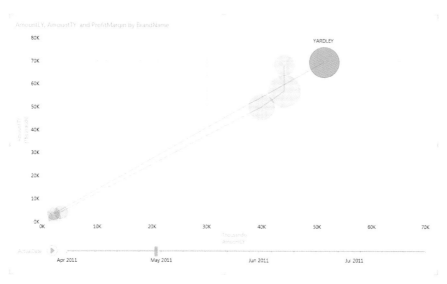

FIGURE A-4 *An animated Bubble chart in Power View*

HTML5

HTML5 (using such adjunct technologies as JavaScript and CSS, and libraries such as JQuery and D3) is a developer's tool and not at all an end-user
technology. HTML5 is used when developing visualizations that are simply
not possible using any of the other tools. A prism map is a good example
and is shown in Figure A-5. An interactive version of this is available at at
`http://www.pwinfographics.net`.

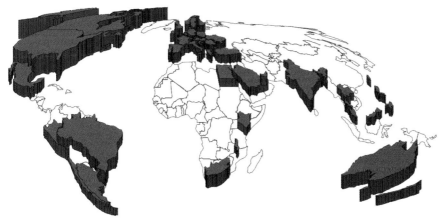

FIGURE A-5 *A prism map shown on a world outline*

MATCHING A VISUALIZATION TO A TOOL

In Table A-1, you can see whether a tool has a visualization type built in, the ease of development (which can sometimes be achieved even when the visualization is not built in), how customizable the visualization is, and finally, where appropriate, the location in this book where you can find how to implement this visualization in that particular tool.

TABLE A-1 The ease of developing Visualizations in each tool

VISUALIZATION	TOOL	PREDEFINED CHART TYPE	EASE OF DEVELOPMENT	CUSTOMIZABLE	CHAPTER
Indicators	PerformancePoint	Yes	●	●	10
Indicators	Reporting Services	Yes	●	●	
Indicators	Excel/Excel Services	Yes	●	●	10
Indicators	Power View	No	N/A	N/A	
Indicators	HTML5	No	●	●	
Scorecards	PerformancePoint	Yes	●	●	10
Scorecards	Reporting Services	No	●	●	
Scorecards	Excel/Excel Services	No	●	●	10
Scorecards	Power View	No	N/A	N/A	
Scorecards	HTML5	No	●	●	
Timelines	PerformancePoint	No	N/A	N/A	11
Timelines	Reporting Services	No	●	●	11
Timelines	Excel/Excel Services	No	●	●	11
Timelines	Power View	No	N/A	N/A	11
Timelines	HTML5	No	●	●	11
Line chart	PerformancePoint	Yes	●	●	11
Line chart	Reporting Services	Yes	●	●	11
Line chart	Excel/Excel Services	Yes	●	●	11
Line chart	Power View	Yes	●	●	11

VISUALIZATION	TOOL	PREDEFINED CHART TYPE	EASE OF DEVELOPMENT	CUSTOMIZABLE	CHAPTER
Line chart	HTML5	No	●	●	
Bar chart	PerformancePoint	No	N/A	N/A	
Bar chart	Reporting Services	Yes	●	●	11,12
Bar chart	Excel/Excel Services	Yes	●	○	11,12
Bar chart	Power View	Yes	●	●	
Bar chart	HTML5	No	○	●	
Column chart	PerformancePoint	Yes	●	●	11, 12
Column chart	Reporting Services	Yes	●	●	11, 12
Column chart	Excel/Excel Services	Yes	●	○	11, 12
Column chart	Power View	Yes	●	●	11, 12
Column chart	HTML5	No	●	●	11, 12
Column & Line	PerformancePoint	Yes	●	●	11, 12
Column & Line	Reporting Services	Yes	●	●	11, 12
Column & Line	Excel/Excel Services	Yes	●	○	11, 12
Column & Line	Power View	No	●	●	11, 12
Column & Line	HTML5	No	○	●	11, 12
Scatter plot	PerformancePoint	Yes	○	●	
Scatter plot	Reporting Services	Yes	●	●	11
Scatter plot	Excel/Excel Services	Yes	●	○	11
Scatter plot	Power View	Yes	●	○	11
Scatter plot	HTML5	No	○	●	11
Bubble chart	PerformancePoint	No	○	○	11
Bubble chart	Reporting Services	Yes	●	●	11
Bubble chart	Excel/Excel Services	Yes	○	○	11
Bubble chart	Power View	Yes	●	○	11

VISUALIZATION	TOOL	PREDEFINED CHART TYPE	EASE OF DEVELOPMENT	CUSTOMIZABLE	CHAPTER
Bubble chart	HTML5	No	◐	◐	11
Pie charts	PerformancePoint	Yes	◐	●	12
Pie charts	Reporting Services	Yes	◐	◐	12
Pie charts	Excel/Excel Services	Yes	◐	○	12
Pie charts	Power View	Yes	◐	●	12
Pie charts	HTML5	No	◐	◐	
Scale breaks	PerformancePoint	No	N/A	N/A	
Scale breaks	Reporting Services	Yes	◐	◐	12
Scale breaks	Excel/Excel Services	No	○	○	12
Scale breaks	Power View	No	N/A	N/A	
Scale breaks	HTML5	No	○	◐	
Multiple axes	PerformancePoint	Yes	◐	●	
Multiple axes	Reporting Services	Yes	◐	○	
Multiple axes	Excel/Excel Services	Yes	◐	○	12
Multiple axes	Power View	No	○	○	
Multiple axes	HTML5	No	○	◐	
Radar charts	PerformancePoint	No	N/A	N/A	
Radar charts	Reporting Services	Yes	◐	◐	12
Radar charts	Excel/Excel Services	Yes	◐	◐	12
Radar charts	Power View	No	N/A	N/A	
Radar charts	HTML5	No	○	◐	12
Bullet chart	PerformancePoint	No	N/A	N/A	
Bullet chart	Reporting Services	Yes	○	◐	12
Bullet chart	Excel/Excel Services	No	○	○	
Bullet chart	Power View	No	N/A	N/A	
Bullet chart	HTML5	No	◐	◐	
Pivot table	PerformancePoint	Yes	◐	●	7

VISUALIZATION	TOOL	PREDEFINED CHART TYPE	EASE OF DEVELOPMENT	CUSTOMIZABLE	CHAPTER
Pivot table	Reporting Services	No	●	●	
Pivot table	Excel/Excel Services	Yes	●	●	12
Pivot table	Power View	No	N/A	N/A	
Pivot table	HTML5	No	●	●	
Pivot chart	PerformancePoint	Yes	●	●	12
Pivot chart	Reporting Services	No	●	●	
Pivot chart	Excel/Excel Services	Yes	●	●	12
Pivot chart	Power View	No	N/A	N/A	
Pivot chart	HTML5	No	●	●	
Drill across	PerformancePoint	Yes	●	●	12
Drill across	Reporting Services	No	●	●	
Drill across	Excel/Excel Services	Yes	●	●	
Drill across	Power View	Yes	●	●	
Drill across	HTML5	No	●	●	
Drill through	PerformancePoint (using SSAS)	Yes	●	●	
Drill through	Reporting Services	Yes	●	●	
Drill through	Excel/Excel Services	Yes	●	●	
Drill through	Power View	No	N/A	N/A	
Drill through	HTML5	No	●	●	
Slicers	PerformancePoint	No	N/A	N/A	
Slicers	Reporting Services	No	●	●	12
Slicers	Excel/Excel Services	Yes	●	●	12
Slicers	Power View	Yes	●	●	12
Slicers	HTML5	No	●	●	
Histogram	PerformancePoint	Yes	●	●	
Histogram	Reporting Services	Yes	●	●	

VISUALIZATION	TOOL	PREDEFINED CHART TYPE	EASE OF DEVELOPMENT	CUSTOMIZABLE	CHAPTER
Histogram	Excel/Excel Services	Yes	●	●	
Histogram	Power View	Yes	●	●	
Histogram	HTML5	No	●	●	
Box charts	PerformancePoint	No	N/A	N/A	
Box charts	Reporting Services	Yes	●	●	
Box charts	Excel/Excel Services	Yes	●	●	
Box charts	Power View	No	N/A	N/A	
Box charts	HTML5	No	●	●	
Trend lines	PerformancePoint	No	●	●	
Trend lines	Reporting Services	Yes	●	●	11
Trend lines	Excel/Excel Services	Yes	●	●	11
Trend lines	Power View	No	N/A	N/A	
Trend lines	HTML5	No	●	●	
Clustering	PerformancePoint	No	N/A	N/A	
Clustering	Reporting Services	No	●	●	
Clustering	Excel/Excel Services	No	●	●	
Clustering	Power View	No	N/A	N/A	
Clustering	HTML5	No	●	●	
Decomposition Tree	PerformancePoint	Yes	●	●	7
Decomposition Tree	Reporting Services	No	●	●	
Decomposition Tree	Excel/Excel Services	No	N/A	N/A	
Decomposition Tree	Power View	No	N/A	N/A	
Decomposition Tree	HTML5	No	●	●	
Network map	PerformancePoint (using Visio)	Yes	●	●	14

VISUALIZATION	TOOL	PREDEFINED CHART TYPE	EASE OF DEVELOPMENT	CUSTOMIZABLE	CHAPTER
Network map	Reporting Services	No	●	●	
Network map	Excel/Excel Services	No	N/A	N/A	14
Network map	Power View	No	N/A	N/A	
Network map	HTML5	No	●	●	14
Color wheel	PerformancePoint	No	N/A	N/A	
Color wheel	Reporting Services	No	●	●	
Color wheel	Excel/Excel Services	No	N/A	N/A	
Color wheel	Power View	No	N/A	N/A	
Color wheel	HTML5	No	●	●	14
Tree	PerformancePoint	No	N/A	N/A	
Tree	Reporting Services	No	●	●	
Tree	Excel/Excel Services	No	N/A	N/A	
Tree	Power View	No	N/A	N/A	
Tree	HTML5	No	●	●	
Strategy map	PerformancePoint (using Visio)	Yes	●	●	14
Strategy map	Reporting Services	No	N/A	N/A	
Strategy map	Excel/Excel Services	No	N/A	N/A	
Strategy map	Power View	No	N/A	N/A	
Strategy map	HTML5	No	●	●	
Embedded charts	PerformancePoint	No	N/A	N/A	
Embedded charts	Reporting Services	Yes	●	●	
Embedded charts	Excel/Excel Services	Yes	●	●	15
Embedded charts	Power View	No	N/A	N/A	
Embedded charts	HTML5	No	●	●	
Conditional formatting	PerformancePoint	Yes	●	●	15

VISUALIZATION	TOOL	PREDEFINED CHART TYPE	EASE OF DEVELOPMENT	CUSTOMIZABLE	CHAPTER
Conditional formatting	Reporting Services	Yes	●	●	15
Conditional formatting	Excel/Excel Services	Yes	●	●	15
Conditional formatting	Power View	No	N/A	N/A	
Conditional formatting	HTML5	No	●	●	
Maps	PerformancePoint	No	N/A	N/A	
Maps	Reporting Services	Yes	●	●	
Maps	Excel/Excel Services	No	N/A	N/A	
Maps	Power View	Yes	●	●	
Maps	HTML5	No	●	●	

APPENDIX B

DAX Function Reference

Data Analysis Epressions (DAX), is the language used by both PowerPivot and the Tabular mode of Analysis Services, and will be of great use during your data analysis. This appendix contains a function reference.

UPDATED FUNCTION REFERENCE

Microsoft maintains an updated function reference at `http://msdn.microsoft.com/en-us/library/ee634396.aspx`.

DATE AND TIME FUNCTIONS

Date and time functions, as listed in Table B-1, allow for the manipulation of data stored in *datetime* formats.

TABLE B1 Date and Time Functions

FUNCTION	DESCRIPTION
`DATE(<year>, <month>, <day>)`	Returns the specified date in date-time format.
`DATEVALUE(date_text)`	Converts a date in the form of text to a date in datetime format.
`DAY(<date>)`	Returns the day of the month, a number from `1` to `31`.
`EDATE(<start_date>, <months>)`	Returns the date that is the indicated number of months before or after the start date. Use `EDATE` to calculate maturity dates or due dates that fall on the same day of the month as the date of issue.

FUNCTION	DESCRIPTION
EOMONTH(<start_date>, <months>)	Returns the date, in datetime format, of the last day of the month, before or after a specified number of months. Use EOMONTH to calculate maturity dates or due dates that fall on the last day of the month.
HOUR(<datetime>)	Returns the hour as a number from 0 (12:00 A.M.) to 23 (11:00 P.M.).
MINUTE(<datetime>)	Returns the minute as a number from 0 to 59, given a date and time value.
MONTH(<datetime>)	Returns the month as a number from 1 (January) to 12 (December).
NOW()	Returns the current date and time in datetime format.
SECOND(<time>)	Returns the seconds of a time value, as a number from 0 to 59.
TIME(hour, minute, second)	Converts hours, minutes, and seconds given as numbers to a time in datetime format.
TIMEVALUE(time_text)	Converts a time in text format to a time in datetime format.
TODAY()	Returns the current date.
WEEKDAY(<date>, <return_type>)	Returns a number from 1 to 7 identifying the day of the week of a date. By default the day ranges from 1 (Sunday) to 7 (Saturday).
WEEKNUM(<date>, <return_type>)	Returns the week number for the given date and year according to the specified convention. The week number indicates where the week falls numerically within a year.
YEAR(<date>)	Returns the year of a date as a four digit integer in the range 1900–9999.
YEARFRAC(<start_date>, <end_date>, <basis>)	Calculates the fraction of the year represented by the number of whole days between two dates. Use the YEARFRAC worksheet function to identify the proportion of a whole year's benefits or obligations to assign to a specific term.

FILTER FUNCTIONS

Filter functions, shown in Table B-2, are applied within the `Calculate` function, and are used to select from a range of data.

TABLE B-2 Filter Functions

FUNCTION	DESCRIPTION
`ALL( <table>  | <column1>, <column2>,…)`	Returns all the rows in a table, or all the values in a column, ignoring any filters that might have been applied.
`ALLEXCEPT(<table>, <column1>, <column2>,…)`	Removes all context filters in the table except filters that have been applied to the specified columns.
`ALLNOBLANKROW(<table>  | <column>)`	From the parent table of a relationship, returns all rows but the blank row, or all distinct values of a column but the blank row, and disregards any context filters that might exist.
`ALLSELECTED([<table>  | <column>])`	Removes context filters from columns and rows in the current query, while retaining all other context filters or explicit filters.
`CALCULATE(<expression>, <filter1>, <filter2>,…)`	Evaluates an expression in a context that is modified by the specified filters.
`CALCULATETABLE(<expression>, <filter1>, <filter2>,…)`	Evaluates a table expression in a context modified by filters.
`DISTINCT(<column>)`	Returns a one-column table that contains the distinct values from the specified column.
`EARLIER(<column>, <number>)`	Returns the current value of the specified column in an outer evaluation pass of the mentioned column.
`EARLIEST(<column>)`	Returns the current value of the specified column in an outer evaluation pass of the mentioned column. `EARLIEST` is similar to `EARLIER`, but it lets you specify one additional level of recursion.
`FILTER(<table>, <filter>)`	Returns a table that represents a subset of another table or expression.
`FILTERS(<column>)`	Returns the values that are directly applied as filters to column.

FUNCTION	DESCRIPTION
HASONEFILTER(<*column*>)	Returns TRUE when the number of directly filtered values on *column* is one; otherwise returns FALSE.
HASONEVALUE(<*column*>)	Returns TRUE when the context for *column* has been filtered down to one distinct value only; otherwise, the function returns FALSE.
ISCROSSFILTERED(<*column*>)	Returns TRUE when *column* or another column in the same or related table is being filtered.
ISFILTERED(<*column*>)	Returns TRUE when *column* is being filtered directly. If there is no filter on the column or if the filtering happens because a different column in the same table or in a related table is being filtered, then the function returns FALSE.

INFORMATION FUNCTIONS

Information functions, as shown in Table B-3, return additional information, such as a data type.

TABLE B-3 Information Functions

FUNCTION	DESCRIPTION
CONTAINS(<*table*>, <*column1*>, <*value1*>, <*column2*>, <*value2*>,...)	Returns TRUE if values for all referred columns exist, or are contained, in those columns; otherwise, the function returns FALSE.
ISBLANK(<*value*>)	Checks whether a value is blank, and returns TRUE or FALSE.
ISERROR(<*value*>)	Checks whether a value is an error, and returns TRUE or FALSE.
ISLOGICAL(<*value*>)	Checks whether a value is a logical value (TRUE or FALSE), and returns TRUE or FALSE.
ISNONTEXT(<*value*>)	Checks whether a value is not text (blank cells are not text), and returns TRUE or FALSE.

FUNCTION	DESCRIPTION
ISNUMBER(<*value*>)	Checks whether a value is a number, and returns TRUE or FALSE.
ISTEXT(<*value*>)	Checks whether a value is text, and returns TRUE or FALSE.

LOOKUP FUNCTIONS

Lookup functions, as shown in Table B-4, are used to retrieve values from other tables for calculated columns, or can be used in calculated measures. Note that using related tables will improve performance dramatically, and using calculated measures will offer a processing and size improvement over calculated columns.

TABLE B-4 Lookup Functions

FUNCTION	DESCRIPTION
LOOKUPVALUE(<*result_column*>, <*search_column1*>, <*search_value1*>[, <*search_column2*>, <*search_value2*>]...)	Returns the value in *result_column* for the row that meets all criteria specified by *search_column* and *search_value*. A replacement for VLOOKUP in Excel, LOOKUPVALUE is used only when relationships don't exist.
RELATED(<*column*>)	Returns a related value from another table.
RELATEDTABLE(<*table*>)	Evaluates a table expression in a context modified by the given filters. Returns a set of values.
VALUES(<*column*>)	Returns a one-column table that contains the distinct values from the specified column including the Unknown member.

PARENT-CHILD FUNCTIONS

Parent-child functions, shown in Table B-5, are used to implement parent-child hierarchies in DAX—these hierarchies are often called Ragged hierarchies.

TABLE B-5 Parent-Child Functions

FUNCTION	DESCRIPTION
PATH(<ID_column>, <parent_column>)	Returns a delimited text string with the identifiers of all the parents of the current identifier, starting with the oldest and continuing until current.
PATHCONTAINS(<path>, <item>)	Returns TRUE if the specified item exists within the specified path.
PATHITEM(<path>, <position>[, <type>])	Returns the item at the specified position from a string resulting from evaluation of a PATH function. Positions are counted from left to right. type is an optional enumeration that defines the data type of the result (Text or Integer).
PATHITEMREVERSE(<path>, <position>[, <type>])	Returns the item at the specified position from a string resulting from evaluation of a PATH function. Positions are counted backwards from right to left.
PATHLENGTH(<path>)	Returns the number of parents to the specified item in a given PATH result, including self.

LOGICAL FUNCTIONS

Logical functions, shown in Table B-6, are used for comparisons within a function.

TABLE B-6 Logical Functions

FUNCTION	DESCRIPTION
AND(<logical1>, <logical2>)	Checks whether both arguments are TRUE, and returns TRUE if both arguments are TRUE. Otherwise it returns FALSE.
FALSE()	Returns the logical value FALSE.
IF(<logical_test>, <value_if_true>, <value_if_false>)	Checks if a condition provided as the first argument is met. Returns one value if the condition is TRUE, and returns another value if the condition is FALSE.

FUNCTION	DESCRIPTION
IFERROR(`<value>`, `<value_if_error>`)	Evaluates an expression and returns a specified value if the expression returns an error; otherwise returns the value of the expression itself.
NOT(`<logical>`)	Changes FALSE to TRUE, or TRUE to FALSE.
OR(`<logical1>`, `<logical2>`)	Checks whether one of the arguments is TRUE to return TRUE. The function returns FALSE if all arguments are FALSE.
SWITCH(`<expression>`, `<value1>`, `<result1>`, `<value2>`, `<result2>`…, `<else>`)	Evaluates an expression against a list of values and returns one of multiple possible result expressions. `else` is the result if expression doesn't match any of the value arguments (optional).
TRUE()	Returns the logical value TRUE.

TEXT FUNCTIONS

Text functions, as shown in Table B-7, are used for formatting text.

TABLE B-7 Text Functions

FUNCTION	DESCRIPTION
BLANK()	Returns a blank.
CONCATENATE(`<text1>`, `<text2>`)	Joins two text strings into one text string.
EXACT(`<text1>`,`<text2>`)	Compares two text strings and returns TRUE if they are exactly the same, FALSE otherwise. EXACT is case-sensitive but ignores formatting differences.
FIND(`<find_text>`, `<within_text>`, `<start_num>`, `<NotFoundValue>`)	Returns the starting position of one text string within another text string. FIND is case-sensitive. `start_num` and `NotFoundValue` are optional.
FIXED(`<number>`, `<decimals>`, `<no_commas>`)	Rounds a number to the specified number of decimals and returns the result as text. You can specify that the result be returned with or without commas.

FUNCTION	DESCRIPTION
`FORMAT(<value>, <format_string>)`	Converts a value to text according to the specified format.
`LEFT(<text>, <num_chars>)`	Returns the specified number of characters from the start of a text string.
`LEN(<text>)`	Returns the number of characters in a text string.
`LOWER(<text>)`	Converts all letters in a text string to lowercase.
`MID(<text>, <start_num>, <num_chars>)`	Returns a string of characters from the middle of a text string, given a starting position and length.
`REPLACE(<old_text>, <start_num>, <num_chars>, <new_text>)`	`REPLACE` replaces part of a text string, based on the number of characters you specify, with a different text string.
`REPT(<text>, <num_times>)`	Repeats text a given number of times.
`RIGHT(<text>, <num_chars>)`	`RIGHT` returns the last character or characters in a text string, based on the number of characters you specify.
`SEARCH(<search_text>, <within_text>, <start_num>, <NotFoundValue>)`	Returns the number of the character at which a specific character or text string is first found, reading left to right. `SEARCH` is case-sensitive. `start_num` and `NotFoundValue` are optional.
`SUBSTITUTE(<text>, <old_text>, <new_text>, <instance_num>)`	Replaces existing text with new text in a text string.
`TRIM(<text>)`	Removes all spaces from text except for single spaces between words.
`UPPER (<text>)`	Converts a text string to all uppercase letters.
`VALUE(<text>)`	Converts a text string that represents a number to a number.

Predefined Numeric Formats for the FORMAT Function

Numeric formats, as shown in Table B-8, are used in the format function for formatting numbers.

TABLE B-8 Predefined Numeric Formats

FORMAT SPECIFICATION	DESCRIPTION
"General Number"	Displays numbers with no thousand separators.
"Currency"	Displays numbers with thousand separators, if appropriate; displays two digits to the right of the decimal separator. Output is based on system locale settings.
"Fixed"	Displays at least one digit to the left and two digits to the right of the decimal separator.
"Standard"	Displays numbers with thousand separators, at least one digit to the left and two digits to the right of the decimal separator.
"Percent"	Displays numbers multiplied by 100 with a percent sign (%) appended immediately to the right; always displays two digits to the right of the decimal separator.
"Scientific"	Uses standard scientific notation, providing two significant digits.
"Yes/No"	Displays No if number is 0; otherwise, displays Yes.
"True/False"	Displays False if number is 0; otherwise, displays True.
"On/Off"	Displays Off if number is 0; otherwise, displays On.

Predefined Date and Time Formats for the FORMAT Function

Date and time formats, shown in Table B-9, are used in the FORMAT function for formatting numbers.

TABLE B-9 Predefined Date and Time Formats

FORMAT SPECIFICATION	DESCRIPTION
"General Date"	Displays a date and/or time. For example, 3/12/2008 11:07:31 AM. Date display is determined by your application's current culture value.
"Long Date" or "Medium Date"	Displays a date according to your current culture's long date format. For example, Wednesday, March 12, 2008.
"Short Date"	Displays a date using your current culture's short date format. For example, 3/12/2008.

FORMAT SPECIFICATION	DESCRIPTION
"Long Time" or "Medium Time"	Displays a time using your current culture's long time format; typically includes hours, minutes, seconds. For example, 11:07:31 AM.
"Short Time"	Displays a time using your current culture's short time format. For example, 11:07 AM.

STATISTICAL FUNCTIONS

DAX provides basic statistical functions such as means and counts. These are listed in Table B-10.

TABLE B-10 Statistical Functions

FUNCTION	DESCRIPTION
AVERAGE(<column>)	Returns the average (arithmetic mean) of all the numbers in a column.
AVERAGEA(<column>)	Returns the average (arithmetic mean) of the values in a column. Handles text and non-numeric values.
AVERAGEX(<table>, <expression>)	Calculates the average (arithmetic mean) of a set of expressions evaluated over a table
COUNT(<column>)	The COUNT function counts the number of cells in a column that contain numbers.
COUNTA(<column>)	The COUNTA function counts the number of cells in a column that are not empty.
COUNTAX(<table>, <expression>)	The COUNTAX function counts non-blank results when evaluating the result of an expression over a table.
COUNTBLANK(<column>)	Counts the number of blank cells in a column.
COUNTROWS(<table>)	The COUNTROWS function counts the number of rows in the specified table, or in a table defined by an expression.

FUNCTION	DESCRIPTION
COUNTX(`<table>`, `<expression>`)	Counts the number of rows that contain a number or an expression that evaluates to a number, when evaluating an expression over a table.
DISTINCTCOUNT(`<column>`)	Counts the number of different cells in a column of numbers.
MAX(`<column>`)	Returns the largest numeric value in a column.
MAXA(`<column>`)	Returns the largest value in a column. Logical values and blanks are counted.
MAXX(`<table>`, `<expression>`)	Evaluates an expression for each row of a table and returns the largest numeric value.
MIN(`<column>`)	Returns the smallest numeric value in a column. Ignores logical values and text.
MINA(`<column>`)	Returns the smallest value in a column, including any logical values and numbers represented as text.
MINX(`<table>`, `<expression>`)	Returns the smallest numeric value that results from evaluating an expression for each row of a table.
RANK.EQ(`<value>`, `<column>`, `<order>`)	Returns the ranking of a number in a list of numbers.
RANKX(`<table>`, `<expression>`, `<value>`, `<order>`, `<ties>`)	Returns the ranking of a number in a list of numbers for each row in the table argument.
SUM(`<column>`)	Adds all the numbers in a column.
SUMX(`<table>`, `<expression>`)	Returns the sum of an expression evaluated for each row in a table.
TOPN(`<n_value>`, `<table>`, `<orderBy_expression>`, `<order>`)	Returns the top N rows of the specified table.

MATH AND TRIG FUNCTIONS

DAX does not provide any of the trigonometry functions such as SIN and COS—you will need to use SIN tables to do these types of calculations. The functions DAX does provide are listed in Table B-11.

TABLE B-11 Math and Trig Functions

FUNCTION	DESCRIPTION
ABS(<*number*>)	Returns the absolute value of a number.
CEILING(<*number*>, <*significance*>)	Rounds a number up, to the nearest integer or to the nearest multiple of significance.
CURRENCY(<*value*>)	Evaluates the argument and returns the result as currency data type.
DIVIDE(<*numerator*>, <*denominator*>, <*alternateresult*>)	Performs division and returns alternate result or BLANK() on division by 0. *Alternateresult* (optional) is the value returned when division by zero results in an error.
EXP(<*number*>)	Returns e raised to the power of a given number. The constant e equals 2.71828182845904, the base of the natural logarithm.
FACT(<*number*>)	Returns the factorial of a number, equal to the series 1*2*3*...* , ending in the given number.
FLOOR(<*number*>, <*significance*>)	Rounds a number down, toward zero, to the nearest multiple of significance.
INT(<*number*>)	Rounds a number down to the nearest integer.
LN(<*number*>)	Returns the natural logarithm of a number. Natural logarithms are based on the constant e (2.71828182845904).
LOG(<*number*>, <*base*>)	Returns the logarithm of a number to the base you specify.
LOG10(<*number*>)	Returns the base-10 logarithm of a number.
MOD(<*number*>, <*divisor*>)	Returns the remainder after a number is divided by a divisor. The result always has the same sign as the divisor.
MROUND(<*number*>, <*multiple*>)	Returns a number rounded to the desired multiple.
PI()	Returns the value of Pi, 3.14159265358979, accurate to 15 digits.
POWER(<*number*>, <*power*>)	Returns the result of a number raised to a power.

FUNCTION	DESCRIPTION
QUOTIENT(<*numerator*>, <*denominator*>)	Performs division and returns only the integer portion of the division result. Use this function when you want to discard the remainder of division.
RAND()	Returns a random number greater than or equal to 0 and less than 1, evenly distributed. The number that is returned changes each time the cell containing this function is recalculated.
RANDBETWEEN(<*bottom*>,<*top*>)	Returns a random number between the numbers you specify.
ROUND(<*number*>, <*num_digits*>)	Rounds a number to the specified number of digits.
ROUNDDOWN(<*number*>, <*num_digits*>)	Rounds a number down, toward 0 (zero).
ROUNDUP(<*number*>, <*num_digits*>)	Rounds a number up, away from 0 (zero).
SIGN(<*number*>)	Determines the sign of a number, the result of a calculation, or a value in a column. The function returns 1 if the number is positive, 0 (zero) if the number is zero, or -1 if the number is negative.
SQRT(<*number*>)	Returns the square root of a number.
TRUNC(<*number*>, <*num_digits*>)	Truncates a number to an integer by removing the decimal, or fractional, part of the number.

TIME INTELLIGENCE FUNCTIONS

Time intelligence functions are provided for work with calendar months, and the functions are listed in Table B-12.

TABLE B-12 Time Intelligence Functions

FUNCTION	DESCRIPTION
CLOSINGBALANCEMONTH(<*expression*>, <*dates*>, <*filter*>)	Evaluates the specified expression at the calendar end of the given month. The given month is calculated as the month of the latest date in the *dates* argument, after applying all filters.

FUNCTION	DESCRIPTION
CLOSINGBALANCEQUARTER(*<expression>*, *<dates>*, *<filter>*)	Evaluates the specified expression at the calendar end of the given quarter. The given quarter is calculated as the quarter of the latest date in the *dates* argument, after applying all filters.
CLOSINGBALANCEYEAR(*<expression>*, *<dates>*, *<filter>*)	Evaluates the specified expression at the calendar end of the given year. The given year is calculated as the year of the latest date in the *dates* argument, after applying all filters.
DATEADD(*<date_column>*, *<number_of_intervals>*, *<interval>*)	Returns a table that contains a column of dates, shifted either forward in time or back in time from the dates in the specified date column.
DATESBETWEEN(*<column>*, *<start_date>*, *<end_date>*	Returns a table of dates that can be found in the specified date column beginning with the start date and ending with the end date.
DATESINPERIOD(*<date_column>*, *<start_date>*, *<number_of_intervals>*, *<intervals>*)	Returns a table of dates that can be found in the specified date column beginning with the start date and continuing for the specified number of intervals.
DATESMTD(*<dates>*)	Returns a table that contains a column of the dates for the month to date.
DATESQTD(*<date_column>*)	Returns a table that contains a column of the dates for the quarter to date.
DATESYTD(*<date_column>* [, *<YE_date>*])	Returns a table that contains a column of the dates for the year to date. The *year_end_date* (optional) is a literal string with a date that defines the year-end date. The default is December 31.
ENDOFMONTH(*<date_column>*)	Returns the last day of the month in the specified date column.
ENDOFQUARTER(*<date_column>*)	Returns the last day of the quarter in the specified date column.
ENDOFYEAR(*<date_column>*)	Returns the last day of the year in the specified date column.
FIRSTDATE(*<date_column>*)	Returns the first date in the current context for the specified date column.

FUNCTION	DESCRIPTION
FIRSTNONBLANK(<column>, <expression>)	Returns the first value in the column where the expression is not blank.
LASTDATE(<date_column>)	Returns the last date in the current context for the specified date column.
LASTNONBLANK (<date_column>, <expression>)	Returns the last value in the column where the expression is not blank.
NEXTDAY(<date_column>)	Returns the next day date from date_column.
NEXTMONTH(<date_column>)	Returns the set of dates in the next month from date_column.
NEXTQUARTER(<date_column>)	Returns the set of dates for the next quarter from date_column.
NEXTYEAR(<date_column>[, <YE_date>])	Returns the set of dates for the next year from date_column.
OPENINGBALANCEMONTH(<expression>, <dates>, <filter>)	Evaluates the expression at the first date of the month, in the current context.
OPENINGBALANCEQUARTER(<expression>, <dates>, <filter>)	Evaluates the expression at the first date of the quarter, in the current context.
OPENINGBALANCEYEAR(<expression>, <dates>, <filter>)	Evaluates the expression at the first date of the year, in the current context.
PARALLELPERIOD(<dates>, <number_of_intervals>, <interval>)	Returns a table that contains a column of dates that represents a period parallel to the dates in the specified dates column, in the current context, with the dates shifted a number of intervals either forward in time or back in time.
PREVIOUSDAY(<date_column>)	Returns a table that contains a column of all dates representing the day that is previous to the first date in the dates column, in the current context.
PREVIOUSMONTH(<date_column>)	Returns a table that contains a column of all dates from the previous month, based on the first date in the dates column, in the current context.
PREVIOUSQUARTER(<date_column>)	Returns a table that contains a column of all dates from the previous quarter, based on the first date in the dates column, in the current context.

FUNCTION	DESCRIPTION
PREVIOUSYEAR(<*date_column*>)	Returns a table that contains a column of all dates from the previous year, given the last date in the dates column, in the current context.
SAMEPERIODLASTYEAR(<*dates*>)	Returns a table that contains a column of dates shifted one year back in time from the dates in the specified dates column, in the current context.
STARTOFMONTH(<*date_column*>)	Returns the first day of the month in the specified date column.
STARTOFQUARTER(<*date_column*>)	Returns the first day of the quarter in the specified date column.
STARTOFYEAR(<date_column>[, <*YE_date*>])	Returns the first day of the year in the specified date column.
TotalMTD(<*expression*>, <*dates*>, <*filter*>)	Evaluates the specified expression for the interval that starts at the first day of the month and ends at the latest date in the specified dates column, after applying all filters.
TotalQTD(<*expression*>, <*dates*>, <*filter*>)	Evaluates the specified expression for the interval that starts at the first day of the quarter and ends at the latest date in the specified dates column, after applying all filters.
TotalYTD(<*expression*>, <*dates*>, <*filter*>)	Evaluates the specified expression for the interval that starts at the first day of the year and ends at the latest date in the specified dates column, after applying all filters.

Index